QUID PRO QUO

WHAT THE ROMANS REALLY GAVE THE ENGLISH LANGUAGE

PETER JONES

Atlantic Books
London

First published in hardback in Great Britain in 2016 by Atlantic Books,
an imprint of Atlantic Books Ltd.

This paperback edition first published in Great Britain in 2017 by Atlantic Books.

1 2 3 4 5 6 7 8 9

A CIP catalogue record for this book is available from the British Library.

E-book ISBN: 978-1-78239-932-2
Paperback ISBN: 978-1-78239-933-9

Printed in Great Britain by Clays Ltd, St Ives plc

Atlantic Books
An Imprint of Atlantic Books Ltd
Ormond House
26–27 Boswell Street
London
WC1N 3JZ

www.atlantic-books.co.uk

QUID PRO QUO

Peter Jones was educated at Cambridge University and taught Classics at Cambridge and at Newcastle University, before retiring in 1997. He has written a regular column, 'Ancient & Modern', in the *Spectator* for many years and is the author of various books on the Classics, including the bestselling *Learn Latin* and *Learn Ancient Greek*, as well as *Reading Virgil: Aeneid I and II*, *Vote for Caesar*, *Veni, Vidi, Vici* and *Eureka!*

Also by Peter Jones

Vote for Caesar

Learn Latin: The Book of the
Daily Telegraph QED *Series*

Veni, Vidi, Vici

Eureka!

CONTENTS

PREFACE

Take the word 'adrenalin'. This hormone, one of the most important in the body, is found in a gland located *on top of the kidneys*. The Latin stem *renal-* meant 'to do with the kidneys' and *ad* meant 'near'. Hence 'adrenalin'. But no Roman would have recognized the word. It was invented, using Latin stems, in 1901.

Take 'microbe'. This derives from two ancient Greek words, *mikros* ('small, short') and *bios* ('life'). No Greek would have recognized it. It was invented, using Greek stems, in 1881. And a very incompetent invention it was too, microbes being millions of years old.

English is full of such predominantly technical words, invented over the past 400 years. They were designed, in particular, to provide the specialized vocabulary required for the then developing disciplines of science and medicine, and the naming of flora and fauna. Indeed, if all of them were taken into account, you could say that English was 90 per cent Graeco-Latin!

Many such invented words will feature in chapters 12 and 13 because medicine and botany are so interestingly rich in them. Otherwise, and with the occasional exception, the subject of this book is English words derived, with minimal change, from Latin and ancient Greek words *used by the Greeks and Romans themselves*, whether in the same sense as we use them or not – words such as 'plasma', 'electron', 'fornicate', 'prune', 'cement', 'agony' and 'poet'. In this respect my debt to the magnificent *Oxford Latin Dictionary*, edited by Peter Glare and his team, is very great indeed.

But it is not simply a book of words or lists of words, though there are a few summarizing lists here and there. The words have also been selected in order to give the reader some sense of the culture and history of the ancient Roman world, and of Rome's connection with the ancient Greek world too. For the Romans took over and latinized many ancient Greek words, just as we have taken over and anglicized many Greek and Roman ones.

So the book has another great pleasure to offer: an easy introduction to the ancient Greek alphabet, the source of the Latin alphabet and ours too. As you will find, nearly half the Greek alphabet is almost identical with English.

It will work as follows: where a Latin word which we use derives directly from Greek, the Latin word will be quoted, its Greek original given in English letters, and then in Greek letters ('transliterated', in other words). For example, our 'stomach' derives, via Latin *stomachus*, from Greek *stomakhos* (στομαχος). A full Greek alphabet – a crisply economical twenty-four letters, as opposed to English's absurdly bloated twenty-six – is provided on p. 23. It should prove a pleasantly harmless way to become acquainted with this enormously influential alphabet that in the eighth century BC first introduced to the West the independent representation of vowel sounds alongside consonants.

My grateful thanks are due to Alan Beale for much general linguistic help, and to Professors Philip van der Eijk and Kenneth Saunders for consultations on medical matters.

Peter Jones

www.classicsforall.org.uk

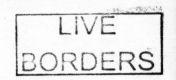

THE LATIN LANGUAGE

HISTORICAL SURVEY:
500 BC–AD 1700

The Latin language is so called because it was spoken in a region of Italy called Latium, by people calling themselves *Latini*. It was only one of a number of Italic languages being used across Italy. One of these Latin-speaking towns was *Roma*, populated by *Romani*.

We know of twenty-two languages in all across Italy from this early period, and scholars speculate from other less secure evidence (such as strange-looking proper names) that there may have been as many as about forty. But from about 500–280 BC, by conquest and alliance, Romans came to control most of Italy, taking Latin with them wherever they went. By the first century BC, virtually all of Italy was speaking Latin. Indeed, by the first century AD, Latin was referred to as *sermo Italus*, 'the Italian language'. Latin *sermo*, 'speech, language, conversation, gossip', giving us 'sermon', seems to have been connected with a root meaning 'link up, join'.

A common form of ancient Greek had also become standard across much of the Mediterranean by this time (though not for poetry). That is why the New Testament was written in that language (and the gospels are probably accurate in saying that Jesus could speak Greek when he needed to, though Aramaic was his first language). Since Greek language and culture exerted a lasting influence over the Romans, the children of elite families also learned the literary, 'classical' Greek of the eighth to fourth centuries BC as part of their education.

By the first century AD, the Romans were also the dominant people of an empire stretching from Britain to Syria and from the Rhine–Danube to North Africa, and Latin became embedded in areas of Western Europe such as Gaul and Spain, which Rome held. Over hundreds of years, Latin in these areas gradually morphed into today's so-called 'romance' languages (French, Spanish, etc.).

'Classical Latin' is the Latin of high literature – Catullus, Cicero, Virgil, Tacitus, for example – composed in the first centuries BC and AD. This 'elite' Latin in its *written* form changed remarkably little. Even in the Middle Ages, the educated still tried consciously to copy it. By about AD 1000, it had become an artificial language, but it was still learned at school for certain purposes, following fixed rules. So it remains today. Anyone who knows classical Latin will not find much difficulty in translating the Latin of the church, the Middle Ages, the Renaissance or later.

But 'Vulgar' Latin – the sort used by the man on the forum omnibus – was far more malleable (*vulgus*, 'crowd, mob, common people', though even Cicero said that he spoke very differently from the way he wrote). It survives mainly in graffiti scribbled on the walls of Pompeii and other cities. This *spoken* 'sub-elite' Latin developed very differently in different areas. Indeed, it became so far removed from the elite version that by the third century AD it may well have been impossible for somebody using the elite language to understand the other (and vice versa)! It was from this common Latin that the different romance languages emerged.

The reason for Latin's long survival in the West is that Latin was the language of the universal Catholic church. So it was the language of St Jerome's translation of the originally Greek Bible (called the 'Vulgate', though not written in Vulgar Latin); the liturgy was in Latin; and it was the church that delivered education.*

Consequently, when the Roman Empire in the West collapsed in the fifth century AD, Latin was at the heart of religion, education and learning. It remained in that position across Europe till at least the sixteenth century. So, during the scientific and cultural revolutions of the fourteenth to eighteenth centuries, it was to Latin and ancient Greek that scientists, thinkers and artists turned when they needed new words to describe the new phenomena with which they were dealing. As a result, Latin and Greek are deeply embedded in our scientific – especially botanical and medical – terminology, and our educational and cultural language in general.

But our everyday English language is also rich in Latin. When the Romans conquered these islands in the first century AD, the British

---

* Many words used by St Jerome in his translation of the Bible into Latin became anglicized and common currency in English – for instance: *creatio*, *evangelium*, *justificatio*, *angelus*, *testamentum*, *gratia*, *redemptio* and *sanctificatio*.

language was Celtic, but Latin never took on here as it had done in Europe. In the fifth century AD the Romans left these islands to try to defend the Roman Empire in Europe against Germanic incursions from the north. As a result, invaders from Holland (Frisians), north Germany (Saxons) and Denmark (Angles, from Angeln, and Jutes) moved into England.

We call these Germanic invaders the Anglo-Saxons. Their language ousted both Celtic and what Latin there was, to become the basis of today's English. So English is basically a Germanic language. But because the Anglo-Saxons had already been in contact with the Roman Empire, their language already contained some Latin.*

When these islands were Christianized from the sixth century AD, more Latin was brought in by the church, together with some Greek.

But the big change came after 1066, when the French-speaking Normans under William Duke of Normandy conquered these islands (the 'Norman Conquest'). French is a dialect of Latin, and the English vocabulary expanded massively during those 350 years of French influence.

That is why the English vocabulary contains so many words of different origins for the same ideas. Contrast Germanic 'king, kingly' with Latin-based 'sovereign, royal, regal'; Germanic 'faithfulness' with Latin 'fidelity'; Germanic 'get' with Latin 'obtain'; Germanic 'hug' with Latin 'embrace'; and Germanic 'come' with Latin 'arrive' (from the Latin *ad ripam*, 'to the riverbank'!). There are also many

---

* Here are some examples of Latin already embedded in the Anglo-Saxon which came into England during the fifth century AD: 'wine' (from Latin *vinum*), 'wall' (*vallum*), 'street' (*strata*, 'laid flat'), 'beer' (*bibere*, 'to drink'), 'sack' (*saccus*), 'sock' (*soccus*).

hybrid words, combining a classical stem with an Anglo-Saxon ending; for instance, Latin *horrificus* giving English 'horrify<u>ing</u>'. By the time of Chaucer's *Canterbury Tales* (*c.* 1380), the English language was already rich in words brought in from Norman French. By about 1600 (the period of Shakespeare and the Authorized Version of the Bible), a language recognizable as modern English had emerged.

THE BIRTH OF ROMANCE?

Pope Gregory V died on 18 February 999. On his tomb it says that he spoke *Francisca*, *vulgari*, et *Latina voce*, and so taught the people 'in three languages'. If *Francisca* means 'French', this is the first written evidence we have of the separation of Latin into romance languages – French, *vulgari*, i.e. Italian, and Latin. But *Francisca* may mean 'German', because the Franks were a Germanic people and Gregory V a German pope.

TWO FOR THE PRICE OF ONE

When after 1066 Anglo-Saxon started to be infused with Norman French, those French words over time began to change. Thus Latin *pauper*, 'poor', had already become Old French *povre*; this was absorbed into Anglo-Saxon (at this time Anglo-Norman would be more accurate) and over time became English 'poor'.

That was one route by which Latin-based words came into English. But there was another: when a Latin word was lifted directly from Latin into English. To stay with *pauper*: law reports were written in Latin and Latin *pauper* was used in them to refer to the poor. Over time, that word came into ordinary English too.

Another example is, indirectly via French: Latin *fragilis* → Old French *fraile* (modern French *frêle*) → English 'frail'; directly from Latin, 'fragile'.

There is even a triple borrowing: Latin *ratio* → French *raison* → English 'reason'; via French, *ration* → 'ration'; and directly from Latin, 'ratio'!

All in all, perhaps about 10,000 Latin- and Greek-based words entered the English language throughout the Norman period. We continue, of course, to take over foreign words, such as 'spaghetti' from Italian and 'curry' from Tamil *kari*.

DOGMATIC DEBATE

In 1546, after fierce debate, the Council of Trent decided that Latin *alone* was to be used for the Mass and the sacraments,* whatever language was spoken by the church congregation.† The reason was that sacred acts required time-honoured ritual, couched in time-honoured language, however meaningless it might be to participants.

One result was that, when Jesuit missionaries opened up China in the seventeenth century, Chinese priests had to learn Latin. The problem was that they could not *pronounce* it. This surely rendered the rite invalid: so could not the Chinese have their own liturgy? No, said Rome: such was the sacred essence of Latin – and the fear of

---

* It was during the Council of Trent that St Jerome's Vulgate Bible became accepted as authentic and it was decreed 'that no one is to dare or presume to reject it under any pretext whatever'.

† 'Decide' is from Latin *decido*, 'I detach by cutting': a decision is the cut-off point.

schism if any concessions were made – that all demands for a Chinese liturgy were rejected.

ENGLISH FOR THE ENGLISH

From the fifteenth-century Renaissance in Europe (p. 118), even more Graeco-Latin words flooded into English, and many Englishmen reacted strongly against the trend. In 1557 Sir John Cheke, first Regius Professor of Greek at Cambridge, moaned:

> I am of this <u>opinion</u> that our tongue should be written clean and <u>pure</u>, <u>unmixed</u> and <u>unmangled</u> with borrowings of other tongues, wherein if we take not heed by time, ever borrowing and never <u>paying</u>, she shall be fain to keep her house as <u>bankrupt</u>. For then doth our tongue <u>naturally</u> and praisably utter her meaning, when she borroweth no <u>counterfeitness</u> of other tongues to attire herself withal.

The underlined words are, of course, Latin-based, but that was not quite Cheke's point. His central concern was that pure Latin words were flooding directly into English – words such as alias, arbiter, circus, delirium, exit, genius, interim, radius, agenda, census, curriculum, lens, pendulum, rabies, squalor and tedium. This trend continued, but at a slowing pace, into the nineteenth century (when words such as consensus, omnibus and referendum made their grand entrance).

ROMANS, OUT!

In 1573 Ralph Lever set about replacing Latinate words with honest English ones. Here are some delightful examples, one of which has actually survived:

- Conclusion: endsay
- Condition: ifsay
- Negation: naysay
- Definition: saywhat
- Proposition: shewsay
- Affirmation: yeasay

Happily, none of these projects came to anything, and the vast vocabulary of English, uniquely drawn from both Germanic and Graeco-Latin stems, helps to make it the rich, flexible language it is.

HANDY 'AND'Y

It is not just in its vocabulary that Latin had a powerful effect on English. It often affected the very structure of the language. In 1384 John Wycliffe produced his controversial translation of Jerome's Vulgate Bible from Latin into English. Part of the Christmas story read as follows:

> Forsooth they, <u>seeing</u> the star, joyed with a full great joy. And they, <u>entering</u> the house, found the child with Mary his mother; and they <u>falling down</u> worshipped him. And, <u>their treasures opened</u>, they offered to him gifts, gold, incense and myrrh.

This is as literal a translation as one could find. In particular, note the underlined participles and the final participial phrase – all pure Latin.

But this was not the style of English prose, as Sir Thomas Malory's *Le Morte d'Arthur* (1485), which brings together tales of King Arthur drawn from French and other sources, clearly shows. The Latinate style did not appeal to the great William Tyndale either. His version of the above passage in his 1534 translation of the Bible, derived from both the Greek and Hebrew, reads as follows:

> When they saw the star, they were marvellously glad: and went into the house and found the child with Mary his mother, and kneeled down and worshipped him, and opened their treasures and offered unto him gifts, gold, frankincense and myrrh.

Farewell participles, and welcome 'when' clauses and sequences of main verbs strung together with 'and'. This is English as she oughta be wrote. King James's Authorized Version of the Bible (1611) got the message:

> When they saw the star, they rejoiced with exceeding great joy. And when they were come into the house, they saw the young child with Mary his mother, and fell down and worshipped him: and when they had opened their treasures, they presented unto him gifts: gold, and frankincense, and myrrh.

Here 'when' clauses dominate, and there is again no sign of Latinate participles. So Latin *vocabulary* may have infiltrated the language, but Latin *prose style* was to affect English only in certain registers.

CLASS AND CLASSICS

By the eighteenth century, most Latin texts had been translated and the local languages, not Latin, were the main vehicle of learning in schools. In America, where the English educational model was followed to begin with, Latin was soon dropped. But European schools plugged on with it, irrespective of practical use, for it had become a sort of bourgeois certificate of authenticity. Its sheer uselessness confirmed it as the ultimate symbol of the noble, liberal education, fit for the truly free man. It was his passport into the elite (*líber*, 'free', →'liberty'; not to be confused with *liber*, 'book', → 'library'). You did not actually need to *know* any Latin: you just needed to have learned it.

LATIN LANGUAGE OF POWER

There was a time when *not* knowing Latin excluded, indeed defined, the unfit. One did not want the masses, especially the working masses, to get ideas above their station. As a result, it was a proud moment for a working-class family when a son of theirs became the first family member to conjugate *amo amas amat* ('I love, you love, he/she/it loves' – the first exercise in Latin they would probably have encountered). Latin, then, became a language of power, bolstering the prestige of those who used it and commanding the respect of those who did not, all the more effectively for being unintelligible.

PROTECTING THE INNOCENT

Latin served another function: it saved people from embarrassment. So when doctors talked about bodily functions, they did so in the decent obscurity of a dead language. In 1758, for example, the Swiss doctor

André Tissot wrote an important medical treatise on masturbation not as sin but as disorder. It appeared under a Latin title: '*Tentamen de morbis ex manustupratione*' ('Investigation into illnesses caused by masturbation'). Even when Tissot translated it into French, the more 'shocking' passages were still left in Latin.

This practice continued well into the twentieth century. Harvard's famous 'Loeb' series of Latin and Greek texts printed the classical language on the left-hand page and the translation on the right. But sexual content was either bowdlerized in translation or, in extreme cases, the original language was repeated where the translation should have been. Indeed, in the first Loeb edition of the often obscene Roman poet, Martial, the Latin was translated into Italian! This was most useful to inquisitive schoolboys. They immediately knew where the filthy bits were and could concentrate all their energies on understanding them. Holidays in Rome were never the same, either.

DROPPING LATIN

Up until 1959, anyone who wanted to study any subject at Oxford or Cambridge had to have passed the Latin (or ancient Greek) examination at O level (the public exam at age sixteen, now GCSE). On 17 May 1959, by 325 votes to 278, Cambridge University decided to drop this compulsory entrance requirement. Oxford followed suit shortly afterwards.

The consequence was a flight from Latin in many state schools. But private schools kept it on. Their staff understood that Latin gave pupils an educational advantage, whichever university the pupils were considering. This was not a decision to be taken lightly. Private schools, unlike state schools, exist only by virtue of their success in the market, and in the 1960s and 1970s Latin was touted as the worst sort of regression to the 'bad old days'. But this long view, far from working against them, in fact enhanced these schools' desirability in the eyes of pupils and parents.

That debate is now past. State schools are for the most part relaxed about the 'elitist' tag pinned by a generation of knee-jerk head teachers on anything to do with the ancient world. How on earth can a mere school *subject* be elitist? Only humans wear that tag. So schools now feel free to ask: 'Is this language, its history and culture, objectively worth studying in its own right?' More and more are answering: 'Yes.' Who, after all, does not long to be a member of the elite?

A PRESCRIPTIVE LANGUAGE

Since Latin is no longer a spoken language, it cannot change. Its linguistic rules, variations and all, are therefore fixed: one can be dogmatic about what counts as grammatically 'right' or 'wrong'. Ancient Roman grammarians and others took this view too. They argued fiercely about 'proper' style and usage even when the language was still being spoken and therefore in a constant state of flux – as indeed did ancient Greeks about Greek.

Perhaps as a result of this, classicists in particular have the unfortunate habit of applying this prescriptive mindset to living languages like English. Since all of these are in a constant process of change, they can for the most part only be described. That is not to deny that there is such a thing as illiteracy: employers, for example, do not warm to applications for jobs written by graduates who cannot spell CV.

The point is that there are conventions – that is, broad *agreements* – about matters such as spelling, for example. On these, all newspapers and publishers establish their own conventions and expect them to be followed. They have been *agreed*: that is why they are important. But they are still conventions, not prescriptions, and will change over time.

ALPHABET SOUP

The English language is alphabetic – it uses relatively few signs to indicate all the vowels and consonants necessary to make up the appropriate sounds.

Our alphabet originated with the consonantal alphabet of the Phoenicians (a Semitic people from the region that we now know as Lebanon). In the eighth century BC Greeks turned this into a consonant-and-vowel alphabet of twenty-four letters – a hugely influential achievement.*

This alphabet was adopted by the Romans and other Italian language groups from Greek colonists who arrived in Italy in the eighth century BC. It was adapted by them and has since become the standard script of the Western world.

Many languages do not use an alphabet. Chinese, for example, is a sort of picture language. Each character represents one syllable, which can be built up into a word. You need to memorize over 2,000 such characters just to read a newspaper. The early ancient Greek script called Linear B (1500–1200 BC) was a 'syllabary'. This consisted

---

* 'Alphabet' derives from the first two letters of the Greek alphabet – alpha (α, a) and beta (β, b).

of about ninety signs representing syllables, e.g. ba be bo, da de do, and so on. So Knossos, an important town in Crete at the time, came out as 'Ko-no-so'.

PIE CHART

To keep things simple: most European languages show such strong linguistic similarities with each other that they must be connected. The reason is that they all derive from a single language, which we call Proto-Indo-European (PIE). 'Indo-' comes into it because the Indian language Sanskrit is also part of this group (as is Persian, the language of Iran).

The following chart shows the family connections, with examples of verbal similarities:

PROTO-INDO-EUROPEAN

↓	↓	↓	↓
Latin	**Greek**	**Sanskrit**	**Germanic**
pater	*patêr*	*pitar*	*Vater*
mâter	*mêtêr*	*mâtar*	*Mutter*
três	*treis*	*trayas*	*drei*
septem	*hepta*	*sapta*	*sieben*
↓ ↓ ↓			↓
Fr Ital Span			Anglo-Saxon
			↓
			English
			father
			mother
			three
			seven

In other words, Latin, Greek, Germanic and Sanskrit are similar *not* because they derive from each other, but because they all derive from the same ancestor – PIE: they are the offspring of father PIE, and English is the offspring of Germanic via Anglo-Saxon. French, Italian and Spanish are the offspring of Latin.

DERIVATIONS AND STEMS

In this book, there will be much talk of the derivation of English words. Ultimately, of course, nearly all of them derive from PIE. But for our purposes, we shall distinguish three routes by which English words have come into being.

(i) They were *borrowed* directly from the ancient languages; for example, *drama* (δραμα) was borrowed directly from the Greek.

(ii) They were *introduced* into English, often via Norman French; for example, 'derivation' came into English via the fourteenth-century French *dérivation* – it derives from Latin *de*, 'from', and *rivus*, 'river' (picture a stream, with small rivers flowing from it).

(iii) They are *descended* from Germanic; for example, Old Germanic *der* and *unta* (modern German *und*) descended, via Anglo-Saxon, into English and became 'the' and 'and'.

Sometimes it would be over-complicating, or it is not possible, to say what the specific connection or derivation of a word is. In such cases, 'related to' will appear.

Latin words regularly have two different 'stems'. For example, the Latin for 'I sit', *sedeo*, has one stem *sed(e)*- (giving us 'sedentary') and another stem *sess-* (giving us 'session'); the Latin for 'king' is *rex*, and its stem is *reg-* (from which we get 'regal', for example). These will be indicated in the text as you meet them.

PRONOUNCING LATIN?

In Latin, as in ancient Greek, every letter counts. So the Latin for soldier, *mîles* (î = a long vowel, 'ee') is not pronounced like English 'miles' but 'meeless' – note the soft 's'. But how do we *know* how classical Latin was pronounced? There is a great deal of evidence, as the following examples show.

LATIN 'C' HARD OR SOFT?

Take it as read that we know how ancient Greek was pronounced. Greeks wrote the name of the Roman orator Cicero as *Kikerôn* (the *-ôn* being a Greek ending), not *Siserôn*, and Caesar as *Kaisar*, not *Saisar*. So 'c' was pronounced hard, as in our 'k', not as in our 's' or in modern Italian 'c'.

Those who sing church music will know that Latin tends to be pronounced as a sort of modern Italian (for example, Latin 'c' as in 'church'). This is because in 1912 Pope Pius X decided to try to impose a standard pronunciation which reflected modern Italian pronunciation.

LIPS, TEETH AND THROAT LATIN
'T', 'D', 'B', 'P', 'R'

Ancient grammarians are full of useful information:

- One grammarian says that 't' and 'd' should be distinguished by the position of the tongue: 't' with the tongue against the back of the teeth, and 'd' with the tongue against the ridge of the gum (try it!).
- Another describes 'b' and 'p' as a 'sound exploded from the lips' and hints that the difference is one of muscular tension. In both cases, they seem to be describing something like the sounds those letters represent for us.
- A third grammarian tells us that 'r' was trilled or rolled in Latin. This pronunciation is supported by the early satirist Lucilius, who describes it as resembling the 'growling of a dog'.

ILLITERATE LATIN HINTS
'N', 'M' AND 'GN'

Illiterate inscriptions can be suggestive:

- We find *in pâce*, 'in peace', written *im pace*; and *in balneô*, 'in the bath', written *im balneô*. Presumably Romans slurred 'n' to 'm' before a 'p' or 'b'.
- Even more surprising, we find *ignês*, 'fires', written '*ingnês*', and there is other evidence to suggest that 'gn' was pronounced 'ngn'. So the 'gn' in Latin *magnus*, 'large', sounded roughly like English 'ha*ngn*ail'.

THE BIG ONE: 'V' OR 'W'?

Romans did not have 'w' but they did have 'v'. But was it pronounced as we pronounce it, or as a 'w'/'ooa' sound?

In a dialogue attacking divination, Cicero tells the following story. Marcus Crassus was about to set out on the expedition to Parthia (which was to end in both his and his army's destruction). A man on the quayside was selling figs from Caunus (southern Turkey) and therefore shouting '*Cauneâs*' ('cow-nay-arse')! Cicero comments that Crassus should have listened to the omen. Had he done so, he would have realized the man was shouting '*Cave nê eâs*', 'beware lest you-go!', 'don't go!'*

So, if 'v' was pronounced as our 'v', there is no way '*cau-*' could sound the same as '*cav-*'. Therefore 'v' was really a sound like 'w'/'ooa'. Greeks also transcribed the Roman name *Valerius* as *Oualêrios*, again suggesting that 'v' was pronounced as a 'oo' or 'w'. Note also that, for Cicero's joke to work, '*nê eâs*' must have been run together into '*nêâs*'.

There is another amusing piece of evidence. An ancient grammarian points out that, when you say the Latin for 'you', *tû*, your lips point towards the person to whom you are speaking (as 'you' does in English). But 'you' plural is '*vôs*'. That does not work unless 'v' is pronounced 'w'. QED!†

Conclusion: when Julius Caesar came, saw and conquered, he said, 'waynee, weedee, weekee' (*veni, vidi, vici*).

---

* Old schoolboy alert: in the past we shouted 'KV!' to warn of the approach of a teacher. We did not realize we were saying – and mispronouncing – *cave!*, 'Look out!', which in Latin would have been pronounced 'ca-way' (→ *cave canem!*, 'Beware of the dog!').

† *Quod Erat Demonstrandum* – 'which was to-be-proved' (and now has been).

THE GREEK ALPHABET

Throughout this book, ancient Greek will appear. Greek words will be given first in English letters ('transliterated') in italics, and then in Greek letters, e.g. *bombos* (βομβος);[1] *krisis* (κρισις); *drama* (δραμα); *historia* (ιστορια);[2] *eukaluptos* (εὐκαλυπτος);[3] *Atlas* (Ἀτλας);[4] *Apollôn* (Ἀπολλων); *Homêros* (Ὁμηρος); *Oidipous* (Οἰδιπους); *ôideion* (ᾠδειον);[5] *angelos* (ἀγγελος).[6]

Where no suggestion is made, pronounce the letters as in English:

a	α A	alpha 'h*a*t'	n	ν N	nu	
b	β B	beta	x	ξ Ξ	xî	
g	γ Γ	gamma	o	o O	omicron 'h*o*t'	
d	δ Δ	delta	p	π Π	pî	
e	ε E	epsilon p*e*t	r	ρ P	rhô	
z	ζ Z	zêta '*sd*'	s	σς Σ	sigma	
ê	η H	êta '*air*'	t	τ T	tau	
th	θ Θ	thêta	u	υ Y	upsilon 'p*u*t'	
i	ι I	iôta 'h*i*t'	ph	φ Φ	phî	
k	κ K	kappa	kh	χ X	khî 'lo*ch*'	
l	λ Λ	lambda	ps	ψ Ψ	psî	
m	μ M	mu	ô	ω Ω	ômega '*or*'	

1. 's' appears as σ except at the end of a word, when it appears as ς.

2. All words *starting* with a vowel indicate whether that vowel is preceded with an 'h' or not by means of a 'breathing'. So: ὁν = *on* ('smooth breathing'); ὁν = *hon* ('rough breathing').

3. *Diphthongs* place the breathing on the *second* vowel: οὐκ = ouk; αἱ = *hai*.

4. The breathing is placed *in front of* single capital vowels, e.g. Ἀλκαιος (Alkaios); note 3 applies to diphthongs, e.g. Εὐριπιδης (Euripidês).

5. In some cases, an iota following an omega, for example, is printed below the omega: not ωι, but ῳ, e.g. ᾠδη = *ôidê*, 'song, ode'.

6. Greek *gg* (γγ) was pronounced as English 'ng' and is transliterated as 'ng'.

POLITICS

INTRODUCTION

As far as the West is concerned, Romans invented the idea both of republicanism and of empire, and it is mainly to Roman models rather than Greek, or any other, that Western governments and historians have traditionally looked when it came to thinking about their own political systems.

The republican system has entrenched three basic ideas into Western political thought: that citizens have the right to govern themselves; that they have the right to outsource that government to those elected by them and to change that government if they see fit; and, consequently, that the authority which the government wields is ultimately dependent on the will of the people. The result is that anyone who wants to stay in government has to do so in the people's interest, and no one else's.

Given the power that this potentially hands to the people – the ultimate model here was provided by fifth-century BC Athenian direct democracy – the system has increasingly developed means to try to ensure that it does not descend into mob rule; and over time the sense has developed that, however sovereign the people are, the state must to all intents and purposes hold the whip hand, but in accordance with the *law*. In other words, the judiciary, not any particular government of whatever stripe, has become the final guarantor and protector of the people's freedoms and power.

What this all adds up to is that the purpose of and justification for government, and the sole grounds on which it survives in the form it does, is the *public good*. As we look around the world today, we in the West have cause to feel eternally thankful that, for all its fallibilities, strains and tensions, we have inherited such a system.

'Empire' is derived from Latin *imperium*, 'the right to give orders' – and the right to enforce obedience to them. That is why holders of *imperium* during the Republic, such as the consuls and praetors, were accompanied by attendants called *lictores*, each carrying a bundle of rods tied around an axe, a symbol of power and the means of its enforcement. These were called the *fasces* (whence 'fascist'), and signalled their ultimate authority.

These *fasces* continued to symbolize power under the Empire too, but there was a difference. When Augustus became the first emperor in 27 BC, he became *princeps*: 'first citizen', literally 'one who has taken first place' (*primus*, 'first' + *-ceps*, 'one who takes', → our 'principle').* So his rule became known as the principate (*principatus*). He was also known, as were all subsequent emperors, as *imperator*. But the *imperium* he possessed came with a difference: it

---

* It is something of a tautology to talk about *first* principles: there cannot be second ones.

was *maius imperium*, 'greater *imperium*' – greater than anyone else's. (Our 'majesty' derives from that *mai-* form: Latin *maiestas*, 'the *greater* standing, dignity of a god or man'.)

Armed with this, as the Roman historian Tacitus saw, 'Augustus drew into his own person the functions [see *munia*, p. 66] of the Senate, *magistratus* [p. 38] and the laws'; and the historian added *nullo adversante*, '[with] no one objecting'. In other words, Augustus was, effectively, by universal acquiescence, a monarch, and proved the point by ensuring that his successor would come from within his extended family when he died in AD 14.

Not only that. Over the period of the Republic, Romans insisted that there be not one but two heads of state: hence, always two consuls who changed, in theory at least, every year. They would not tolerate the idea of too much power in the hands of one person. But with an emperor there was now one head of state, who also reconstituted, and made himself head of, the army. For the first time, it became a professional body, with terms and conditions of service, answerable only to him. Rome was now a military state, its people, army and law under the *imperium* of one man, and its empire too, which Rome continued to expand (Rome had been running provinces since 241 BC,* after it conquered Carthage in the first 'Punic' War over control of Sicily). When Augustus was asked how he was, he would reply, 'I and the army are well.'

Empires can be run well or badly. The Roman Empire in the West, which (technically) lasted till AD 476, must have been doing

---

* Incidentally, we have no idea what the derivation of the Latin *provincia* is.

something right, given that its army of about 300,000 controlled an empire of about fifty million people over an area of about two million square miles. Its light regulation – basically, pay us our taxes and permit our army to station itself where it will – and the enormous economic benefits it brought on the back of long periods of peace were all part of its secret. In AD 212 the emperor Caracalla declared that all free men in the Roman Empire would become full Roman citizens and all free women have the same rights as Roman women.

For all that, the association between empire and conquest turned out to be an unhappy one. The British argued that their conquests in America (1607–1789) did not make an empire but a 'protectorate'. Yet they could hardly claim the Americans were 'fellow citizens'; one commentator argued it was nothing but an exercise in domination, commerce and population settlement. Napoleon's empire did not exactly improve the image. The empire of the British Raj in India (1858–1947) uneasily both centralized and decentralized power.

At the end of the day, it came down to a balance between power and liberty. Was the empire an indivisible whole, run by one central authority, over a free citizenry, as in the Roman Empire, or not? Such an entity could claim justification. But in these days of the nation state, the closest we can get to that construct is the confederation of free states, reaching free agreement on the nature of that confederation (*con/cum*, 'with, joined' + *foedus* [*foeder-*], 'treaty'). The days of empire are gone.

LATIN ITALIANS

'Latins' (*Latini*) was the name give to those Italians who lived in the tribal region called *Latium*. Since it was there that Rome was built, Romans were also *Latini*. And their language was *lingua Latina* – 'the Latin tongue'.

The country that we call Italy was in Latin *Italia* (and still is). In early times (around the eighth century BC), Greeks dominated the south, Etruscans the centre, and Celts the north of the country. But by the first century BC, Rome controlled the lot and Latin had become the universal tongue, and it was then, under the first emperor Augustus (27 BC–AD 14), that the whole country began to be called *Italia*.

The derivation of *Italia* is not certain, but the current favourite is that Greeks arriving in the deep south were impressed by the area's fertility, particularly its calves – for which we are told the Greek name was *witalos* (→ Oscan dialect *viteliu* and Latin *vitulus*). That, we are told, became *Italia*.

Another story is that an early king called Italus, master of the toe of Italy, expanded his power over the region and began to call it after himself.

PROTECTING THE SECRET NAME OF ROME

Romulus and Remus were sons of the war god Mars; they were suckled by a wolf. Romans were rather pleased by this story about their origins because it explained their love of war. What it did not do was explain why Rome was called *Roma*. So when they learned that

Greeks associated *Roma* with the Greek word for 'strength', *rhômê* (ῥώμη), they were happy to accept the connection.

However, Pliny the Elder said that Rome 'had another name, which it is sinful to mention except in ceremonies of sacred mysteries. When Valerius Soranus gave away the name which was kept secret for excellent reasons of state security, he soon paid the penalty.' Infuriatingly, Valerius did not tell us. But he did write a (now lost) work about guardian protective spirits (*Tutelae*, p. 119); he might well have named the protective spirit of Rome there.

Anyway, later Romans tried to guess what this name might be. The Greek *Erôs* (Ἔρως, 'Love') was one suggestion, because in Latin that was *amor*, i.e. *Roma*, reversed; *Flora*, a goddess of flowers, was another; and *Diva Angerona* another: she was a goddess whose statue in Rome had her mouth bound, or her finger to her lips.

EVOKING THE DEITY

But why should Romans need a secret name for their protective deity? The theory was that, before one attacked a city, one would invite the gods who protected it to leave, assuring them that they would be given an honoured welcome by the conquering army. This process was called *evocatio*, from the Latin *evoco*, 'I summon out'. But you could do that successfully only if you knew their names. A deity whose name was not known could not be evoked and would presumably stay and defend his/her city to the last.

THE CITY OF ROME

The Latin for 'city' was *urbs* ('urban', etc.); it also stood for 'Rome' (compare 'the City', which means the financial zone of London). According to Romans, only city-dwellers could be *urbanus*, 'urbane' (i.e. sophisticated, witty, smart). The Greek king Pyrrhus once heard that people had been talking disrespectfully of him at dinner. Challenging them, he was told it was nothing to what they would have said, had not the wine run out. Pyrrhus fell about laughing at this '*urbanus* justification of their drunken behaviour' (for which the Latin was *crapula*, which led to our 'crapulous').

FROM REPUBLIC TO EMPIRE

We always think of Rome as the ultimate top-down society. But that was not the way it presented itself. From 509–31 BC, Rome was a republic.

Res publica, whence our 'republic', meant literally 'the public's possession/property/business'. A sense of common ownership of the state underlay the term. Army standards and many inscriptions were marked 'SPQR', or *Senatus Populusque Romanus* ('The Senate and the Roman People'), confirming the relationship between ruler (the *Senatus*) and ruled. Cicero talked of the Roman *people* as 'master of kings, conqueror and ruler of all nations'.

From 31 BC to its technical demise in AD 476 in the West (not the East), the Roman Empire was the *imperium Romanum*, the 'command' or 'dominion' exercised by the Romans through the Roman emperor – *imperator* (→ 'imperial').

PEOPLE AND *PLEBS*

This sense of common ownership of the state emerges in the Latin *populus*, an almost political term implying 'people as the state'. Our idea of a state – derived from Latin *status*, 'posture, stature, condition, situation, rank' – is an entity *distinct* from those who inhabit it. Our 'state' has an absolute authority and powers and an identity all of its own; these remain constant, however much the population changes. This was not the Roman idea at all.

Plebs, on the other hand, was related to Greek *plêthos* (πληθος), 'crowd' (→ our 'plethora', literally 'crowds') and Latin *plenus*, 'crowded, full'. It always meant a general 'body of people'. So in Latin there was no such thing as a single 'pleb'; one pleb would be a *plebeius*, 'plebeian'.

PLEBISCITES

Politically, the *plebs* were those whose tribes in early Rome (traditionally 753–508 BC) did not provide advisers to the king. When the last king was driven out and Rome became a republic, those 'patrician' advisers, as they were called (from *pater* [*patr-*], 'father'), formed the Senate; and the early years of the new republic were characterized by conflict between the patricians and the *plebs* on the subject of political and social equality. The historian Livy made a plebeian protest to a patrician:

> Why don't you pass a law to stop a plebeian living next to a patrician, or walking down the same street, or going to the same dinner party, or standing beside you in the same forum?

The establishment in 494 BC of special plebeian assemblies with their own tribunes evened up the game. In 287 BC resolutions passed by the assembly of the *plebs* were given the formal force of law, making them binding on all citizens. Such a law was called a *plebiscitum*, *scitum* meaning 'resolution, decree, ordinance'. The *sci-* stem here meant 'get to know, ascertain' (→ 'science'), and therefore 'approve'. The resolution, in other words, had been thoroughly worked over by the plebeian assembly and approved by it, giving it its official status.

By the time of the Late Republic, plebeian families were on a par with everyone else. Famous Romans of plebeian family included Pompey and Cicero. It was all part of the state's slow movement towards a political and social order acceptable to all.

DREGS OF THE WORLD

That said, all was not necessarily peace and light between the various groupings. For the historian Tacitus, the *plebs* were *sordida* (see p. 218); for the statesman Cicero, in a letter referring disparagingly to Romans unsupportive of his generally traditional viewpoint, they were the *faex urbis*, 'scum of the city'. *Faex* (*faec-*) meant 'lees, suspended solid matter or impurities', and is the source of our 'faeces'. Romans, as all people everywhere at all times, were used to making judgements about, and so discriminating *between*, people, places, actions, and so on, and deciding some were good and some bad.

DISCRIMINATION

Discrimen, the source of our 'discrimination', was originally a spatial and temporal term. It meant a separating line, or structure, partition;

a parting in the hair (!); an interval in time. It then came to mean 'point in which things differ' and so the 'power of making distinctions'. The judgement a Roman made could be negative or positive, but *discrimen* in itself was a quite neutral term (in fact it comes from *discerno*, 'I distinguish', source of our 'discernment').

'Discrimination' as a condemnatory term came into use in the slavery debates in the late nineteenth century, and now seems the dominant sense of the word. Indeed, today's use of 'discrimination' seems to signal another meaning of the Latin *discrimen*: 'crisis, dangerous situation with much at stake'.

ORDER, ORDER

Our word 'order' derives from Latin *ordior*, 'I place in rows'; the noun *ordo* (*ordin-*) originally meant a thread on a loom, and then a row of something, e.g. seats at the games. The word *ordo* went on to cover 'a rank, standing, position, an assigned position, class, spatial arrangement; connected sequence, order of succession, professional body'.

All these were words suggestive of ordered rules and structures. And when you *order* someone, you are telling them to get themselves in the right position or rank, the position that the rules, or at least your rules, would demand that they be in – all part of the endless search for 'systems so perfect that no one will ever need to be good' (T. S. Eliot). Roman enthusiasm for order was epitomized in their class system and in their commitment to legal process (see p. 79).

THE CLASS SYSTEM

From early on in the Republic, it seems, Romans were divided into seven classes (singular *classis*, source of our 'class') by wealth, i.e. the property they owned, to determine:

(i)   into which *classis* they fell for voting purposes;
(ii) into which military rank they fell, by the amount of weaponry they could contribute; and
(iii) how much they had to pay, if necessary, in property tax each year.

The consequence of this *classis* system was an attempt to place an *ordo* on society, in which power resided with those in the top *classes*. When the patricians and the *plebs* came to argue about their relative places in society (see p. 32), it was 'a battle of the orders'.

THE ASSIDUOUS EQUESTRIAN

Only the rich owned horses, Latin *equus* (plural *equi*). If you were one of those, it is likely that you were in the top 1 or 2 per cent of Roman society and owned property worth 400,000 sesterces. As such, you were classified as an *eques* (plural *equites*), traditionally translated 'knight'. It was from this grouping that senators would be chosen, as long as you had property worth one million sesterces.

If you thought an 'assiduous' person was diligent and hardworking, a Roman would only partly agree. *Assiduus* meant 'settled on the land, landowning', i.e. very rich. Since Romans liked making distinctions, the term was contrasted with those at the very bottom of the heap: the *proletarii*. These were the poorest in society, who were good for only one thing – producing *proles*: children.

There is an important point here: from Roman times until relatively recently, the economic well-being of children depended mostly on how much land (if any) their parents left them by inheritance. Today, by contrast, education and training are for most people the wealth-providers.

SUFFRAGE AND VOTES

The Latin for a vote was *suffragium*, whence our 'suffrage(tte)'. Its derivation is quite obscure. In time, it also took on the meaning 'influence on behalf of a candidate for election', and even 'bribe'! On hearing of the death of his young friend Avitus, Pliny the Younger mourned the lost potential and remembered 'the time he took up the senator's broad [purple] stripe in my house, my first, and now last, *support for his election*, our talks and discussions'.

Our 'vote' derives from Latin *votum*, which bore no relation to voting at all: it meant 'vow, offering, prayer, pious wish'. Well, perhaps *some* relation.

THE NORM

Normality is a condition much to be desired, and the purpose of Rome's imposition of *ordo* was to encourage it. *Norma* in Latin meant 'right-angle, square', used by builders, carpenters and surveyors to get things correctly and so securely lined up. It came to be used as an image to describe standard patterns of behaviour or practice, rules and regulations. Cicero could always use it against opponents: he mocked a descendant of the famously rigorous Cato the Elder for always ignoring the world's complexities and 'reducing life to the fixed *norma* of a system'. At the same time, Romans like Cicero always felt a deep respect for *mos maiorum*, 'ancestral custom, convention', hallowed by age, not system.

Today, big companies dodging taxes would say they were playing by the strict *norma* of the law; we might quote *mos maiorum* and talk of fairness, or the right way to do things.

'O TEMPORA, O MORES'

'The times [we live in]! The values [we live by]!' Cicero's famous exclamation was uttered during his assault on Catiline, who was threatening to overthrow the Roman state. *Mos* (*mor-*) meant 'the way we do things, way of life; inherited customs, traditions, conventions; habit, character, disposition; style'. It is the source of our 'morals, morality'. Cicero was linking time and ethics, a wish for a stable world whose values did not change.

In Latin, *mos* was associated with ancestors: *mos maiorum* meant 'traditions of the ancestors' (*maior* gives us 'major', literally 'greater': one's ancestors were defined as 'greater men'). There was something time-honoured about *mos*. In 92 BC, the censors summed it up: 'Everything new, that is done contrary to the *usage and the customs of our ancestors*, seems not to be right.' Vague that utterance may be, but it sums up the *aura* ('breeze, air, breath, aroma') around the idea of *mos*. It was felt to be the glue that held society together: consensus was at the heart of it.

Good Latin word, *consensus*: it derives from *consentio* (*consens-*), 'I share in a feeling, am in harmony/unison/sympathy with'.

MAGISTRATES

A *magistratus* bore no relation to our 'magistrate'. He was an elected official. *Magis* meant 'greater'; *magister* meant 'greater person' (usually 'teacher'); and the *-atus* ending indicated an office or function. So a *magistratus* was a 'person in a greater office, with greater official power'. It is ironic that our elected officials in Parliament are called 'ministers', the Latin *minus* meaning 'lesser'.

SENATUS

Senatus is a term that seems to imply rule by the old: it derives from *senex*, 'old man' + *-atus*, an ending indicating office or function (→ our 'consulate'). Senators were also referred to as *patres*, 'fathers'. But one could become a senator by the age of about thirty, and there seems to have been an unwritten agreement that by about sixty one was allowed to go back to private life (there was no concept of 'retirement').

Pliny the Younger wrote to his friend Pomponius Bassus: 'It is our duty to commit our youth and adulthood to our country, but our last years are our own. The laws themselves suggest this, in permitting one greater in years to withdraw into leisure [*otium*, see p. 106].' What age that might have been is not clear: sources suggest sixty to sixty-five. But there was no compulsion about it, though the physical and mental infirmities of old age, especially in the ancient world, probably encouraged the elderly not to make fools of themselves before their younger colleagues.

Romans, of course, grew as decrepit and enfeebled in old age as we do. Latin *decrepitus* derives from *crepo* (*crepit-*), 'I clatter, creak, crack, crackle', and the *de-* prefix here means 'completely'. 'Houses *creak* before they fall down', said the philosopher Seneca. So do humans.

TRIBUNE

It may be that Latin *tribus*, 'tribe', was connected with Latin *tres*, 'three' (→ our 'tri-' prefix, as in 'tripartite', 'tripod' and 'trident' with its three teeth [Latin *dens, dent-*]). If so, the word finds its origin in the three traditional ethnic divisions which made up early Rome. A *tribunus* was originally a leader of one of those tribes; and when the plebeian assembly was set up (see p. 33), a *tribunus* of the *plebs* was appointed to act as its official representative with legal powers to protect the *plebs* from consular might and to veto senatorial legislation (Latin *veto*, 'I forbid'). Today a 'tribune' is seen as a champion of people's rights.

AEDILE

The Roman *aedilis* was the *magistratus* in charge of cleaning, repairing and overseeing the streets, markets and buildings of Rome. *Aedes* was Latin for a 'room' or 'temple', and in the plural (same word) a 'house' or 'home' (a collection of rooms). So the *aedile* was a 'houseman'. *Aedes* seems to be associated with a Greek word meaning 'flame, burn' – perhaps referring to the centre of the home, the hearth (see p. 61). Latin *aedifico* meant 'I build', from *aedes* + *fico*, 'I make'. We get 'edifice' from this word, and also 'edify', in the sense of building character (see p. 132).

FESTIVE SPECTACLES

One other area of responsibility for the *aedile* was the organization of the games during Roman holidays, i.e. festivals for the gods. *Festus* was the word for a holiday in a god's honour (giving us 'festival', 'feast', etc. – it is related to *fanum*, 'shrine'). Putting on magnificent shows on such occasions was a sure-fire vote-winner with the people, and could do the up-and-coming *aedile* a great deal of political good. *Spectaculum* was the word used of a sight or spectacular performance (*specto*, 'I watch, spectate'). The seven wonders of the world were all *spectacula* (plural).

QUAESTOR

Quaero (*quaest-*) in Latin meant 'I try to find, look out for, seek'. It provides us with 'question', 'enquire', 'inquisition' and so on. Originally, it seems that the *magistratus* known as *quaestor* was part of a criminal investigation board, but over time his role became a mainly financial one. *Quaestors* often accompanied provincial governors abroad to run their finance offices, but could also serve in a judicial capacity too.

PRAETOR

The *praetor* was the *magistratus* who 'led, went ahead' (*prae-eo*, 'I go in advance'). It was primarily a military term, as in leading the attack, and was in fact the original word for what was to become *consul*, the top office of all. The praetor's main function in Rome became judicial: he ran the legal services.

We talk today of leading politicians having a 'praetorian guard'.

This refers back to the Roman emperor's highly prestigious special force garrisoned in Rome to 'go before' and so protect the emperor's person, and also to act as his eyes and ears in case of trouble.

CONSUL

The top *magistratus*, of whom there were always two (Romans, after their experience of kings, traditionally feared single rulers), was *consul*. Its derivation is not entirely certain, but it may be connected with *consilium*, a noun meaning 'discussion, advice, decision, diplomacy, strategy, good sense'. All these were activities or qualities vital for a head of state who had to co-operate with the other consul (→ our 'counsel'). In war, they were in supreme military command; in peace, they had extensive administrative and legal powers.

Do not confuse 'counsel' with 'council'. The source of 'council' is Latin *concilium*, 'assembly, association, company', itself derived from *concilio*, 'I bring together, unite', as in 'conciliation'. *Reconcilio* meant 'I bring back into agreement, harmony; re-establish, restore'. Cicero wrote to a friend, whose decrees had seemed to attack the interests of the ever-sensitive *publicani* (see p. 105), begging him to 'do all in your power to *reconcile* them to you, or at least mollify them'. He knew what political trouble these tax-collectors could cause if anyone tried to protect the provincials from their depredations.

CURATOR

In today's world, a 'curator' is someone who selects/organizes/ arranges/displays anything, from a lobster roll to stuff on the web (where everything is now 'content', implying it contains something, and 'content strategists' toil selflessly night and day in the urgent task of 'curating' it all).

In the ancient world a *curator* was someone with a proper job incurring heavy responsibilities: he was in charge of public works. There were *curatores* of the corn and olive-oil supplies, the river Tiber, public funds, public buildings, roads, aqueducts and public games. A senatorial decree (AD 11) for maintaining the water supply survives, showing the powers and duties of such boards. This system was adopted across the Empire, to the great benefit of local communities.

Curatores could also be appointed to deal with specific crises. In AD 79 Mount Vesuvius erupted, laying waste to the land all around it. The emperor Titus appointed *curatores* chosen from among ex-consuls 'to take charge of the restoration of Campania'. Some of the work was funded by the sale of the property of those who died and left no heirs. Our 'volcano' derives from the Roman god of fire *Vulcanus*; and 'crater' via Latin *crater(a)* from Greek *kratêr* (κρατηρ), meaning a large bowl in which wine was mixed with water for distribution into cups, and also the mouth of a volcano.

Cura in Latin is the origin of our 'care' (compare 'manicure', care for the *manus*, 'hand'). A 'sinecure' is a job or position *sine cura*, 'without care', i.e. money for old rope. 'Sincere' is often held to derive from *sine cera*, 'without wax', i.e. the real thing (the reference is to the Roman habit of mending broken pots with wax and selling them on as if new). This is not true, alas ('alas', from Latin *a, lassum* via French, 'ah, weary, wretched!', → 'lassitude').

THE IMAGE OF THE NOBILITY

One indication of the control that the wealthy exerted over Roman society was the regularity with which their families held the consulship. Such families were called *nobilis*, meaning 'generally known' and so 'renowned, famous'. Over any reasonable period of time, 70 to 90 per cent of consuls would come from noble families.

This caused real problems for any *novus homo* ('new man', → 'novel', 'innovate'), i.e. of non-noble family. Cicero was one such, becoming consul in 63 BC and boasting about it for ever more. But the noble families were well aware of their superiority.

In 63 BC Cicero was attacked by Metellus Nepos, of the very noble Metelli family. Cicero, as consul, replied in kind. Then Nepos' brother Metellus Celer stepped in with a letter, as follows:

> I would have expected, given our mutual interests and our restored good-will, that I would not be damaged with such derision, nor would my brother Metellus be threatened in his person and property by you because of what he said. Even if respect for him himself was not enough to restrain you, the dignity of our family and my services to you and to the state ought to have been enough to hold you back... Since you have done all this quite unreasonably and without the benignity due to our ancestors, do not be surprised if you live to regret it. I had not expected such inconstancy in you towards me and the members of my family.

Ouch! There are parallels between ancient Romans and the modern Mafia.

EXPERIENCE OF HIGH OFFICE

Over time Romans became relatively relaxed about the background of those who held office. The only condition was: were they and their families committed to the Roman way of doing things? So emperors came from all over the Empire. Septimius Severus (emperor AD 193–211) was of North African descent and shpoke Latin with a shlight local acshent, so he may have pronounched hish own name Sheptimius Sheverush. It did not hold him back.

Our 'office' derives from Latin *officium*, which basically meant a 'beneficial act or service carried out as an obligation or duty' (*ops* [*op-*], 'help, resources' + *-ficio*, 'I make'). It expanded into meaning one's 'job, function, task', but that sense of duty about it was never entirely lost. Cicero's dialogue *De officiis* ('On Duties') was a discussion of the proper obligations of the state and the individual.

Unlike today's politicians, Roman 'magistrates' (see p. 38) had in theory to be elected to, and work their way through, a series of highly practical administrative posts in order to reach the top, i.e. become consul. Anyone who reached the top would, at one stage or other, have had to run the city of Rome; learned financial administration at home and possibly abroad; and overseen Rome's legal services. From the moment they put their foot on the lowest rung, they would also have been a member of the Senate. So by the time they reached the top job, they would have built up a huge range of contacts and experience in responsible positions, all highly relevant to the functioning of the state.

Our words 'experience', 'experiment' and 'expert' all derive from the Latin *experior* (*expert-*), 'I try out, put to the test', related to the Greek πειρα (*peira*), 'an attempt', which gives us 'empirical' ('based on experience'). Romans were put thoroughly to the test before being entrusted with the job of high office.

ROMAN PRIORITIES

The great Scipio Africanus, conqueror of Hannibal, gave a sense of how a Roman *nobilis* conceived of the route to power. It all began from *innocentia*, 'freedom from guilt, integrity'. He said:

> *ex* [from] *innocentia nascitur* ['is born'] *dignitas, ex dignitate honor, ex honore imperium* ['the right to give order and expect to be obeyed'], *ex imperio libertas*

The verb *nascor* (*nat-*) meant 'I am born, come into being', and is the source of our 'nature, native, nativity', etc. *Dignitas* meant 'fitness for a task; rank; respect'; *honor* meant 'marks of esteem', especially 'high public office'; and *libertas* that freedom which meant you were your own master and no one could tell you what to do.

One of the things Romans feared about Julius Caesar was that in his position as *dictator* his power became such that the *libertas* of the wealthy classes was being terminally threatened. Latin *dictator* derives from *dicto*: 'I say repeatedly; I dictate' (implying 'and you listen and take it down'). A *dictator* was a legal *magistratus*, appointed in Rome only at times of emergency. But Caesar's ambition seemed to extend well beyond that. As Cicero saw when he wrote to his friend Atticus in 54 BC, well before Caesar became *dictator* for life in 44 BC and was assassinated a month later: 'Hurry back to Rome and experience the empty husk of our old Roman republic! See bribes being openly paid and sniff the smell of dictatorship.'

AMBITION

Getting to the top of the greasy pole (i.e. consul) was every ancient politician's aim. To reach that goal in a world where communications consisted of talking face to face or writing (see p. 155), he had to spend a long time on the hoof.

Latin *ambitus* derived from *ambio*, 'I go round and round, canvassing for support'. Cicero said of elections that 'the public are moved by favours, yield to pleas and elect those by whom they are most assiduously canvassed'. But there was a sting in the tail: *ambitus* did indeed mean 'desire for advancement', but also 'bribery, corruption, graft'. Cicero pointed out the difficulties when such cases came to court: 'for on a charge of *ambitus*, it is rarely given that generosity and kindness can be distinguished from graft and hand-outs.'

Someone standing for election was a *candidatus*, whence our 'candidate'. It derives from Latin *candidus* (our 'candid') meaning 'white, fair, lucky, good-natured, innocent': Roman candidates wore specially whitened togas. In late October 54 BC Cicero wrote to his friend Atticus saying, 'all the *candidati* for consul are being prosecuted for *ambitus*'!

A CIVILIZED WORLD

Whatever the trials and tribulations of the wealthy, for the average Roman in the forum what counted was citizenship. This was automatically conferred if you were the son or daughter of a Roman father and mother; or of parents with the right to produce citizen children, e.g. a Roman father marrying a foreign woman who enjoyed such a privilege.

The Latin for 'citizen' was *civis* (→ 'civic', 'civilization'). Appropriately enough, it is linguistically associated with Proto-Indo-European words meaning 'home, family, marriage'. Citizenship bestowed on sons a range of rights, including voting rights and standing for office; and on daughters no political rights but the right to marry a citizen, demand a divorce, own property, engage in business and partake in various features of public life, especially religious rituals. 'Divorce' derives from *divortium*, 'where a road, river branches; turning point; incompatibility' – it comes from the same source as 'diversion', which could be one way of looking at it.

Romans saw property rights as central to the workings of a civilized, united world. 'Property' derives from *proprius* – 'one's own absolutely or in perpetuity'. Cicero said:

> There are those who pose as friends of the people, and who for that reason try to have laws passed to drive owners out of their homes, or propose that money given as a loan should be given as a gift to those who borrowed it. Such people are undermining the foundations of the republic. First of all, they are destroying harmony, which cannot exist when money is taken away from one party and handed over to another; and second, they do away with fairness, which is utterly subverted, if the rights of property are not respected. For, as I said above, it is the special function of the state and the city to guarantee to every man the free and undisturbed control of his own particular property.

CENSORS AND CENSUS

We tend to associate 'censor' with 'censorship'. For a Roman a *censor* was primarily an official appointed to ensure the official state *ordo* was kept. Every five years, all free males were required to present themselves before the censors. There they publicly stated their full name, age, name of their father/*patronus* (see p. 71), place of residence, occupation and amount of their property. On that basis they would be assigned to a *classis*. Their wives and children would not be included in the registration, though their existence would be stated.

Further – and more in line with our view of a censor – the censors had a duty of moral oversight of the population. Anyone who did not seem to be living up to the required standards, in public or in private, had a note made of it and put by his name: *nota*, 'distinguishing mark, brand, stamp; grade, class'. We would call it a *stigma*, Greek στιγμα taken straight into Latin, meaning a 'tattoo with a hot needle on runaway slaves and criminals; general mark of condemnation'. A senator who did not come up to scratch was removed from the Senate.

Since censors had a detailed understanding of individuals' situations, they also leased out government contracts for work, and had control over state-owned assets and collected revenue from them. Such contracts would go to private partnerships of the wealthy (see p. 103). No surprise that *censor* derives from *censeo*, 'I give as a considered opinion, evaluate, assess'.

DELEGATING POWER

In Julius Caesar's account of his conquest of Gaul, one man (apart from Caesar) stood out above all others for his military ability: Titus Labienus. He had made a career in politics up to the rank of *praetor*, but joined Caesar's army in the rank of *legatus*; indeed, he is the only *legatus* named by Caesar during his first campaign in Gaul (in 58 BC), and pulled off brilliant victories throughout the campaign, as Caesar reports.

The post of *legatus* was no demotion (indeed, in 52 BC Caesar made Labienus governor of part of Gaul). It had developed from the second century BC, when it became the custom for a provincial governor or general to take with him to his province senators to act as back-up when he needed it. Derived from *lex* (*leg-*), 'law', the *legatus* (→ our 'legate', 'legation') was someone legally commissioned to act on his leader's behalf, either in charge of troops or ships, or as an ambassador or envoy.* He was a man, in other words, to whom a governor's or general's powers were *delegated*, i.e. legally entrusted away from (*de-*) the governor himself. Such positions were much sought after by young senators making their way up the greasy pole. In Gaul, Labienus was effectively Caesar's second-in-command. Under the emperor Augustus, the position of *legatus* became one of great authority, e.g. imperial governor.

---

* A 'legacy' is something *legally entrusted* to you in a will.

DIPLOMAS

One of the roles the *legatus* fulfilled was that of what we call a diplomat (a term that emerged in the eighteenth century). The Greek δίπλωμα, Latin *diploma*, meant 'folded in two'. It could be found in the works of the philosopher Aristotle describing the parallel streams of the Milky Way, and in the medical writings of Soranus evoking the position of the foetus in the mother's womb. It was usually an official letter of some sort. It could be a receipt for the payment of taxes. It could be a licence to use the public postal system. Mostly, though, it was a recommendation of this sort: 'I am pleased to inform you that the bearer of this letter is a *bona fide* Roman citizen and would be pleased if you would allow him to go wherever he wants.' In other words, it was a passport.

PROTOCOL

Nowadays, a protocol is usually a record of an original diplomatic agreement, or a document forming the basis of a legal treaty, or a set of official procedures. It derives from Greek *prôtokollon* (πρωτοκολλον) – the *first* of the glued sheets of a scroll (*prôtos*, 'first', *kollô* [κολλω], 'I glue'). In the ancient world, it listed and authenticated the content of the scroll. The emperor Justinian (*c.* AD 482–565), concerned about forgery, passed a law stating:

> We also add to the present law that lawyers shall not draw up
> legal summaries on any other sheet than the one [called the
> *prôtokollon*] which bears at the head the title of 'Our Most

Glorious Count of the Imperial Largesses'; the date of the execution of the document; and whatever else it is customary to write there. Lawyers must not abridge the protocol.

The connectivity protein 'collagen' and 'collage' all derive from *kollô* (see p. 148).

SOCIETY

INTRODUCTION

Romans had a strong sense of the importance of their past and its influence upon the present. They believed that the values of their ancestors (*mos maiorum*) were also their values and would be their children's too, and were perhaps summed up best in the word *pietas*: commitment to the preservation and glory of family, gods and Rome. Romans had 'always' been like that – and always would be. 'Her men and ancient values kept Rome standing tall', intoned the second-century BC Roman poet Ennius. That at least was the rhetoric.

Key terms underpinned that commitment. One was *virtus*: 'manliness'. The satirical poet Lucilius (second century BC), slamming the customs of his day, put it like this:

> It is *virtus* to know what is right and useful and honourable,
> What things are good, and what are evil...
> To be the enemy and the foe of bad men and manners,
> The defender of good men and manners;

> To esteem these highly, to wish them well, to live in friendship
>   with them;
> And moreover, to consider the interest of one's country first;
> Then those of parents; and finally to put our own interests in the
>   third and last place.

From this flowed good faith towards others (*fides*, being true to one's word and meeting one's obligations) and *gratia*, the regard for others which generated co-operation between individuals and families for mutual benefit; and it resulted in *dignitas*, the respect one gained in the eyes of society from living by these values.

These were, of course, the values of the wealthy great and good, which dominate surviving literature. They were probably shared by the moderately well-off too: doctors, the better rank of soldiers, teachers, architects, merchants, artisans. The poor may have felt differently. As far as we can tell from folk tales, fables, popular sayings and so on, it was a hierachical world, in which gods might be just but did not always show it; the future was quite unpredictable; inexplicable changes of fortune were to be expected; and man's prospects for improvement were pretty limited. Conflict was the natural order of things, for resources and status. Though gods were committed to justice and good faith, man's best hope was looking pragmatically to his own interests, maintaining his position in the pecking order, keeping his friends close and his head down: with luck, success might breed success. It was not a matter of *being* good, but rather of making decisions good enough to enable you at least to survive, and (with luck) thrive, usually by being good *at* something.

This was not a society characterized by opportunity and aspiration – except for the very wealthy, powerful few. What slaves thought of their lot we do not know. Freed slaves, however, who automatically became Roman citizens, showed no inclination not to own slaves themselves.

For the poor living in the city, it was a matter of making a living out of whatever they could turn their hands to: the rich were there to be served – serve them in any way you could. Those who served the rich also need services – all those greasy spoons and eateries, for people on the go. If one had no trade of one's own, one turned to helping a blacksmith, butcher, launderer, carpenter, baker or potter; building; serving in shops or the docks; portering; prostitution; labouring – whatever.

As for peasant life in the country, we do have one (anonymous) Roman account of the day – or at least morning – in the life of a peasant, Simylus, composed about AD 15 not by a farmer but by a cultured poet. He was a poor tenant farmer, with just one acre (most families would hope for anything between two and ten acres). Whatever they could make out of their smallholding, such people would supplement earnings by working during off-peak times, labouring, perhaps acting as tenants on other farms, or working as craftsmen in town.

Simylus wakes early. No switching on a light: he gropes for the fire, puffs its embers awake – he must keep a fire burning all the time if he wants light in the morning and heat or a cooking facility in the day – and fetches grain from his cupboard. This is precious: it must be locked away against need. He grinds it into flour, and calls his slave, an African woman Scybale, to fetch wood for the fire, heat cold water and bake the flour into bread. 'He has no meat-racks, no hard salt ham or bacon slices curing.' This is real poverty. But he has a small garden, and makes a pesto out of garlic, salt, cheese and herbs to put on the bread which Scybale has now baked. Then off he goes to plough his field.

The peasant's aim was to be self-sufficient. To achieve that, he needed a little left over which he could sell or exchange for the other goods and services required for subsistence: buying salt, for example, mending and buying implements, or paying rent or interest on a debt. The poet tells us that Simylus' garden served this purpose: every week he took its produce to market – cabbages, beet, sorrel, mallow, radishes – to make what surplus he could from it.

At the same time, the peasant had to adopt tactics that would see him through periods of unexpected shortage. Since staple cereals like grain could keep for up to two years, Simylus had a store of grain, but kept it locked away, so precious was it. Meat did not play any part in his diet. But if real famine (mercifully rare) did set in, elite city-dwellers would simply commandeer whatever they could, leaving the peasant to the grim consequences of a diet of twigs, tree shoots, bulbs, roots and grasses.

To paint the wider picture, precious metals apart, all the wealth of the ancient world derived from what the land could produce. This fed the population and kept numbers up. Further, even Simylus, at the limit of survival, could produce some surplus; and this surplus could be taxed by local authorities ('10% of annual surplus' spread over a defined area was a typical demand), collected and returned to the central treasury. In the case of the Roman Empire, surplus from its provinces was taxed in cash or kind and used (among much else) to pay for the Roman army. The wealthy, who owned huge acreages of land, made their vast fortunes by renting it out and selling the surplus. So Simylus' activities were replicated across the ancient world, on a smaller or larger scale, and kept the whole system going.

Farming the land was one operation, pasturing another. The encyclopedist Varro described the sort of work this entailed:

> For herds of cattle, use older men; for flocks of sheep or goats, use boys. But in either case, the herdsmen who stay in the mountain pastures should be sturdier than those who return every day to the sheepfolds in the villa. Thus, in the woodland areas you may see young men, usually armed; but close to the villa, boys and even girls tend the flocks...

> The herdsmen must be forced to stay in the pasture all day, to let the herds pasture together during the day, but to spend the night alone, each with his own herd. Neither old men nor young boys can easily tolerate the difficult terrain and the steep and rugged mountains, although herdsmen must endure these hardships, especially herdsmen who follow cattle and goats which love to pasture on sheer cliffs or in thick forests...

> In choosing herdsmen, examine their physique. They should be sturdy, swift-footed, quick, with good reflexes, men who not only can follow a herd, but also can protect it from predatory animals and from thieves; men who can lift loads onto pack animals; men who can run fast and hurl a javelin.

It is easy to become romantic about the farmer's life. There was nothing romantic here for the shepherd or herdsman, out in all weathers, in rough terrain, with little in the way of companionship. This was usually slaves' work, so disagreeable it was.

Quite apart from the danger of thieves, there were Bullingdon Club-style jokers to contend with, in this case the famous emperor and philosopher Marcus Aurelius, who wrote in a letter:

> When my father had got home from the vineyards, I, as usual, mounted my horse and set off along the road, and had gone a little way when I met a flock of sheep, all huddled together in the road, as happens when there is little room, with four dogs and two shepherds; that was all. Then one of the shepherds, seeing our group, said to his mate, 'Keep an eye on those riders. They always like a bit of rustling.' Hearing that, I dug the spurs into my horse and galloped right into the flock. Frightened out of their wits, they ran helter-skelter, scattering in all directions, bleating. The shepherd threw his crook at us. It hit my attendant behind me, but we got clear off.

The ancient world was an unforgiving place.

THE FAMILY

By *familia*, Romans did not quite mean 'family' in our sense. They meant rather 'household', i.e. the relatives, freedmen, slaves and property that were under the control of one man – 'the father of the family', the *pater familias*. He had absolute power over the disposal of the family and its assets. However doddery their father, his sons, however old, remained technically dependent on him until he died. *Familia* was related to *famulus*, 'slave', and *familia* was also used of slave gangs. This hinted at the power that the *pater familias* wielded. That said, in our texts he was more often seen as 'estate holder' than tyrant.

The *pater familias* could also be called the *dominus*, a word derived from *domus*, 'house, home' (→ 'domestic'), with overtones of 'lord and master'. Cicero punned on the connection, saying that 'the *dominus* should bring honour to his *domus*, not the *domus* to its *dominus*'. Our 'danger', amazingly, derives, via French, from *dominus*, relating to the authority of the master of the house and the danger of crossing it.

PATERNAL *GENIUS*

The *pater* also enshrined in his person the 'genius' of the family. For us, a genius is a person of outstanding capacities far beyond the reach of ordinary people, in whatever field of endeavour. For Romans, *genius* derived from a stem meaning 'inborn' and meant primarily the male spirit of the *gens*, or family unit, existing in the *pater familias* and passed down the generations. It was a sort of personal guardian deity. The *genius* of the emperor was worshipped. The emperor Caligula, we are told, could inflict horrific (Latin *horreo*, 'I shudder, shiver, bristle') punishments on those who did not swear by his *genius*. Even places and corporations could be held to have a *genius* within them. Our 'ingenious, ingenuity' derive from Latin *ingenium*, a word emphasizing the 'natural abilities, talent, intellect' born *in* someone.

But whatever a father's *genius*, the key to a successful family was the wife's capacity to produce children.

WOMEN'S FERTILITY

Latin *fero* meant 'I bear, carry, produce', all very relevant to a *fertilis* ('fertile') woman. On her depended the continuance of the family, and so of citizen children, and so of the Roman state and the worship of its gods. Given the high death rate at childbirth and in the first years after, a Roman mother would have to be regularly pregnant to be certain of producing the two to three children that would survive and keep up the population.

Nevertheless, the word for 'blessed', *felix* (→ 'felicitous'), applied to her: it is related to *femina* ('woman'), *fecundus* (our 'fecund'), *fetus* ('foetus') and *fello* ('I suck milk').

Our 'effete' today is used to mean general languid decadence and moral decay; in Latin *effetus* meant literally 'out-wombed', i.e. 'worn out (*ex-*, 'out, away') by bearing offspring'.

ADOPTION

If children were lacking, or had turned out to be unimpressive, it was very common indeed to adopt them from another family to ensure the survival of the line, or to give it a boost. Latin *optio* meant 'the power to choose' and *adoptio* 'choosing someone to come *to* one's family'. As lawyers said, 'adoption imitates nature'; it was as if the adoptee had been born into the family.

What is so striking about Roman adoption is that it had nothing to do with homeless children or those who had lost parents. It was all about helping the family to succeed. So it was adolescents and adults, not babies, who were adopted by agreement with other families. Childless aristocrats, even emperors, used the system.

Augustus, Tiberius, Caligula, Nero, Trajan, Hadrian and Marcus Aurelius were all adopted. The system was clearly not entirely foolproof.

HEART OF THE FAMILY

The religious centre of the family was its *focus* – its domestic hearth, or fireplace. This was not only the place where the cooking was done; it was also the 'focal' point where the personal household deity (*lar familiaris*) was worshipped. As such, *focus* in Latin came to mean 'household, family' as well as a sacrificial hearth or altar. Our phrase 'hearth and home' reflects a similar convergence.

SLAVERY

How many families possessed a slave or slaves is hard to say. They may have made up 30 to 40 per cent of the population. We hear that the fabulously rich Crassus had 800. A slave was a *servus* – its derivation is unknown – and its associated verb *servio* meant 'I serve a master, am politically subject, am subservient to'. Our idea of 'service' (→ 'servitude') does not quite have these connotations, though the old idea of being 'in service' perhaps did. A home-bred slave was a *verna*, which – via *vernaculus*, 'domestic, home-produced, native' – gives us our 'vernacular', one's local language.

MANUMISSION

A *servus* was a person without rights or legal status. That tells us nothing about how a slave was treated. A slave on a *latifundium* (*latus*, 'wide'; *fundus*, 'country estate, farm', see p. 75) or in the mines would endure a dreadful existence. A slave working for a family could be treated well or badly. Slaves *could* reach positions of influence because they owed their position to their master and could therefore (for the most part) be trusted. The emperor Claudius had slaves among his closest advisers. We hear of slaves acting as businessmen on their master's behalf (see p. 63).

There was certainly some incentive for a slave to *behave* well, because manumission (release from slavery) was standard – *mitto* (*miss-*), 'I release, dismiss', *manu*, 'from the (master's) hand/ authority'. The slave then became a 'freedman', i.e. a slave who had been freed (Latin *libertus*, feminine *liberta*), though without political rights; his children, however, became full citizens.

GROWING UP

There is no precise Latin word for 'baby', and there were many different theories about the life stages from then on. For example, the Roman encyclopedist Varro suggested an *infans* (*infant-*), a little child, technically unable to speak yet, covered years zero to seven, after which education began; the pre-pubertal *puer* (non-adult young boy, → 'puerile') and *puella* (young girl) covered years seven to fifteen.* The Roman then became an *adolescens*, from *adolesco* (*adult-*), 'I become mature, grow up', till thirty; a *iuvenis* (→ 'juvenile') till forty-five; a *senior* from forty-five to sixty; and a *senex* from sixty till death. Note the absence of middle age. Another account carved life into seven stages, by seven astrological signs: 0–4: Moon;

---

* Our 'pubescence' comes from Latin *pubesco*, 'I reach physical maturity'.

4–14: Mercury; 14–22: Venus; 22–41: Sun; 41–56: Mars; 56–68: Jupiter; 68–death: Saturn.

'Adultery' has nothing to do with adults. It derives from Latin *adultero* (*adulterat-*), literally 'I [go] to (*ad*) another (*alter*)'. Nor did a Roman *homo* have anything (necessarily) to do with homosexuals. 'Homosexual' (first used 1892) derives from Greek *homos* (ὁμος), 'one and the same, common, joint' + Latin *sexus*, 'gender'. *Homo* in fact is related to Latin *humanus* and meant basically 'human being' (of either sex). That it became strongly associated with males may tell one something about the Roman mindset.

DEATH MASKS

Families rejoiced in their history. It demonstrated that the gods favoured them and gave them hope that they would continue to do so. A well-known tradition of the aristocracy was the preservation of busts and portrait-masks of their ancestors (sometimes derived from death masks). These were called *imagines* (singular *imago*, from *imitor*, 'I copy, imitate') and during family funerals would be displayed with lists of their achievements and paraded in the forum – a useful reminder to those who are concerned about their 'image'. Freedmen who had made good were keen to imitate free Romans and would parade busts of their powerful patrons (*patroni*).

FREEDMEN

If a freed slave had been a member of a wealthy or productive household, he could use his skills to make good in business. If he had the skills needed by the imperial household, he could make good in politics too, in an administrative role. Under the emperor Claudius, some freedmen rose to considerable positions of power, which greatly annoyed the aristocrats. Narcissus, for example, spoke in the Senate, gave leg-ups to promising young men (e.g. the future emperor Vespasian), helped organize the invasion of Britain, and was even put in charge of a big civil-engineering project. Another of Claudius' freedmen was given an honorary praetorship!

FUNERARY RIGHTS

Our 'funeral' derives from Latin *funus* (*funer-*), 'funeral rites, corpse, death'. 'Cemetery' derives from Greek via Late Latin: a *koimêtêrion* (κοιμητηριον) was 'a room for sleeping in'. Romans used *sepulc(h)-rum* for 'grave' (→ 'sepulchre'), from Latin *sepelio*, 'I dispose of a corpse, submerge'; the Latin seems to have been associated with related words meaning 'venerate'.

Incidentally, Latin *postumus* meant 'last born'. But thanks to a Roman misunderstanding, it came to mean 'born after a father's death'. This came about because Romans imagined *postumus* arose from *post* + *humus*, 'after [the father's] burial' (→ our 'posthumous'). Note *humus*, 'ground' → 'inhume' → 'exhume'.

IMMIGRANTS

From earliest times, according to Roman tradition, citizenship had been open to non-Romans too. The explanation was that, when Rome was founded by Romulus in 753 BC, there was a general shortage of men to make a viable state. Romulus therefore welcomed in assorted riff-raff from elsewhere – slaves, exiles, paupers and debtors – with the promise of citizenship. These were 'immigrants', but in the Roman sense: *immigro* meant 'I go and take up residence', not 'I go in the hope of taking up residence'. Pliny the Younger praised the emperor Trajan for allowing new owners to take up residence in his own inherited estates, 'so that great houses no longer fall to pieces and decay'. The Latin *migro* seems to be related to a Greek word meaning 'I change places', which was used to describe moving from place to place, passing into a new condition, e.g. from death to life.

LIBERALS

Rome was remarkably liberal about extending citizenship across its empire in a number of formats from restricted to full status, and in AD 212 Caracalla extended full citizenship to all free inhabitants.

Note 'liberal': in Latin *liberalis* referred to one's status and duty as a free (*liber*) person – 'typical of a free man, obliging, generous'. Cicero said of the Greek sophist Hippias that he had all the accomplishments of a *liberalis* education: 'Geometry, music, knowledge of literature and poetry, the natural world, ethics and politics.'

EXTENDING RIGHTS

Early Rome was soon in conflict with neighbours and began extending control over them, first by conquest and then by assimilation, i.e. giving them some form of legal relationship with Rome. Two legal rights were especially valued.

The right of marriage (*connubium*) opened up Roman citizenship. This allowed a non-Roman woman to become upwardly nubile, marry a Roman male and so produce Roman children. The Latin *nubo* (*nupt-*, → 'nuptial'), 'I marry', was used of a woman, the *con(m)-* prefix meaning 'with'.

The right to engage in commerce with Rome was *commercium* (→ 'commercial'). This was vital for encouraging the expansion of trade across Italy in accordance with proper legal procedures. The Latin stem *merc-* meant 'commodity, price, sale', and was the stem of *mercennarius*, 'working for hire, someone for sale, mercenary'.*

COMMUNITIES

The Latin *munia* meant 'duties, functions'; and *communis* (*com/ cum* = 'with') meant, basically, 'shared, joint, belonging to *or* affecting everyone, sociable, obliging' (→ our 'communal'). The importance Romans placed on the idea of communal obligations and responsibilities was well illustrated by the praise the historian Livy heaped on Rome's greatest enemy Hannibal, who took on Rome in Italy, far from his home in North Africa (Carthage):

> For here he was, carrying on war in the enemy's land for thirteen years, so far from home and with very mixed fortunes, with an army made up not of his own citizens but a mixture of the dregs of all nations; with men who had in common no law, no custom, no language; and differing from each other in character, clothing, arms, religious rites, sacred observances, even one might almost say in their gods. Yet he somehow *bound them together by a single*

---

* The Mercedes brand name derives from Spanish 'Mércedès', the name of the daughter of one of the founders of the company. It means 'Mercies' (→ 'Mary, our Lady of Mercies'), and derives from the *merc-* stem because – through Vulgar Latin – it acquired the meaning 'favour, pity'.

bond, so that no outbreak ensued among the men themselves nor any mutiny against their general.

BRITISH COMMUNITIES

When the historian Tacitus described the Roman takeover of Britain in the first century AD, he said something about the *Britanni* (Celts at the time) that seems to have become part of the DNA of our ancestors the Anglo-Saxons:

> The Britons themselves actively accept enrolment into the army, taxes and other *munia* [e.g. road-building, grain collection] associated with imperial rule, provided that there is no injustice. That they will not put up with, being habituated to obey but not to be treated like slaves.

The British have a reputation for doing their duty as long as it is 'fair'; but they are an independent-minded lot and will not bow to tyrants.

Britannia derived from what the Greek traveller Pytheas (*c.* 320 BC) heard local Britons call it – *Pretannikê* (Πρεταννικη). By the first century BC this had become *Pretannia*, and so ultimately *Britannia*. The word probably meant something like 'painted/tattooed people' – the description the Romans translated into *Picti* to describe the Picts.

MUNICIPALITIES AND COLONIES

Our 'municipal' is based on the *muni*- stem (see p. 66). Latin *municipium* meant a self-governing community in Italy, but one which had been granted a number of Roman citizen rights. This distinguished it from a colony.

A *colonus* meant basically 'farmer', and a *colonia* was a self-governing settlement established outside Rome with land for Romans to work on and live off. Originally, a *colonia* was established to help to control a conquered town; but over time it became a means of providing Roman veteran soldiers with a retirement home and of Romanizing far-flung places across the Empire. The very name of Lincoln reveals its origin: <u>*Lindum*</u> <u>*colonia*</u>, the colony *Lindum*, an ancient British word meaning 'lake'.

IMMUNITY

Immunis meant 'exempted from duties'; *immunitas* boiled down to 'exemption from taxes'. It was a much sought privilege. We know of a letter from Livia, wife of the emperor Augustus, begging him to grant freedom from taxes to the Greek island of Samos. He turned her down. We have his communication to the Samians:

> It is not right to grant the greatest privilege of all without reason and cause. I have goodwill towards you and would be willing to do a service to my wife who is enthusiastic on your behalf, but not so far as to contravene my custom...

DOING FAVOURS

The great and good in any society like nothing better than mingling with other great and good. It creates relationships, back-scratching (or knifing), and – with luck – bonds of friendship and obligation that can be useful to both sides. 'Bonds' indeed: Latin *obligo* (*obligat-*) meant basically 'I tie up, bind'. In the Roman world, this was the way to get on, helping your friends with such things as financial aid, jobs, business deals, court cases, even marriage prospects.

An army commander, for example, would have many junior positions at his disposal. If he gave a position to X on the advice of friend Y, a chain of obligation would be established. The governor of a province likewise could offer jobs and protection; as he went on tour, local bigwigs would be keen to entertain him lavishly and so strike up a relationship. The emperor was the biggest dispenser of patronage of all.

GRACE AND FAVOUR

The world of *obligatio* tied in with that of *gratia* (see pp. 54, 196). What *gratia* hinted at was 'a lively sense of future favours' (ascribed to Sir Robert Walpole), implying a return for services to be rendered at some future date. Power and prestige depended on working these personal connections. Pliny the Younger wrote in this vein to his chum Romatius Firmus:

> You and I were born in the same township, we went to school together, and shared quarters from an early age; your father was on terms of friendship with my mother and my uncle, and with me – as far as the disparity in our years allowed. These are overwhelming reasons why I ought to advance you as far as I can along the path of dignities. The fact of your being a mayor in our town shows that you have an income of a hundred thousand sesterces. So, in order that we may have the pleasure of enjoying your society not only as a mayor but as a Roman knight, I offer you 300,000 sesterces to

> make up the equestrian qualification [see p. 35]. The length of our
> friendship is sufficient guarantee that you will not forget this favour...

A Roman would not have been pleased, however, if you had
congratulated him on his *praestigia*, source of our 'prestige': it meant
'an action intended to deceive or hoodwink, a trick, deceit'. Sometimes
Latin is a little too close for comfort. Its meaning in English derives
from conjuring. 'The prestige' is the conjuror's final and most baffling
trick (→ 'prestidigitator', someone nimble-fingered, like any good
magician). The term was extended to any outstanding performance
of any sort. The French used it to describe Napoleon's incredible
escape from Elba in 1815 to start his war against England and her
allies all over again.

PRIVILEGE

Privilege through family connections was deeply rooted in Roman
society. But in Cicero's day, a *privilegium* – literally, a law (*leg-*)
relating to an individual (*privus*) – was always one passed *against* him;
only later was it more of a 'privilege' in our sense, of a special right,
a prerogative. In a famous case in 62 BC, one Clodius, disguised as a
woman, broke into a secret female ceremony. Clodius' enemy Cicero
claimed that a special *privilegium* had already been brought against
Clodius: that if he ever did such a thing, he would be sent into exile.
In fact, said Cicero, Clodius bribed his way out of the charge and
boasted about what he had pulled off. Since it was Julius Caesar's
house where this ceremony was taking place, Caesar divorced his
wife, saying: 'Caesar's wife must be above suspicion.'

PATRONS AND CLIENTS

Given the huge disparity in power in the ancient world, it is not surprising that the weak looked to the great and good for help. But it was in the great and good's interest as well: it enabled them to get support among those at the lower end of society with whom they would normally have no dealings.

This relationship was expressed in terms of 'patronage': the *patronus* (compare *pater*, 'father') was an influential person protecting the interests of his *cliens* (plural *clientes*); his *cliens* was a dependant of some sort (a term possibly connected with the Latin for 'inclined'), rendering services to his *patronus*.

At this lower level, it was a matter of social welfare: the landowner who provided the tenancy of a farm to a poor family, the politician who wanted to be accompanied around Rome by large groups of followers and would give them meals and a small allowance to do so.

The satirist Juvenal depicted the miserable existence of the poor *cliens*: first thing in the morning he presents himself at his *patronus*'s house and picks up his pathetic allowance; then he heads down to the forum and hangs around the law courts in case the *patronus* needs support; then he follows him home and hopes for a dinner invitation. Fat chance. So off he goes to buy a cabbage and something to cook it with, while the *patronus* lolls about on his own at dinner, not a guest in sight, hoovering up the best that the woods and sea can offer.

PARASITES

It was easy for rich Romans to see this sort of *cliens* as a parasite – a Greek word *parasitos* (παρασιτος) taken directly into Latin as *parasitus*.

It meant in Greek 'one who eats (*sitos*, 'food') beside (*para*)', either as a guest, but more likely as a scrounger, earning his corn by flattering the host. But given the patron's often supercilious attitude to his clients, it is he who exploited them rather than the other way round.

Supercilium in Latin meant 'eyebrow'. Seneca urged people not to worry about the 'eyebrow', presumably raised in contempt, of any slave calling out guests' names as they entered a room for a banquet – what did a slave's opinion count for?

THE WORLD OF WORK (1): SHOP AND MARKETS

A city of a million people, Rome had few natural resources except water and superb volcanic building material. So Romans brought in raw materials from all over the world – foodstuffs, wood, leather, metals, cloth, precious stones, etc. – to use or turn into products that the wealthy and others required in the greatest city in the world. Inscriptions in Rome list some 150 different trades. Many of these would sell their own products through their own shops.

Rome, then, was a city of shopkeepers. The Latin for 'shop' was *taberna* (whence our 'tavern'), which meant basically 'wooden hut' (related to *trabs*, 'tree-trunk'), then a wayside inn, and a shop; and a 'shopkeeper, innkeeper' was *caupo*, from which our 'cheap' derives.

As well as markets – for instance, the *forum vinarium* for wine and *forum piscatorium* for fish – where farmers would come from the country to sell their goods, usually once a week, *tabernae* lined the streets of Rome – ground-floor single rooms, often with living quarters and workshops attached.

The term covered all manner of shops: retail, small-scale manufacture, inns, cook-shops, brothels (*lupanaria*, from *lupa*, 'she-wolf', whence 'lupine'). We hear of shops dealing in such goods as cheese, leather, books (*libraria*), charcoal, felt and perfume (*unguentaria*), but archaeologically it is often difficult to determine what any specific shop sold. There seem to have been plenty of takeaways, selling prepared foods such as bread, hot sausages, pastries and chickpeas. They even had 'greasy spoons' (*uncta popina*, 'oily ['unctuous'] cook-shop' – a place where, presumably, you could just pop in).

We also know shopkeepers advertised their wares keenly, spilling out onto the walkways to do so. This was banned by the emperor, and the Roman satirist Martial wrote:

> The barber, innkeeper, cook, and butcher keep within their own
> doors. What was recently one great *taberna* is now the city of
> Rome again.

We also hear of retailers visiting the wealthy at home. The poet Ovid objected to this: these people always arrived when your mistress was in the mood for being showered with gifts!

BUYING AND SELLING

Latin had no specific word for 'shopping' as a leisure activity, only buying and selling.* That does not mean they did not go shopping, any more than they did not smile because their only word for that relates to a verb meaning 'to laugh'. There is a story from Alexandria

---

* Latin *emo* meant 'I buy', which gives us the phrase *caveat emptor*, 'let the buyer beware' (see also p. 22). Latin *vendo* meant 'I sell', whence our 'vendor'.

of ladies shopping for shoes and going through all those in the shop, commenting on style, fit and colour – or were they actually shopping for dildos? Martial told of people window-shopping, gazing longingly at antiques and so on, all quite out of their range.

THE WORLD OF WORK(2): FARMING

Shopping was high on the list of the farming community, the most admired Romans of them all. A farmer was an *agricola*: *colo* (*cult-*), 'I farm, cultivate' + *ager* (*agr-*), 'field'. Another term was *colonus*, 'cultivator', a farmer or tenant farmer, looking after a farm for someone else. They were also 'colonists', i.e. people who took over conquered territory and made a life for themselves as farmers there. Many veteran soldiers went for this option on retirement (see p. 68).

In his work on *agricultura*, Cato the Elder provided farmers with the following shopping list and the best sources for them:

> Tunics, togas, blankets, patchwork, and shoes should be bought at Rome; caps, iron tools, scythes, spades, mattocks, axes, harnesses, ornaments, and small chains at Cales and Minturnae; spades at Venafrum; carts and sledges at Suessa and in Lucania; storage jars and pots at Alba and Rome; tiles at Venafrum... oil mills at Pompeii, and at Rufrius' yard at Nola, nails and bars at Rome, buckets, oil vessels, water carriers, wine urns, other bronze vessels at Capua and Nola...

It is difficult for anyone in today's world to appreciate what serious farming meant in the ancient world. Cato's treatise runs to over 150 pages of closely written instructions.

THE FOUNDATIONAL FARMER

The farmer comes across as the model of the ideal Roman. Cato the Elder saw them as the moral and military backbone of the nation:

> And when our ancestors would praise a worthy man, their praise took this form: 'good *colonus*', 'good *agricola*'. One so praised was thought to have received the greatest commendation... It is from the *agricolae* that the bravest men and the sturdiest soldiers come. Their calling is most highly respected, their livelihood is the most dependable, it arouses the least hostility, and those engaged in it are least inclined to be disaffected.

The Latin for 'farm' was *fundus*. The very word emphasizes its central importance in Roman eyes: it meant 'bottom, basis, foundation', whence our 'fundament(al)'. The farmer and his farm were felt, as Cato the Elder suggested, to be the rock on which Rome was built.

THE IMPORTANCE OF EXAMPLE

Because farming was of such central importance, Romans constantly turned to it as an example or paradigm (Greek *paradeigma* [παραδειγμα]) of how the world should be. The poet Virgil wrote a complete work on farming, his *Georgics*, from Greek *geôrgos* (γεωργος), 'farmer' – one who works (*erg-*) the land (*gê*): hence 'Farmer George'. In it he drew constant parallels between farming, nature and the state.

The Latin for 'example' was *exemplum*. It derived from Latin *eximo* (*exempt-*), 'I take out, extract' (→ 'exemption'): an *exemplum* drew out wholesome lessons from both the past and the contemporary world (*con/cum*, 'simultaneous' + *tempus* [*tempor*-], 'time'). Pliny the Elder gave a powerful *exemplum antiquitatis* ('from antiquity') in his story of a farmer who was a freed slave, Gaius Furius Chresimus (Chresimus [Χρησιμος] was his slave name, Greek for 'useful'). He had made a tremendous success of his farm, and was accused by jealous neighbours of using magic to lure away other people's crops. When the time came for the verdict:

> Chresimus brought all his agricultural implements into court and produced his farm servants, sturdy people, well looked after and well clad, his iron tools of excellent make, heavy mattocks, ponderous ploughshares and well-fed oxen. Then he said: 'These are my magic spells, citizens. But what I cannot show you, or produce in court, are my midnight labours and early risings, my sweat and toil.' This procured his acquittal by a unanimous verdict. The fact is that cultivation depends on expenditure of labour, and this is the reason for the saying of our forefathers that, on a farm, the best fertilizer is the owner's eye.

This approach to the past had implications for the Roman concept of history (see p. 156). If analysis of the past consisted to a large extent in mining it for *exempla*, positive and negative, there was much of significance that the historian would ignore or miss.

THE WORLD OF WORK (3): HANDIWORK

Manufacturing today evokes images of vast factories, smoke billowing from multiple chimneys, daily churning out objects by the thousand. This bears little relationship to pre-industrial ancient manufacturing.

In Latin *manu factus* (or *manufactus*) had a very specific meaning. Cicero, reflecting on mutual helpfulness as the key to civilization, said:

> What we call 'inanimate' is for the most part the product of man's labour. Without *manus* ['hand, manual labour'] and *ars* ['technique'] we would have none of them – no health-care, no navigation, no agriculture... no exports or imports... no quarrying of iron, copper, gold and silver... no houses... no aqueducts, canals, irrigation works, breakwater or harbours *manu factos* ['made by hand', artificial as opposed to natural].

Lucretius, arguing for a world made of atoms, pointed out that the atoms were not all completely identical since, like ears of corn, for example, 'they are the products of nature, not *manu facta* to a set pattern'.

Today, 'made by hand' implies a product not made by machine and so untouched by human hand. In the ancient world, 'made by hand' was the only way anything could be made, though machines could help.

JUSTICE

INTRODUCTION

Roman law has been a benchmark of Western law for some 2,500 years. Its greatest virtue is that it was entirely secular, free of religious influence of any sort. There were therefore no holds barred as to its interpretation. Its categorization of the civil (as opposed to criminal) law in three distinct areas – *personae*, *res*, *actiones* (persons, things and actions) – has also been very influential, as has its acknowledgement of the fledgling notion of international law in its *ius gentium* ('law of nations'), *ius legationis* ('law of diplomacy') and *ius belli* ('law of war').

One of its main differences from modern law is that people were not equal before it. The law treated you differently if you were free or slave and, within the 'free' category, whether you were higher or lower class, and whether you were subject to another, as a wife to a husband, a sibling to a father, or a child to a guardian. Status was all as far as the law went. Another difference was the absolute power over life and death (*patria potestas*) which a father had over all his family.

Roman education was designed to prepare the rich and privileged for the job market. This meant the teaching of rhetoric, the art of persuasive public speaking and writing, which would prepare students for life in the law and politics (see p. 155). Two of the key features of the training were exercises known as *suasoriae* and *controversiae*. In the former, pupils were given an incident from myth or history to argue over: did Hannibal, who laid siege to Rome for a while but then gave up, make the right decision? Should Caesar have accepted the kingship offered him by Marc Antony? In the latter, pupils were given tricky legal cases, many clearly invented, to debate, for example:

> A man who had been disinherited by his father went to study medicine. His father fell ill but, while other doctors gave up on him, the son was called in, and said he would cure him if he drank the medicine he gave him. The father drank some and said that he had been poisoned: the son drank the rest. The father died, and the son is accused of parricide.

In a famous letter to his friend Atticus, Cicero showed what such training could achieve when he debated with himself what to do about tyrants. On 12 March 49 BC, as civil war was about to break out between Pompey and Caesar (whom Cicero regarded as a tyrant), he reflected:

> Should a man remain in his country under tyranny? Should he do everything in his power to overthrow it, even if the very existence of the state would be put at risk? Should he watch out for the person who does the overthrowing, in case *he* becomes tyrant [Cicero means Pompey]? Should he try to help his country under tyranny

only by word and seizing opportunities when he can, rather than by war? Is it the mark of a statesman to withdraw and keep his head down under tyranny, or rather run any risk in the cause of freedom? Should he make war on his country and blockade it under tyranny? Should he run the same risks as his friends and benefactors, even if they do not seem to him to have made intelligent decisions about the matter [Pompey again]? If a man has brought great benefits to his country and has incurred considerable suffering and hostility in so doing [Cicero here thinks of his own past services], should he then voluntarily agree to risk all for his country, or should he rather be allowed to think of himself and his family first and to give up his opposition to those in power?

These would be just the questions that would be asked in a *suasoria* about tyranny.

As for the actual shaping and development of Roman law, whatever part orators may have played, a central role was played by jurists. Technically, Roman law was made up of *leges* agreed by the Senate and passed by the people, laws passed by the people's assemblies, decrees, magistrates' edicts, decisions of the emperor and jurists' answers. These jurists were freelance legal consultants. One did not have to be a senator or pass an exam to become one. It was simply a matter of earning people's respect for the legal advice you offered them. Here Cicero described Servius Sulpicius Rufus:

> Servius did his service in the city here with me, giving legal
> opinions, preparing documents, and giving advice, a life full of

> worry and anxiety. He learned the civil law, worked long hours,
> helped many people, put up with their stupidity, suffered their
> arrogance, swallowed their cantankerousness. He was at the beck
> and call of others, not his own master. A person wins widespread
> praise and credit with others when he works hard at a discipline
> which will benefit so many.

This flattery was needed – Servius was a friend of his – but Cicero was speaking as defence counsel against the prosecution counsel: Servius! Later in the speech, Cicero put the knife in:

> Many men would have greatly preferred to become professional
> orators, but when they did not make the grade, they sunk to yours.
> As Greek musicians (so they say) sing to the pipe if they cannot
> sing to the lyre, so we see that those who do not succeed as orators
> degenerate to giving legal opinions.

But whatever Cicero's real feelings, the jurists' work was of high importance. In the English system, the law is made by Parliament, and judges interpret and apply it in court proceedings. Their interpretations become precedents for later judges to follow, unless those interpretations are overturned. In the Roman system, it was jurists who interpreted and argued over the law; their opinions were then preserved for others to argue over, and the final authority on them was the emperor. *Gaius' Institutes* (*c.* AD 150) is one collection of such jurists' opinions. In AD 530 the Eastern Roman emperor Justinian published his massive *Digest*, most of it legal opinions datable to AD 100–250, drawn from some 2,000 books of opinions.

To give a taste of the jurists' debates: the *lex Aquilia* on unlawful killing was proposed by Aquilius in 287 BC and duly became law. It covered a wide range of potential damages. Here jurists discussed the issue of legal liability:

> The question is asked whether an action under the *lex Aquilia* will succeed if a lunatic causes damage. Pegasus says not, for he asks how there can be any accountable fault in one who is out of his mind; and he is undoubtedly right. Therefore a case brought under the *lex Aquilia* will fail in this instance, just as it fails if an animal has caused damage, or if a tile has fallen. The same must be said if an infant has caused damage, though Labeo says that if the child is over seven years of age he could be liable under the *lex Aquilia* in just the same way as he could be liable for theft. I think this is correct, provided the child is able to distinguish between right and wrong...

When the Roman Empire in the West collapsed in the fifth century AD, the legal systems of the German peoples that had overrun it took precedent, but Roman law was still studied by schools and in the church ('canon', i.e. church, law was Roman-based). But in the eleventh century, Justinian's *Digest* began to be studied at the world's first university in Bologna, as a training in legal argumentation. This became a standard feature in later universities too, all of them attracting fine minds from across Europe. The result was that the new graduates (as *doctores iuris*, 'doctors of law') took this Roman understanding of the law back home with them – and Roman law was reborn, to become dominant in the West again. 'Roman law' now meant law as it was understood by its contemporary post-Bologna interpreters, who began to align Roman law with the reality of the medieval world; and it was this law that was taken to the Americas from the fifteenth century. The values of Roman law became supranational, deeply embedded across the West, defining what 'justice' meant and how it was to be understood.

Much has changed since then, but the outlines of Roman law are still visible in the continental system. England, of course, was the exception. Here the Roman example was rejected by Henry III (1234) and local laws ('common law'), interpreted by judges in courts and the king, held sway, becoming over time national law, the first such body of national law in Europe.

THE LANGUAGE OF LAW

Latin ius (*iur-*), that which was sanctioned or ordained, seems to have been originally associated with the idea of health, or purification. A healthy society was one where justice held sway. *Ius* was the stem of *iustus*, 'just', *iustitia*, 'justice', and *iudex* (*iudic-*), 'judge'. He was one who spoke (*-dex*) justice, and in so doing gave a *iudicium*, 'judgement'. The *iur-* stem provides us with 'jury'.

Lex (*leg-*) was the law as the legal machinery of state, a regulation, a rule, a condition of existence (whence 'legal', 'legitimate', etc.). '*Silent... leges inter arma*', said Cicero: 'The laws fall silent in the presence of weapons.' And violence was what the law was designed to prevent. As Cicero said elsewhere, one of the instincts of nature was *vindicatio*, whose linguistic stem was *vis*, 'violence' (see p. 261). *Vindicatio* meant 'championing a wronged person', or 'avenging a wrong'; Cicero talked of it 'repelling violence and insult from ourselves and those dear to us' – all well and good at one level but in fact a major cause of taking up arms. At the heart of Roman law was the desire to *remove* revenge from the private to the public sphere and bring it under the law.

PREJUDICE

'Prejudice' originally had a quite innocent meaning. It derived from *prae-*, 'before, in advance' + *iudicium*, 'judgement', and referred to the preliminary action that had to be taken before a case could be heard, or to a previous ruling that could act as a precedent. For example, Cicero discussed the case of a weathy Roman who lost a hand in an attack by armed robbers. He brought an action for 'injury' (see p. 89), but the defendant asked that any *praeiudicium* should not turn that into a capital charge, i.e. that the main trial should not be prejudiced by an earlier judgement in a lesser court.

EDICTS AND ALBUMS

When the praetor (see p. 40) entered his year of office, he verbally announced his *edicta*, 'edicts'. These were the 'legal provisions he intended to observe' during his term (probably virtually identical from year to year). *Edico* (*edict-*) meant 'I speak out, proclaim'. At the same time, he also issued an *album*. This did not set the *edicta* to music; it was the white board (*albus*, 'white' → 'albumen') on which the praetor had written up the *edicta* in black ink. In one of his letters, Seneca rounded on those who split philosophical hairs on matters of moral urgency, asking: 'Is philosophy to proceed with such trivial "ifs and buts" that would repel and disgust even those who sit there examining the *album*?'

LEGAL FORMULAS

Formulas for us are often associated with chemistry. For Romans, they were at the heart of civil law. Latin *formula* meant a set form of words designed to guide a trial. Cicero made the point explicitly:

> There are laws, there are *formulae* established for every kind of action, so that no one can possibly be mistaken as to the nature of the injury done to him or the method of legal procedure to be adopted. For according to the loss, vexation, inconvenience, disaster, or injustice suffered by each individual, public *formulae* have been drawn up by the praetor in precise terms, to which every private action can be adapted.

Civil suits, then, worked as follows. The praetor would summon the parties in the civil action to a preliminary hearing, in which the ground rules of the action were decided. The praetor then appointed a *iudex* to conduct the trial. He would not be a professional, but someone of standing in the community. The praetor had a list of possible judges, but it was up to the parties to decide whom they wanted. The *iudex* would be both judge and jury.

That done, the praetor then drew up the *formula* by which the *iudex* was to conduct proceedings. The purpose of the *formula* was to make the charge as clearly defined as possible; and then to guide the *iudex* into making certain that the right questions were asked to ensure a satisfactory outcome to the case, but without being excessively specific. There had to be room for interpretation and discretion.

A SIMPLE *FORMULA*

Here Cicero put a case at its simplest: an innkeeper had two guests lodging with him, asleep in the same bedroom. At night the innkeeper crept in, took the sword of one of them and killed the other, whose purse he then stole. He replaced the sword in the sheath and crept out:

> Long before dawn the man whose sword had been used to commit the murder got up and called his companion again and again. Deciding that he did not answer because he was sound asleep, the traveller took his sword and the rest of his belongings and set out alone. Not long afterward the innkeeper raises a cry of 'Murder' and with some of the guests goes down the road in pursuit of the traveller who had left earlier. He seizes him, draws the sword from its sheath and finds it stained with blood. The fellow is brought to the city and accused of the crime. In this case the *intentio* is 'You committed murder.' The answer is 'I did not.'

FORMULAE EXPLAINED

The jurist Gaius identified four elements to the *formula*, all words easily recognizable in English, in a case of a stolen silver table. It began by stating: 'Let X be *iudex*.' Then:

1. *demonstratio*: placed at the start, so that the subject matter of the action was clear, e.g. 'If it appears that A deposited a silver table with B...'

2. *intentio*: here A expressed what he was claiming, e.g. '... and that the table was not returned to A by the bad faith of B...'

3. *adiudicatio*: the part of the *formula* which empowered the *iudex* to take action on the property concerned: '... then let the judge condemn B to pay the value of the table to A.'

4. *condemnatio*: the power of the *iudex* to condemn (here stated under 3) or absolve: 'But if it does not so appear, acquit him.'

At the heart of it was the *intentio*. That did not refer to the question of the 'intent' of either party, though that might come into it: it meant the 'statement of the charge, accusation'. In this case, the *intentio* was that B had defrauded A of a silver table.

CRIME...

Our 'crime' derives from Latin *crimen* (*crimin-*) – whence 'criminal' – but its Latin meaning was different from ours: it meant primarily 'accusation, charge'. The brilliant poet Ovid was sent into exile by the emperor Augustus for a *crimen et error*: 'a charge [brought against him] and a mistake'. *Not* a crime.

... AND PUNISHMENT

Across the whole range of court procedures, punishments could range from flogging and removal of rights, to execution, exile and compensation for victims (*compenso* [*compensat-*], 'I balance, make good, counterbalance'), but not long-term imprisonment, for which the finance was not available. Selling into slavery was preferable.

ALLEGATIONS

In the course of his prosecution of Verres, the corrupt governor of Sicily, Cicero uncovered a plan of Verres' to make big money out of a contract for the repair of a temple that in fact needed no repair. The cost of this 'repair' fell on the shoulders of a young boy, because his father had won the contract for the repairs but had died. It should have cost 40,000 sesterces; but Verres put the contract up for sale, bid for it himself at fourteen times the actual cost (all to be taken from the boy's estate) and made a packet out of it. All that was done was to take down and re-erect four pillars using the same stone, whitewash others and repoint others. The boy's guardians had done all they could to stop this blatant thievery, making endless *allegationes* to (note: not against) Verres and his various sidekicks, but to no avail. But that was the original meaning of an *allegatio*: acting as an intermediary, making an intercession or representation on behalf of someone else.

INJURY

The Latin *iniuria*, from which our 'injury' derives, was a combination of *in-* (indicating 'negative') + *ius* (*iur-*): it meant 'unlawful conduct'. Its original meaning was physical harm. As the story was told:

> One Lucius Veratius, who was a famously wicked, cruel and brutal man, used to amuse himself by slapping free men in the face. A slave followed him with a purse full of *asses*. As often as he slapped anyone, he ordered twenty-five *asses* to be counted out at once, according to the provision of the *Twelve Tables*.

The *Twelve Tables* was the name of Rome's earliest penal code, and twenty-five *asses* a trivial sum of money. As the story pointed out, 'who is so poor that twenty-five *asses* would stop him inflicting any *iniuria* he wanted to?'

This was *iniuria* in a different sense: Veratius was humiliating people. So the praetor produced a new edict on the matter, extending the scope of *iniuria* and allowing judges to adjust the penalty to circumstances. The result was that *iniuria* now covered defamation and various sorts of harassment, such as shouting abusively at someone in their own home, stalking and so on. *Physical* assault did not need to have been carried out.

Once that had been enacted, it became possible to argue that if a woman was harassed – for instance, by being called a whore – her husband had been injured too because his honour had been demeaned. Anyone who injured someone else's slave could be said to have disrespected the owner. As Cicero defined it: 'By *iniuria* is meant doing violence to someone, to his person by assault or to his sensibilities by insulting language or to his reputation by some scandal.'

Iniuria, then, went to the heart of the Romans' sense of self-worth. It assaulted their reputation, directly or indirectly. No Roman would be prepared to put up with that.

PUNISHMENT BY STATUS

One question arising from the law of *iniuria* was: when it came to punishment, was A's reputation worth more than B's? And if so, should not the penalties differ? We may guess the Roman answer.

The result was that, under the Empire, when it came to handing out sentences, the law divided humanity into three categories: *honestiores*, *humiliores* and slaves. The *-ior* suffix to an adjective in Latin marked a comparative, 'more, rather'. So the *honestiores* were 'those of more honour, distinction, merit'; the *humiliores* – Latin *humus*, 'earth, soil' – 'the more humble, lowly, abject'. So a law on wills stated:

> Anyone who knowingly and with wrongful intent forges... a will is liable under the law: *honestiores* are to be deported to an island, *humiliores* are either sent to the mines or are crucified.

Or take a law on murderers:

> Capital punishment is usual these days, except for those whose status is too high to sustain the statutory penalty. These are deported to an island, while *humiliores* are usually either crucified or thrown to beasts.

A law on treason laid down that *humiliores* should be thrown to the beasts or burnt alive, *honestiores* capitally punished.

The issue here was public degradation. The *honestior* did not evade punishment, but expulsion, deportation and/or confiscation of goods did not propel him into the popular limelight, let alone humiliate him there. Even if he was sentenced to capital punishment, an execution was a comparatively quick and clean death, in the face of which he could win credit by exhibiting proper Stoic fortitude. The *humilior*, on the other hand, was sent to the mines, crucified, thrown to the beasts (*ad bestias*) or burnt at the stake – the first a slow death sentence, the last three carried out in public, before mocking crowds in the arena.

SERVITUDE

There were more ways than one of being a slave (*servus*) in the Roman world. One of these was owning property attached to a condition by which the owner was duty-bound to give certain rights to a neighbour, e.g. a right of way, a right to draw water and so on. The technical term was *servitus*. The jurist Ulpian clarified the law:

> The following are the four *servitutes* of country estates, namely: the right of walking, the right of driving cattle, the right of way, and the right to conduct water. The first is the right a man has to pass or walk, but not to drive a beast of burden. The second is the right to drive a beast of burden, or a vehicle; and therefore a party who has just the right to walk, does not have the right to drive cattle; and he who has the latter privilege has also that of walking, even without a beast of burden. The third is the right of passing, driving cattle, or walking, since all are included in this right of way. The last is the right to conduct water over someone else's land.

But how did it work in practice? In a letter to his friend Atticus, Cicero mentioned his neighbour Marcus Aelius. Cicero had the right of *servitus* over Aelius' property, and had wanted to use it in order to draw some water from his land. But he decided it was not worth the hassle:

> Please set M. Aelius' mind at rest. Say that I had thought that a few water conduits at the edge of the farm, underground at that, would be subject to some kind of *servitus*; but do tell him that I don't want to go ahead with it now and would not worry him for

the world. But do it in the nicest possible way, as you said to me, so that his mind is set at rest. I don't want him to suspect that I am at all put out.

Cicero, here at the height of his fame (44 BC), did not want to create a rift with his (presumably) lowlier neighbour. Good relations were more important. Whatever the law said, however self-important Roman aristocrats appeared to be, real life had a habit of intruding.

THE CONTRACTUAL AGREEMENT

'A man's word is his bond', it used to be said in the City. No longer, one imagines. The lawyers have seen to that. But it was standard practice in Rome. Here is the jurist Gaius:

> A verbal obligation [*obligatio*] is created by question [*interrogatio*] and answer [*responsio*] in such forms as: 'Do you solemnly promise it will be given? I solemnly promise'; 'Will you give? I will give'; 'Do you promise? I promise'; 'Do you promise on your honour? I promise on my honour'; 'Do you guarantee on your honour? I guarantee on my honour'; 'Will you do it? I will do it.' The words 'solemnly promise' in a verbal obligation are peculiar to Roman citizens; but other forms belong to the *ius gentium* ['law of nations'] and are consequently valid between all men, whether Roman citizens or not.

Not all agreements needed such specific wording. Indeed, any sort of 'consensual' *pactum* could be made: as Cicero said, a *pactum* was 'anything agreed between people'.

LEGAL STRAWS

The word for 'solemnly promise' was *spondeo* (*spons-*), which is what our 'sponsor' should do. When one made such a promise, one expected a response to it (*respondeo*), Latin for 'I reply'. *Respondeo* may well have had legal connotations in origin: as a lawyer said, 'Where one of the parties present asks a question, and departs before a *responsio* is given him, he renders the *stipulatio* void.'

Stipulatio was indeed the general word for 'binding promise'. Its origin may possibly be found in *stipula*, 'straw, stubble'. The seventh-century encyclopedist Isidore said: 'The ancients, when they promised each other something, would break a straw that they were holding. In joining this straw together again, they would acknowledge their pledge.' Our word 'contract' derives from Latin *contraho* (*contract-*), 'I draw together', i.e. 'reduce in size', but also 'I bring together, establish a formal relationship between'.

WILLS

It is surprising that, under law of contract, written documentation (*tabula*, p. 233; or *instrumentum*, literally 'equipment designed for a specific purpose', → 'instruction') rarely came into it. It was largely a matter of 'good faith', *fides*: 'the condition of having trust placed in one; guarantee; credibility' (→ 'fidelity'), though written documentation did become more common during the Empire.

The main exception was, not surprisingly, the will, *testamentum*, from *testor* (*testat-*), 'I invoke as witness, solemnly declare'. In this example, Antonius Silvanus, a cavalryman in a Thracian regiment, made his son Marcus his heir. He had to do this because, as a soldier, he could not marry. His son was therefore illegitimate. But if Marcus did not agree to become his heir:

> let him be disinherited. In that case, let my brother... Antonius be my heir, and let him accept my estate in the next 60 days. If he is not my heir, I give him as a legacy 750 *denarii*. I name as curator of my goods in camp − for their collection and restoration to Antonia Thermutha, mother of my heir − Hierax, son of Behax, elite soldier of the same troop, the squad of Aebutius, so that she may guard it herself until my son and heir comes into his own and receives it from her... [further legacies and finally] As for my slave Cronio, I wish him to be free after my death so long as he handles everything correctly and hands it over to my heir or procurator, and that the manumission tax [see p. 62] be paid out of my estate. Let fraud be absent from this will.

A list of witnesses, some of whom participated in the ritual, then follows.

On the larger picture, it may be that, at the level of something like negotiations between friends, family or the great and good, it would have smacked of distrust to demand proof in writing, let alone securities or interest. In another context, oaths of agreement sworn in the name of gods were often felt to be needed between bitter enemies but certainly not between friends and acquaintances. It was just not 'the done thing'. That culture may have spread more widely.

However that may be, we do have records of written agreements; and in the case of disputes there is evidence for *testatio*, 'a sworn statement', made by a third party to a transaction. Not that that guaranteed anything. The first century AD educationist Quintilian pointed out that '*testatio* is often in conflict with oral evidence'.

EVERYDAY LAW

The law is an intellectual as well as a social construct, and Roman law a formidable example. But Roman jurists never forgot that the purpose of the law was to serve the people. When they argued over it, it was to everyday life that they turned for their *exempla* (p. 75). *Aequitas*, 'fairness', and *utilitas*, 'practicality', were words always on their lips, and the relationship between blame (*culpa* → 'culpable'), intention (*voluntas* → 'voluntary, volition') and guilt (*noxa* → 'noxious') uppermost in their thoughts. Their works are full of tiles falling off roofs, dogs off leads, medicines wrongly prescribed, and shopkeepers getting into fights over stolen lamps. All human life was there.

CUI BONO?

Most of our well-known legal Latin sayings emerge from reports of legal cases, written (but not pleaded) in Latin, from the medieval age onwards. *Cui bono* is an exception. It meant 'to whom [is it for] a good', i.e. 'who stands to gain?' When in 52 BC Cicero was defending Milo, killed in a gang war by Clodius, he said:

> So how can it be proved that Clodius had laid an ambush against Milo? In fact, it is enough, in dealing with such an audacious, such a wicked monster, to show that he would have had a strong incentive

to do so, and great expectations and great advantages in the event of Milo's death. So let that maxim of Lucius Cassius Longinus Ravilla [137 BC] – 'Who stands to gain?' – be applied to the parties now before us.

BUSINESS

INTRODUCTION

I n the pre-industrial ancient world, there were, effectively, no such things as 'jobs', with terms of employment, annual holidays and wages. For virtually everyone, bar the rich, soldiers (while soldiering) and city-dwellers, survival meant never-ending working on the land, day in, day out, year in, year out, in order to eat (see pp. 55–6). It was, literally, life or death. Popular morality rammed home the point. Aesop contrasted the ant, who worked to prepare for the winter, with the grasshopper, who sang the summer away and paid the price.

Industrial manufacture on the scale we understand it barely existed. There is something of an exception with the large-scale production of pottery which we hear about in Gaul. A red-gloss pottery produced at Arretium in Italy suddenly became extremely popular. So pottery production was set up in Lyon, southern Gaul and North Africa, all of it stamped 'Arretine'. That said, it was not all produced in one gigantic factory, but spread among local potteries, none employing more than about twenty people.

But that was unusual. Business in the ancient world meant trade, farming, moneylending and winning state contracts. At one end of the scale, trade consisted of town markets and local trade, with farmers large and small buying and selling their goods and services. At the other end, it meant what is today called Monte Testaccio, 'The Hill of Pots'. This consists of the now broken *amphorae* (clay storage jars) – they could be used only once – which brought olive oil from southern Spain to Rome. It has been estimated that some 4 billion kilograms (4.5 million tons) of olive oil were imported in the first two centuries AD. About 2 million tons of grain were imported annually, and about 1.8 million hectolitres of wine (40 million gallons).

Further, as the Roman Empire expanded, its trade expanded too. No fewer than 120 ships made the Red Sea–India run in the 20s BC; in 25 BC an Indian embassy visited the emperor Augustus in Spain. We know of a Syrian trader, Barates, working and marrying in South Shields, 4,000 miles from home, serving the army that guarded Hadrian's Wall. We hear of one Alexandros making a journey to Sri Lanka and the South China Sea, perhaps Hanoi and Java. Roman goods have been found in Iceland, Sweden, Norway and Vietnam, though that does not prove that Romans traded there, only that people who traded with Romans traded there.

As for the aristocrats, their wealth lay in their huge estates and the gigantic profits they could make from working them efficiently with slave labour. This not only generated the cash they needed to climb the greasy pole of power, but – if the estate was properly looked after – it brought prestige and social status too.

All this trade was greatly facilitated by cash: the economy was 'monetarized', though naturally barter and payment in kind continued. But since Rome had no economic policy and understood little about money supply and its effects, shortages of coins occurred. When Vitellius launched his bid to become emperor in AD 69, the historian Suetonius tells us:

> So short of money was his household that it is generally agreed that he had no money at all for the journey to Germany, and had to rent a garret for his wife and children whom he was leaving behind in Rome, and let out his own house for the remaining part of the year. He also took the pearl ear-ring from his mother's very ear to pawn it for the expenses of the journey. Nor could he get away from the crowd of creditors who waylaid him (and who included the people of Sinuessa and Formiae, whose public revenues he had illegally seized), until he threatened them with prosecution for personal insult, on the grounds that an ex-slave who was claiming a particularly large sum had kicked him...

The jurist Gaius understood the problem:

> We know how the prices, particularly of wine, oil and grain, vary from community to community and region to region. It may seem that money has one and the same value everywhere; but in some places it can be found more easily and at a low level of interest, while in others it is more difficult to come by and at a substantial rate of interest.

But this problem was offset by the existence of basic systems of credit, moneylending and banking, both at the modest local, everyday level and on the very large scale too. This came about when groups of very wealthy people (*equites* and senators, the latter using third parties) got together to set up trade deals of the sort described for olive oil and wine above, and to bid for major state projects such as building roads and aqueducts and collecting taxes.

The role of the *negotiator* was important here. They set up deals and financed them. They played a major part, for example, in supplying the Roman armies with arms, food and equipment. Some started to specialize: we hear of *negotiatores* in wine and olive oil. But there is another point here. The wealthy did not want the hassle of doing 'business' all day long, let alone the risk of getting it wrong and losing their wealth. So it often paid them to hand everything over to *negotiatores*, for an agreed price. On one occasion, Pliny the Younger sold them the rights to pick and sell his grape harvest while it was still on the vine 'and prospects seemed good'. But the harvest failed, threatening them with ruin. Far from leaving them in the lurch, however, Pliny established a complex system of rebates to those who had put the money up.

A monument from Rome's port of Ostia illustrates just what involvement in the world of business meant to one man, Gnaeus Sentius Felix. It was set up by his son and described what he had done for Ostia. As well as serving as town mayor and treasurer he was:

> senior official of the guild of superintendents of sea-going ships, co-opted without payment into the guild of the Adriatic sea shippers...
> He was patron of the... bankers, of the wine-dealers from the city of

Rome, of the corn-measurers, and of the corporation of the rowers, and of the ferryboat-men... and of the citizens from the forum and the public weigh-house, and of the freedmen, of the public slaves, and of the oil-dealers, and of the young cabmen, and of the guild of the catchers and sellers of fish.

However much landowning aristocrats tended to sneer at commerce, people such as Felix were at the heart of the extraordinary prosperity that Rome brought to its empire.

BUSINESS PARTNERSHIPS

The Latin *socius* meant 'ally, comrade, companion'. This derives from Latin *sequor*, 'I follow, accompany' (our 'sequence', etc.). The Latin for a business partnership or consortium was *societas* (our 'society', 'social'): a body of people united by a common purpose, especially in business (or crime).

We hear of Cato the Elder, famous for his ascetic lifestyle, being attacked for engaging in shipping finance, putting together a *societas* of fifty partners and ships and – through a third party – taking a share in it and reaping the profits:

He used to loan money in the most criticised of ways, that is in shipping, as follows. He required his many borrowers to form an *association*. When there were fifty partners and as many ships, he took one share in the company through his front-man and freedman, Quintio. Quintio dealt with the business and accompanied the ships on their voyages. In this way the risk did not fall on Cato entirely, but only a small part of it, and the profits were large.

MARINE DANGERS

Sailing the high seas (Latin *mare*, → 'marine') was indeed a risky business. The shipping season was basically March to September. People sailed by day, stopping over by night, though trading vessels did navigate by the stars if necessary (*navigo*, 'I drive [*ago*], by ship [*navis*]', our 'navy'). They did not venture far from the coast either (Latin *costa*, 'rib, side'), in case of a storm. The steersman was a *gubernator* (from which our 'governor', 'government'); *gubernator* derives from Greek for 'steersman', *kubernêtês* (κυβερνητης), whence too 'cybernetics', the study of control systems.

THE SHIP OF STATE

The image of the 'ship of state', with a great leader at the helm (or not), was a common one in the ancient world. Horace began a poem which turns out to refer to the ship of state as follows:

> O ship! Will new waves carry you out to sea
> Again? What are you doing? Make boldly
>> For the harbour [*portus*]. Don't you see how
>>> Your side is stripped of oars,
> Your mast is crippled by the swift sou'wester,
> The yardarms [*antennae*] are groaning...
>>>> (trans. David West)

Portus, 'harbour' + the prefix *ob*, 'towards', lies at the root of our 'opportune': your boat has come safely *into harbour*, laden with goods for sale. Yardarms were the horizontal 'arms' or spas fixed onto the mast of a sailing ship, from which the sails were hung.*

PUBLICANS AND SINNERS

One important *societas* consisted of *publicani* (*publicanus* meant 'state-authorized'). These were in fact private-sector businessmen who bid for state contracts, e.g. to build an aqueduct, work a mine, provide supplies to the legions, collect harbour dues and so on.

The most famous example is probably that of the *publicani* gathering taxes in the province of Asia (modern Turkey). Rome calculated how much tax it needed to gather from a province – in this case, one-tenth of agricultural produce. *Societates* would then be invited to bid to collect that sum. The winners paid the whole sum up front as a 'loan' to the state treasury, and so received interest on it from the state (though only when the work had been completed). The aim of the *publicani*, however, was to collect more than the state required, generating pure profit on top of the interest. That was where the big financial gains lay. It was for this reason that the Bible connected these 'publicans' with 'sinners', because of the reputation they gained for ruthlessly exploiting their position.

Publicans these days run public (drinking) houses, or pubs, so called because they are licensed to sell alcohol to the public. They first came to be called publicans instead of 'pub landlords' in Victorian times.

---

* 'Horizontal' is from Greek *horizô* [ὁρίζω], 'I mark out a boundary'; in the case of our 'horizon', between earth and sky.

NO PEACE FOR THE BUSY

The leisured lifestyle of the wealthy, living off the products of their extensive holdings in land and property, was only for the very few. Such people looked down on those working for a living (see the attack on Cato for 'working', p. 103), but there was no such feeling among the workers about a job: for them it was a matter of life or death, and the more flexible and multi-skilled they were, the better.

While the rich enjoyed their *otium* ('leisure'), the workers were denied it: all they had was *negotium* ('not-leisure'), which meant 'business, pains, difficulty, trouble', and businessmen, engaged in commercial activity, were *negotiatores* (→ 'negotiate'). By the first century BC, Roman traders and dealers were all over the Empire. Cicero talks of Gaul being stuffed with *negotiatores*, wielding their account books and providing the coin with which to do business.

HARD COIN

There was a temple to *Moneta* in Rome where money was coined. Our 'money' derives from it. Romans also used *moneta* to mean the die stamp. Since coins were actually worth their weight, there was a temptation to debase them in hard times. Pliny the Elder said that Marc Antony 'mixed the silver *denarius* with iron, forgers put bronze in *moneta*, others reduced the weight of a coin'.

Our 'coin', again, derives from the technicality of its production. The Latin *cuneus* meant 'wedge', and the die which stamped the coins was wedge-shaped. 'Coin' derives from *cuneus*. Given the importance of the weight of ancient coins, it is no surprise that weight features in the names of our coins too – our 'pound' derives from the Latin *pond-* stem, meaning 'weight' (our 'ponderous', etc.).

We keep coins in purses. This derives, via Late Latin, from Greek *bursa* (βυρσα), 'ox hide', and gives us 'bursar', 'purser', and the French *bourse*, 'stock exchange'.

MONEY

The Latin for 'money' was *pecunia* (→ 'pecuniary', 'impecunious'), based on *pecu*, 'flock, herd, farm animals'. Basically it meant 'wealth, possessions', and only in time came to mean 'cash' (from Latin *capsa*, 'box, container', where cash should be kept). Filthy lucre derives from Latin *lucrum*, 'material gain', and the slang 'spondulicks' possibly from Greek *sphondulos* (σφονδυλος), 'vertebra', slang (apparently) for a stock of coins.

Land was the primary source of wealth in the ancient world: you could grow crops on it (arable farming – *aro*, 'I plough'), feed animals off it (pastoral – *pastor*, 'shepherd') or dig minerals out of it. There were plenty of businesses in the ancient world, most small and some relatively so. But industry, capitalism and stock markets as we know them did not exist, nor did investment for long-term capital growth. Incidentally, 'invest' may derive from a fourteenth-century Italian usage of the Latin *investio*, 'I clothe', in the sense of giving one's capital a new form.

Note that 'mineral' and 'mine' (the other source of wealth) are connected, but neither term is classical. The Latin for a 'mine' was *metallum* (our 'metal'), from the Greek *metallon* (μεταλλον). This derives from the verb *metallô* (μεταλλω), 'I search out, investigate'.

And 'investigate' derives from Latin *vestigium*, 'footprint', *in* which you follow.

DISCREDITABLE

Private moneylending was widespread, with credit depending on money supply. But there was little state regulation of money-lenders. So it is not surprising that our 'credit' (*creditum*, 'something lent', i.e. a loan or a debt) derives from Latin *credo*, 'I trust, have confidence in'.

But because of the attitudes of the rich towards work, lending to all and sundry rather than your own friends and acquaintances was always rather frowned upon. The story is told of Cato the Elder, asked about the best way to exploit one's property. He replied, 'Raising livestock successfully.' And the second best way? 'Raising livestock quite successfully.' And the third? 'Raising livestock unsuccessfully.' The fourth? 'Crops.' Asked 'What about moneylending?', he replied: 'What about murder?'

DEBT

The Latin *debeo* (*debit-*) give us our 'debt' and 'debit'. Its root meaning was 'I am under an obligation to pay/give/do something for someone else'. So it spanned the meanings 'I owe' (e.g. of money) and 'I ought' (e.g. of moral obligation) – in the same way English does, e.g. 'I *owe* it to you, so I *ought* to do it.' 'Owe, ought' derive from a Germanic stem.

LENDING AND ECONOMICS

Romans had no sense that lending was a good, productive thing in itself. Indeed, Latin did not have a verb meaning precisely 'to lend'. Instead, Romans talked of giving money *mutuus* – 'reciprocally, belonging to each other', source of our 'mutual'.

That word derived from *muto*, 'I give and receive'. So it was made quite clear in the words used that this was a *quid pro quo**(literally 'what for what', or 'tit for tat'), with firm obligations on both sides. Credit crunches were not uncommon (especially if people started hoarding coins rather than circulating them), when interest rates could shoot up; if you lent to people whose credit rating was poor, the same would happen.

In fact, 'economic activity' and 'growth' in our sense did not figure actively in Roman thinking. Latin *oeconomicus* derived directly from the Greek *oikonomikos* (οἰκονομικος) and meant 'relating to household (*oikos*) management (*nomos*)'. That was about as far as economic thinking went.

INTEREST

Our old-fashioned term for (usually an exorbitant rate of) interest, 'usury', derives from *usura*, 'a sum paid for the *use* of money provided by someone else' (Latin *utor* [*us-*], 'I use').

But dodgy deals were rife. In 193 BC, interest rates between *Romans* were restricted. So Romans who had lent money to other Romans would contact a friendly non-Roman *socius* (see p. 103) and

---

* The derivation of 'quid' = £ is unknown.

make *him* the lender. This was just a technical matter of transferring the loan from his loan book to the *socius*'s loan book, so that it was now under the *socius*'s name. Being non-Roman, the *socius* could charge any interest rate he liked. Result: he and his Roman chum both made a handsome profit. 'Profit' and 'proficient' both derive from Latin *proficio* (*profect-*), 'I make headway, gain results, increase in size or extent'.

As a result, debt was increasing at an intolerable rate. Eventually, the Roman authorities got wise to this *fraus*, a Latin term which combined the ideas both of hurt and deception (our 'fraud'). So they fixed a day when all *socii* had to declare loans made to Roman citizens. When it was discovered just how gigantic the sum was, the Romans passed a law that *socii* could lend to Romans only on the same terms as Romans could. So that little 'offshore' scam was halted.

BRUTAL BRUTUS

In 88 BC, anyone lending *in Italy* could not charge more than 12 per cent per annum. So lenders looked to lend abroad, when they could charge whatever they liked. Many lenders, as well as lending their own money, borrowed yet more money in Rome at 12 per cent and then lent it out at 17 per cent. This is known as 'gearing up' and is common practice still. Cicero talked of the rich 'sending out their ex-slaves [freedmen] to lend to and pillage the provinces'.

Brutus (one of Caesar's assassins) was one such. In 50 BC, he was lending money to the poverty-stricken people of Salamis, a town in Cyprus, and charging an interest rate of 48 per cent a year! Cicero, the provincial governor of that year, refused to collect it because he had imposed a fixed rate of 12 per cent. But Brutus persuaded the Senate to force Cicero to do so. That, incidentally, was how Cicero found out that it was Brutus who was lending the money: very often the great and good liked to hide their moneylending operations behind a third party, e.g. one of their slaves or freedmen.

Such high rates of interest raised serious questions of solvency. The Latin *solvo* (*solut-*) meant 'I loosen, release, untie' and by extension 'destroy the binding force of', e.g. a marriage or any other contract. So in Rome, if you managed to *release* yourself from debt, you would have been untied from the contract – *solutus* – and so found the 'solution' to your problem. Today, being 'solvent' means 'able to pay what you owe'.

Our term 'interest' derives from Latin *interest*, 'it is advantageous, beneficial', which in the Middle Ages (via French) came to refer to a legal claim, or right.

BONUSES

Whether bonuses are a good thing or not, 'bonus' itself derives from the Latin for 'good' – *bonus*, with its adverbial form *bene*, 'well'. *Bonus* in Latin had a wide range of meanings, none specifically financial but still reflecting what makes a 'bonus' desirable, e.g. 'satisfying to the appetites, senses', 'good of its kind, effective', and 'morally good', so justifying it. 'Bonus' was probably stock exchange slang (1773), though grammatically inept: *bonus* meant 'good person'. *Bonum*, the neuter form, 'good thing', would have been preferable.

MONOPOLIES

'Monopoly' is a relatively rare example of a Greek word, turned into Latin, which does exactly what it says on the tin in the Greek, Roman and modern worlds. Greek *monopôlion* (μονοπωλιον), Latinized to *monopolium*, derived from Greek *monos*, 'sole, only' + *pôleô*, 'I offer for sale', and meant '[right of] monopoly'. A Greek historian described how the Sicilian island of Lipari became fabulously wealthy, and one reason was because it had a *monopôlion* in alum, a form of iron sulphate widely used in dyeing and medicine. The Roman emperor Tiberius took a great interest in regulating business, 'laying before the Senate matters for consultation on taxes and monopolies'.

Apparently, there was also a monopoly on the use of hedgehog skins in the carding of woollen stuffs, which people tried to exploit or get round. Pliny the Elder said: 'There is no subject on which the Senate has more frequently passed decrees, and there is not one of the emperors who has not received from the provinces complaints respecting it.' Bizarre to us, but not in the light of a world where every one of roughly fifty million inhabitants of the Roman Empire wore clothing made from wool. They stood to gain from maintaining a grip on one of the processes.

CAPITAL

For us 'capital' can be anything from an exclamation meaning 'Excellent!' to a capital letter or city or punishment. In business terms, 'capital' means 'store of money'. 'Capitalism' is all about private people (not the state) setting up businesses or providing services in order to make money (capital), either to keep it, or to make even more of it by putting it back into expanding and developing the business. Indeed, 'capital' is also the source of our 'cattle', once the main indicator of a person's wealth.

All these meanings derive from Latin *caput* (*capit-*), 'head (of a person, animals, etc.), summit or top, leader, matter of importance'. Apparently the financial connection was made around AD 1200: it referred to the sum of money loaned out (the main, or 'capital', part), as opposed to the interest one had to pay to borrow it.

FOMENTING REVOLUTION

Capitalism was not a feature of the Roman economy, nor was private business *per se* ('in itself') of political concern. No one was out to overthrow it, let alone to 'ferment revolution', as a left-wing politician recently wanted to do. What he meant was 'foment revolution', Latin *fomentum*. This meant 'soothing application, poultice, dressing', or 'remedy'. It derived from *foveo*, 'I warm, nurture, support', and that is what the politician was so keen to do: nurture capitalism's overthrow. *Fermento* in Latin meant what it does for us: 'I cause x to ferment', by turning sugar to alcohol, for example.

Revolutio was not in fact a classical Latin word at all, but it does derive from one, *revolvo* (*revolut-*), 'I roll something back to where it came from' (on *volumen*, see p. 147), 'I bring round again' (of the seasons, etc.). So a *revolutio* would change nothing: it would merely take you back to the beginning. That, presumably, would mean the Bolshevik revolution (1917).

BILLS AND BULLS

'We are worth no more than *bullae*', said Petronius – 'bubbles'. Little did he know... for *bulla* is the origin of our 'bill'. It meant not just a bubble but also a 'boss, knob, stud' for ornamental purposes. In later Latin it was used of an official document carrying a raised, knob-like wax seal (→ papal 'bulls', a letter with a lead seal attached to it). Over time it became applied to official papers demanding money; and (via French) 'bulls' became 'bills'.

Bulla is also the source of 'bullet' (via French *boule*, a small ball), and 'bulletin', a small official document.

ACCOUNTS AND CONTRACTS

An 'account' in Latin was the plural of that catch-all word *tabula* (see p. 233) – *tabulae*. Accounts could be fiddled then as now (for 'calculations', see p. 126). Cicero told of an estate bought for the woman Caesennia by her dodgy agent Aebutius. He said that no evidence of the transaction was available – no, said Cicero, because Aebutius had stolen her account books, and kept in his own possession the moneylender's account book, in which the price on the debit side had been duly carried over to the credit side!

Meanwhile, a contract was a *locatio*. This came from *loco*, 'I put in a given position' (→ our 'location'), but also 'I give out a contract for work'. Cicero again reports that Verres, the corrupt governor of Sicily, fiddled things so that 'large sums of money were paid over personally to him, that had been falsely entered into the books as paid in connection with *locationes* that never existed'.

EDUCATION AND PHILOSOPHY

INTRODUCTION

When Christianity became Rome's official religion in the fourth century AD, it was the end of paganism, but not of pagan education, even after the break-up of the Roman Empire in the West in the fifth century AD. The point is that a romanized education had long been standard across the Empire, and because it fulfilled society's *secular* needs, Christians had no problems with it. It both accustomed provincials to the Roman ways of doing things, and opened up, for those who wanted it, a route into the Roman political world.

The church was only too keen to take over an established, empire-wide system perfectly designed to help it spread its message among the young. After all, if Pliny the Elder was to be believed, the Roman system had already shown what could be done. Here he described Italy as:

> a land which is the nurseling and mother of all other lands, chosen
> by the divine might of the gods, to make heaven itself more
> glorious, to unite dispersed empires, to temper manners, to draw
> together in mutual comprehension by community of language the
> warring and uncouth tongues of so many nations, to give mankind
> *humanitas* and, in a word, to become throughout the world the
> single fatherland of all peoples.

Changes in the system were made, of course, with much more emphasis on Christian teaching – the Latin Bible, the church fathers (for example, St Augustine). But pagan methods were still the focus. The priority here was given to what the Middle Ages called the *trivium* (*tres*, 'three' + *via*, 'road'), the three 'branches' of literary/ philosophical education – grammar (see p. 121), rhetoric (p. 155) and logic; and teaching still concentrated on line-by-line technical linguistic analysis (see p. 121). The *quadrivium* (four 'branches') – music, arithmetic, geometry and astronomy – referred to mathematical education.

Cicero's treatises on rhetoric were a key text; collections of passages were made from authors like Virgil and even Ovid that exemplified ancient wisdom about life and psychology in line with Christian teaching; and stories were told of pagan Romans, such as the ascetic Cato the Elder, who set good Christian examples. The justification for this was provided by St Augustine, who said:

> If the philosophers chanced to utter truths useful to our faith, as
> the Platonists above all did, not only should we not fear these

truths, but we must also remove them from those unlawful
usurpers [i.e. pagans] for our own use.

St Basil used another image: rose bushes produce glorious flowers for picking, but we must avoid the (pagan) thorns. And that was what Christians did. Ancient philosophy was predominantly concerned with reasoned reflection about the morally good life, often springing from beliefs about the nature of the world and always open to question. The gods, being a product of nature, were not a driving force behind this moral existence; there was certainly no equivalent of an ultimate authority, such as the Bible. When the Christian Tertullian said, 'I believe *because* it is impossible', he was rejecting the whole intellectual classical tradition. But that tradition was still behind the highly respected pagan education, and there was much that could be assimilated to Christianity – for example, Plato's view of a morally good deity and Aristotle's views of logic and language and the relationship between the natural and the metaphysical world. Thereby hangs a tale. First Aristotle wrote about 'The Natural World', *ta phusika* (τα φυσικα); and *after* that he wrote about the metaphysical world, *ta metaphusika* (τα μεταφυσικα), which meant literally 'After [my book about] The Natural World'!

A central figure in the development of Christian education was Alcuin, from York (*c.* AD 735–804). Widely learned in classics, he was recruited by Charlemagne, who ruled much of Europe from AD 771 to 814, to help establish schools in all monasteries and cathedrals in his European 'empire' and raise the standards of education among the clergy. The result was the copying and editing of texts on a huge scale, ensuring the survival of large numbers of Greek and Roman authors.

A major shift occurred in the European Renaissance, from the late fifteenth century onwards. This saw a gradual movement away from technicalities to 'humanism', which used classical authors to help pupils understand people and man's place in the world. The move was prompted partly by the re-emergence of Greek in the West.

This came about because, from the twelfth century, scholars in the Greek East in Byzantium became fearful of assaults by the Ottoman Turks. So they moved west, especially into Italy, and brought their precious Greek manuscripts with them, which had not been available in most of the West since the end of the Roman Empire there. Scholars had been aware of the Greeks' achievements, of course, because Latin literature was full of them (see p. 143); but their works had disappeared.

There was also renewed interest in, and so a search in libraries for, Latin authors, especially those like Cicero, with their interest in the best forms of government and man's duties and responsibilities. In his *Education for Boys* (1450), the future Pope Pius II declared that, in reading these works of practical wisdom by the ancient and modern authors, 'through zeal for virtue you will make your life better, and you will acquire the art of grammar and skill in the use of the best and most elegant words, as well as a great store of maxims'.

New interest in classical painting, sculpture and architecture accompanied this general revival. As a result, the learning of Latin and reading of Latin authors were embedded in school curricula all over Europe for around the next 400 years. For the rest of the story, see p. 7ff.

EDUCATION

The Latin *educatio* meant the rearing of young or breeding of animals; it derives from the verb *educo*, 'I support the growth of', used of offspring, animals and plants. It was not used of systematic education in our sense largely because there was no such thing in Rome. Teaching was done by parents – we hear that Cato the Elder taught his son reading, law and athletics, to throw a javelin, fight in armour, ride a horse, box, endure heat and cold, and swim – and private tutors. The *litterarius* ('letters man') taught basic reading and writing and numbers; then for the pupil aged about nine, the *grammaticus* polished up those skills, teaching mainly poetry and Greek; then at around the age of fifteen, the *rhêtôr* (Greek ῥήτωρ, Latin *rhetor*: see p. 155) taught the arts of political and legal persuasive argument. Much of this would involve the use of history and its precedents, myth and its examples, philosophy and so on. Repetition and learning by heart from a young age were strongly emphasized.

Interestingly, the Latin word *tutor* had nothing to do with teaching; he was a guardian or protector, originally someone appointed to look after a person considered unable to manage their own affairs. The term derives from *tutus*, 'safe', from the verb *tueor* (*tuit-*), 'I catch sight of; watch over, protect'. Our 'intuition' derives from *intueor*, 'I fix my gaze upon, consider, contemplate', though nowadays it means 'instant understanding, without proper thought'.

SCHOOLS FOR LEISURE

Since education was designed for those committed to public life, it was largely the domain of the elite (*eligo* [*elect-*], 'I extract [of weeds];

I pick out, select'). First, it had to be paid for; second – and far more significant – you had to have the time to indulge it. When most of the population had to make their own living as best they could, whether off the land or in some form of private endeavour, a structured education was largely irrelevant: it was all hands to the pumps on the farm or in the forum (see p. 55). Only the wealthy, living off the profits of their land, could afford the luxury. Our 'school' reflects this, being derived from the Greek for 'leisure' – *skholê* (σχολη). For Romans, the word for 'elementary school' was *ludus*, 'sport, play, show, frivolity' (whence 'ludicrous', and so on).

PUPILS, PUPPETS AND POPPETS

Pupils may often feel like captives of their tyrannous teachers, and they would be right, at least linguistically. The emperor Nero knew the feeling. Madly in love with Poppaea, he could not divorce his wife Octavia because of his mother's disapproval. Poppaea rounded on him, calling him a *'pupillus*, dependent on someone else's orders, in control neither of your empire nor your freedom!'

Latin *pupa* meant 'girl, doll', and the diminutive forms *pupilla* and *pupillus* were used, respectively, of girls and boys under the care of a guardian, as Poppaea accused the emperor of being. So our 'pupil' is an appropriate name for one under the care of a teacher. Another term for 'pupil' was *discipulus*, 'one who learns', requisitioned by the church, as in 'disciple'. That comes from *disco*, 'I learn', as in *disciplina*, 'instruction, branch of study, orderly conduct'. This could become physical. Romans had no problem about this as long as it was purposeful. Tacitus said disapprovingly of the Germans that they were accustomed to kill their slaves not to maintain discipline and strict standards (*severitas*) but out of impulse and rage (*ira*).

When we talk of inculcating good habits, for example, we are using the Latin *inculco* (*inculcat-*). Its root meaning was 'I stamp in with the heel' (*calx* [*calc-*], 'heel'). That will show them!

EYEING PUPILS

The diminutive *pupilla* had in Latin another meaning, at it does in English: 'pupil' as in 'pupil of the eye', the hole in the centre of the iris which looks black but through which light can hit the retina. Apparently it is so called because when you look in another person's eye, you see a diminutive reflection of yourself. Pliny the Elder commented that 'when a man lets go of a bird, it will usually make straight for his eyes because it sees there an image of itself which it knows and wants to reach'.

Vulgar Latin spelled *pupa* '*puppa*', and because it meant 'doll' as well as 'girl', it is the source of our 'puppet' and the endearment 'poppet'.

LEARNING YOUR GRAMMAR

The pupil confronted with a Latin text was trained to analyse it in minute technical detail. This would include everything from dividing words up into syllables (see p. 149), pronouncing them properly and parsing them, to writing them, analysing the metre of a poem, reading aloud and so on. Outlandish words were chosen for this exercise, e.g. *knaxzbikh* (κναξζβιχ) – whatever that meant. Our 'parse' derives from the question: '*Quae pars orationis?*' 'What part of speech?' Only much later in a pupil's education were texts mined for anything other than technicalities, such as historical and moral content, and then only for the purpose of learning to produce a really persuasive speech.

DOSITHEUS' *GUIDELINES*

There survives from the fourth century AD a collection of material, some produced by one Dositheus, some ascribed to him, some by others, illustrating how Latin was taught to Greek speakers.

It consisted of a series of *colloquia* (→ our 'colloquial'), simple everyday 'conversations' in Latin translated into Greek word for word; explanations of the alphabet; discussions of grammar, such as the case system, i.e. nominative, accusative and so on; lists of different types of noun; conjugating verbs, from Latin *coniugo*, 'I marry up' (the different parts); vocabulary lists; words with multiple meanings; and passages from Latin authors.

One manuscript shows that Romans transliterated Latin into Greek to help Greeks learn Latin, just as this book transliterates Greek into English before giving the Greek. So Latin *feliciter* ('good luck!') is transliterated as φιλικιτερ (*filikiter*).*

THE CASE SYSTEM

Latin and Greek are 'inflected' languages (Latin *inflecto*, 'I bend, modify'). That meant many of the words changed their shape to

---

* Note the confusion of 'i' and 'e', due to some merging of these sounds at this late date.

reflect the job they did in the sentence (English 'I' and 'me', 'he' and 'his', etc.).

Nouns changed their endings to do this. So Latin *servus* meant that 'slave' was the subject of the sentence; *servum* that he was the object; *servi* meant 'of the slave'; and so on. So *servus servum servi video* would mean 'the slave sees the slave of the slave' – and so on. These different forms of the noun were called 'cases', and when you listed them in order, you 'declined' them.

CASES OF FALLING OVER

The terms for grammatical cases derive from Latin, though Greeks, of course, had got there first. Aristotle's word for 'case' was *ptôsis* [πτωσις], 'falling, modification', whence Latin *casus* (*cado* [*cas*-], 'I fall') and so 'case'. This 'falling' image was taken literally: the ancients envisaged the nominative, *nominativus* – the 'naming' case (or subject of a sentence) – as 'at the top', and the other cases falling away from it sideways (whence Greek *egklisis* [ἐγκλισις], 'leaning' = *declinatio*, 'declining', whence our 'declension').

The vocative, *vocativus*, 'for calling', was used for addressing people. The genitive, *genitivus*, 'giving birth', was the equivalent of Greek *genikê* [γενικη], 'generic' (represented by English 'of'). The dative, *dativus*, 'giving', corresponded to Greek *dotikê* [δοτικη], 'giving' (English 'to' or 'for'). The accusative – *accusativus*, 'accusing', from *aitiatikê* [αἰτιατικη], 'produced by a cause, effected' – indicated the direct object of a sentence. The ablative case – *ablativus*, 'that from which something is taken away' (English 'by, with or from') – was unique to Latin and first mentioned by

Quintilian. The Roman antiquarian Varro (116–27 BC) called the ablative the 'sixth case' or the 'Latin case'.

NUMBERS

We owe our alphabet to the Greeks and Romans. It is a relief that we owe our numerals to the Arabs. You try multiplying XXXVI by MDCCCXCVIII.

Below is a chart with basic Greek and Latin words for numbers, many of which will be familiar. It will help to explain primary, secondary and tertiary education, decimal, the mile (a thousand paces), September to December, the octave, Pentecost, quarts, Deuteronomy (*nomos* [νομος], 'law'), the Septuagint, quarantine (from *quadraginta*, the number of days a potentially infected person would be kept isolated) and trivial (Latin *trivium* was where three roads met, basically a street corner, a place of no importance). Juvenal satirized know-all women who banged on about politics, soldiering and world affairs:

> How cities are tottering, lands subsiding,
> and tells everyone she meets all about it *at every street corner.*

Scientists will recognize 'proton' and 'deuterium', whose nucleus is called 'deuteron'. But not 'neutron': this derives from Latin *neutrum*, 'neither', given a Greek ending (*-on*) to look like the others.

Geometricians will know the Greek for 'corner', *gônia* (γωνια). This gives us all those geometric shapes with different numbers of corners, such as pentagon, hexagon and polygon ('many-cornered': *polu* [πολυ], 'much, many').

Really big modern numbers have been given modern help from the ancient Greeks, or at least from their vocabulary. Numbers in the millions are *mega* (μεγα, 'big'); in the billions they are *giga* (γιγας, 'giant'); and in the trillions they are *tera* (τερας, 'monster').

Incidentally, Latin *secundus* is so called because it follows *primus* (Latin *sequor* [*secut-*], 'I follow').

	Greek	Latin		Greek	Latin
1	α' heis (hen-)	I unus	1st	prôtos	primus
2	β' duo	II duo	2nd	deuteros	secundus
3	γ' treis	III tres	3rd	tritos	tertius
4	δ' tessares	IV quattuor	4th	tetartos	quartus
5	ε' pente	V quinque	5th	pemptos	quintus
6	ς' * hex	VI sex	6th	hektos	sextus
7	ζ' hepta	VII septem	7th	hebdomos	septimus
8	η' oktô	VIII octo	8th	ogdoos	octavus
9	θ' ennea	IX novem	9th	enatos	nonus
10	ι' deka	X decem	10th	dekatos	decimus
11	ια' hendeka	XI undecim	11th	hendekatos	undecimus
20	κ' eikosi	XX viginti	20th	eikostos	vicensimus***
21	κ' heis kai eikosi	XXI viginti unus	21st	prôtos kai eikostos	vicensimus primus
30	λ' triakonta	XXX triginta	30th	triakostos	tricensimus
40	μ' tessarakonta	XL quadraginta	40th	tessarakostos	quadragensimus
50	ν' pentêkonta	L quinquaginta	50th	pentêkostos	quinquagensimus
60	ξ' hexêkonta	LX sexaginta	60th	hexêkostos	sexagensimus
70	ο' hebdomêkonta	LXX septuaginta	70th	hebdomêkostos	septuagensimus
80	π' odgoêkonta	LXXX octoginta	80th	ogdoêkostos	octogensimus
90	Ϙ' ** enenêkonta	XC nonaginta	90th	enenêkostos	nonagensimus
100	ρ' hekaton	C centum	100th	hekatostos	centensimus
500	φ' pentakosioi	D quingenti	500th	pentakosiostos	quingentensimus
1,000	'ω khilioi	M mille	1,000th	muriostos	millensimus

*   This letter is *vau*, a form of *digamma* (w), which dropped out of the Greek alphabet. It was used only to represent the number six.

**   This letter is *koppa*, used in an early form of the Greek alphabet but replaced by *kappa* (κ). It is the source of the Latin, and so our, letter q.

*** The *-ensimus* ending can appear as *-esimus*.

COMPUTING MATHEMATICAL CALCULATIONS

It was Pythagoras (it seems) who first suggested that there was a mathematical harmony to the universe, as if number and ratio in some sense lay at the root of everything. From this came the idea of the cosmic 'harmony of the spheres' (see p. 246). The Greek *mathêma* (μαθημα) meant basically 'lesson, learning', and then 'mathematical science'; *arithmos* (ἀριθμος) meant 'number, counting' and then 'arithmetic'.

The Romans took over both these words (*mathêmaticus, arithmêticus*) but also gave us 'calculus'. For Romans, *calculus* meant 'small stone, pebble' (also used for juggling), but specifically a pebble used to make calculations on a counting board, and so 'reckoning, account'. *Calculatores* were people who taught arithmetic. The poet Martial urged *calculatores* and teachers of shorthand to forget about pupils during the sweltering, mosquito-ridden days of summer: 'They'll learn enough if they just keep well.'

For 'making a calculation', Romans used *computo* (*computat-*), 'I calculate, reckon up'. A 'reputation' derives from *reputo*, 'I reckon up, reflect on, consider'; another meaning (somewhat ironical these days) is 'I make allowances for expenses', which the reputable are always very careful not to massage.

DIGITAL WORLD

Pliny the Younger mentioned a court case he conducted about a contested inheritance, and said at one stage he had to do some calculating (*computo*), and 'practically demanded pebbles and a board' (*calculos et tabulam*) to do it. He also talked of a man 'moving his lips, twiddling his fingers...' as he does his sums (*computat*). Nothing new about the digital world, then (*digitus*, 'finger').

VOTING PEBBLES

For us, 'calculus' has a very specific mathematical meaning and was first used in the 1660s. The Greek for 'pebble' was *psêphos* (ψηφος), and pebbles were used for voting in the courts. Hence our 'psephology', the study of voting, or elections.

GRAMMAR SCHOOLS

Our 'grammar' derives ultimately from Greek *gramma* (γραμμα), 'letter of the alphabet', a noun formed from *graphô* (γραφω), 'I write' (whence the 'graphite' in your pencil). From this Greeks created *grammatikos* (γραμματικος), an adjective meaning 'good scholar, grammarian, critic'. Romans turned this into a noun, *grammatica*, meaning 'the study of literature and language, including its explanation critically and grammatically'. This emerged in Old French as *gramaire*, and so our 'grammar'.

The original grammar schools from the sixth century AD – *scolae grammaticales* – taught Latin mainly to train people for the church, and Latin (with Greek) remained at the heart of grammar school curricula for another thousand years: it was *the* language of education. In the process Latin grammar came to be thought of as providing the definitive systematic account of the rules of language, to which every language should conform, however uneasy the fit (see p. 16).

It ought to be said here that in Rome the top teachers of language and literature at the advanced level could command gigantic salaries.

After all, it was the key to political success. One such teacher (born in slavery) was bought for 700,000 sesterces, another was paid 400,000 sesterces a year to teach.

THE GLAMOUR OF GRAMMAR

Not many pupils would think of grammar as an alluring subject, but words have always been felt to hold some mysterious, even bewitching power (see p. 14); and the Scottish word 'gramarye', derived from 'grammar', meant 'magic, enchantment' and then 'magical beauty'. Many consonants readily change to 'r' (called 'rhotacism', after the Greek letter *rho*, for example 'got a lot of' becomes 'gorra lorra'). So 'gramarye' became 'glamer', with the spelling 'glamour' the final result.

THE COURSE OF LIFE

Our 'curriculum' was taken over from Latin *curriculum*. *Curro* meant 'I run' (→ our 'current'), and *curriculum* meant 'running, race, racetrack' and also 'course of action, way of behaving'. But, rather like most modern school *curricula*, Latin *curriculum* had nothing to do with education. Nowadays, your *curriculum vitae* is supposed to reveal how you have run the race of life.

THE LANGUAGE OF GRAMMAR

Ancient Greeks invented much of the grammatical terminology that we still use today. The Greek words were translated into Latin by excited Roman grammarians. The Roman encyclopedist Varro was among the enthusiasts: his reaction to Greek research was to write the twenty-five-volume *De lingua Latina* ('On the Latin language'), of which five books survive. These terms came into our language via Norman French. The chart below gives some examples.

Greek	Latin	English
onoma, 'name'	*nomen*	noun
rhêma, 'what is said'	*verbum*	verb
epi-rrhema, 'in addition to what is said'	*ad-verbium*	adverb
ant-ônumia, 'in-place-of noun'	*pro-nomen*	pronoun
sun-desmos, 'binding together'	*con-iunctio*	conjunction
pro-thesis, 'placing before'	*prae-positio*	preposition
metokhê, 'sharing' (i.e. the function of a verb and noun/adjective)	*participium*	participle

The language of tense (past, present, etc.), voice (active, passive, etc.), transitive/intransitive, mood (imperative, subjunctive, etc.), case names (nominative, accusative, etc.) and so on all originated in the classical world.

GROVES OF *ACADEME*

Looking back at his past, the Roman poet Horace (first century BC) talked of a brief spell of 'higher education' in Athens 'seeking truth in the groves of Academus' (*silvas Academi*). It was brief because, following the assassination of Julius Caesar in 44 BC, civil war broke out between Caesar's supporters Octavian and Antony (the eventual winners) and the assassins Brutus and Cassius. Horace joined the losing side.

But who, or what, was Academus? He was the mythical Greek hero *Akadêmos* (Ἀκαδημος; alternatively *Hekadêmos*) and was said to have originally owned the area, about a mile north-west of Athens.

His bit part in myth was very small: when Theseus and Peirithous had stolen the young Helen (later of Troy) from Sparta with a view to one of them marrying her, *Akadêmos* revealed her whereabouts to Helen's brothers, the gods Castor and Pollux. In the sixth century BC, the area was walled in, trees were planted and it became a public park. Plato bought a piece of property nearby and taught there or in the park: hence Plato's *Akadêmeia*, our 'academy', 'academic' and so on.

PHILOSOPHY IN LATIN

Horace went to Athens to finish off his education, as did many other Romans, including the Roman statesman Cicero, and that meant philosophy. There is a good reason why Greeks were the philosophers: they invented the subject and the language. It was Cicero who took the Greek and latinized it, providing us with a range of Latin options.

In some cases, the Greek word was simply written in Latin, such as *philosophia* from φιλοσοφια. The Greek meant 'love' (φιλο-) + 'cleverness, intelligence, learning, wisdom' (σοφια, → 'sophist'). Cicero debated how to translate Greek *sôphrosunê* (σωφροσυνη), 'moderation, self-control': 'Sometimes I call it *temperantia*, sometimes *moderatio*, sometimes also *modestia*. But I do not know whether this virtue could better be termed *frugalitas*...'

SOME PHILOSOPHICAL TERMS

As a result of the efforts of Cicero and others, the following technical terms came from Greek via Latin into English:

- Greek *êthikos* (ἠθικος), 'to do with ethics', became in Latin *moralis* (see p. 37), our 'morals'.

- Greek *philanthrôpia* (φιλανθρωπια), 'love of mankind', became *humanitas*.

- Greek *epistêmê* (ἐπιστημη), 'knowledge', became *scientia*, our 'science'.

- Greek *hormê* (ὁρμη), 'energy, impulse' (p. 283), became *appetitus* (*animi*), our 'appetite'.

- Greek *ousia* (οὐσια), 'unchanging reality', became *essentia*, our 'essence'.

- Greek *poiotês* (ποιοτης), 'what-sort-of-ness', became *qualitas*, our 'quality'.

- Greek *idiôma* (ἰδιωμα), 'special character, unique feature', became *proprietas*, our 'property' in a philosophical sense ('what is the property of electricity?').

But in another sense, *idiôma* meant 'special use of words', as in our 'idiom'. It was formed from *idios* (ἰδιος), 'one's own, private, personal', while *idiôtês* (ἰδιωτης) meant 'private person, layman'. This drifted into meaning 'someone of no professional skill at all, ignorant, uneducated', as it did in Latin *idiota*. And so, 'idiot'!

ETHICS

Many philosophical schools of thought sprang up and became subjects of higher education. Ethical behaviour was at the heart of all of them. This is such a hot topic these days that it is educative to learn that originally the word had nothing necessarily to do with humans at all. Greek *êthos* (ἠθος) meant an 'accustomed place', and in the plural *êthea* (ἤθεα) related to the usual abodes not only of humans but of such things as lions, fish, plants, and even the sun. Herodotus reported that, according to the Egyptians, in the course of its history 'the sun on four different occasions moved *from its accustomed place*, twice rising where it now sets, and twice setting where it now rises'. The term became focused on humans in the sense 'manners, customs', and then 'character'.

This is essentially what Aristotle meant when he talked about ethics. The question for him was what makes a good human being; and by 'good' he meant what we mean by (for example) a good, functioning, successful car. Goodness (in that *practical* sense) of character was one issue – courage, modesty, fairness, and so on; goodness of the intellect was another – knowledge, intelligence, judgement, etc. Man was also a social animal, knowing what was just and unjust, good and bad. That too was all part of being successful.

STOICS

Ancient philosophy was not pie-in-the-sky theory. Its aims were ethical – to show adherents how to lead the good life (Latin *vita beata*, → 'beatitude'); it was also holistic (Greek *holos* [ὅλος], 'whole') because the good life was thought to depend on the physical nature of the universe.

'Stoicism' derived from the Greek *stoa* (στοα), the portico in Athens where from 300 BC its inventor Zeno (a Greek from Cyprus) taught this branch of philosophy. His ideas were based on the belief that (i) in a sense the universe was God, and God was the universe; (ii) to that extent, everything was fated; (iii) the divine element in the world was reason (*logos* [λογος]); and (iv) the whole material world was permeated by *logos* – 'like honey through a honeycomb' – including our souls (Latin *animus*, or *anima*), the divine in us. So if we wanted to align ourselves with the divine – which would presumably make us happy – we should exercise *logos*, the reasoning faculty. *Logos* was the key to a happy life. Material rewards and worldly success were irrelevant.

Logos gives us 'logic' and all the '-[o]logies', which mean 'giving a rational account of'. So 'biology' means giving a rational account of *bios* (βιος), 'life, living things'. The Latin for 'reason' was *ratio* (see p. 10). It meant 'the act or process of reckoning, explanation, (exercise of) reason'. In the chaos after Julius Caesar was assassinated, Cicero wrote despairingly to his friend Atticus: 'We must leave everything to *fortuna*, which counts for more than *ratio* in such matters.'

DANGEROUS EMOTIONS

If *logos* enabled us to lead a happy life, what could stop it? The Stoic answer was: the emotions – anger, fear, pride, grief, desire, even (to take it to extremes) pity and love. Deal with those, and happiness should be yours. But if everything was fated (see above), what chance did you stand? A favourite Stoic image was that of a dog on a long leash tied to a bullock cart. There was nothing the dog could do to stop the bullock going where the bullock wanted. So: the dog could travel its destined course by acting rationally in line with the divine *logos*, and so go freely and happily (though being on a long leash, it had a degree of leeway); or by acting irrationally, it would struggle and be miserable. 'Restrain yourself and endure', said the Stoic thinker Epictetus.

Emotio was not a Latin word, but in the sixteenth century the French invented *émotion*, derived from Latin *emoveo* (*emot-*), 'I shift, dislodge, displace' – which is certainly what the emotions can do to you.

JUSTIFYING SLAVERY

Stoicism was a dogma embraced by many Romans, but it brought its own problems with it. The founder of Stoicism, Zeno himself, argued that all forms of subjugation were evil, and therefore both slavery and empire – the exercise and maintenance of power over other states – were morally wrong. Other Stoics agreed: 'Justice instructs you to spare all men, to respect the human race, to return to each his own, not to touch what is sacred, or what belongs to the state, or what belongs to someone else.' The argument was extended by later Stoics to embrace the idea that humans were naturally bound to one another by a code of law; for one man to use another merely for his own benefit was to break that natural, mutual bond.

Roman Stoics therefore had to reverse the trend of Greek thinking if they were to justify Rome's imperial ambitions. The defence of empire began from the proposition that slavery was in the interests of certain kinds of men who, if left to their own devices, would only damage those interests, for instance by robbery or civil disorder. A properly administered empire, however – that is, one driven by moral concerns – would ensure such injustices did not take place. In certain cases, therefore, the subjugation of a people was justified – on condition that the imperial power acted morally and had the well-being of its subjects at heart.

EPICUREANISM

The belief that Rome had been divinely ordained to rule the world was strong. Virgil in his *Aeneid*, a canonic work of literature for the Romans, described Jupiter as affirming that he 'had given Rome rule (*imperium*) without end'.

Yet Epicurean philosophers saw no room for deities. The Greek Epicurus (*Epikouros*, Ἐπίκουρος) had taken on board atomic theory (Greek *atomos* [ἄτομος], meaning 'unsplittable'). It was invented by the Greek philosopher Democritus in the fifth century BC. *Atomos* referred to the small, indivisible particles out of which, Democritus speculated, the whole universe, including the gods, was constructed; and their movement through the universe was random and irrational. So there were no such things as controlling gods or providence.

AN ATOMIC UNIVERSE

In his marvellous poem 'On the Nature of Matter', the Roman poet Lucretius (first century BC) showed with almost religious fervour how atomism explained everything without recourse to divine agency – from gods to man, from sex and sight to dreams, thunderstorms and earthquakes. In particular, since from atoms we come and to atoms back we go, the soul or life force (*anima*, → 'animal') must also be made of atoms. It disintegrated in death with us. Therefore there was no afterlife and nothing to fear in death; and further, gods had no interest in the activities of humans. Not that Lucretius used *atomus*: he preferred *semina rerum*, 'seeds of matter', from *semen* (*semin-*), which gives our 'seminal, inseminate' and 'seminar', where ideas are seeded; and *primordia rerum*, 'very beginnings, elementary stages, of matter', whence our 'primordial' (see p. 34 for *ordo*).

By contrast, with intense disgust in his voice, Lucretius described how *religio* persuaded Agamemnon, leader of the Greek army against the Trojans, to lead his very own weeping daughter Iphigeneia as a sacrifice to the altar and personally cut her down, in order to get the wind that would enable the Greeks to sail to Troy: 'Such monstrous wickedness could *religio* incite.'

FROM ATOMS TO MOLECULES

Lucretius was unlucky. His work vanished from sight for hundreds of years, largely because Aristotle's theory that the main constituents of the cosmos were earth, air, fire and water ruled the roost. This was the 'four-element' theory – five if you add *aithêr* (αἰθηρ), the element filling the external universe. But in 1417 a manuscript of the poet was discovered in a library in Germany. Its contents became known to thinkers who had come to see that Aristotle's theory was nonsense and were grappling to find a better one. By the seventeenth century atomic particle theory had started to come to the fore – where it remains to this day.

In 1678 this new particle theory spawned the term *molecula*. It was derived from the Latin *moles*, which, bizarrely, meant 'a gigantic mass' (giving us our 'mole', a huge breakwater to hold back the sea). The *-cula* ending, however, is a diminutive, so *molecula* should mean 'a small gigantic mass'. Naturally, no Roman would ever have envisaged such an idiotic word. Anyway, the result was the gradual development of the idea that atoms combine to form molecules.

SCEPTICS

If people are 'sceptical' about, say, global warming, it is understood that they do not believe it, or have severe doubts about it. That indicates quite a shift from the original meaning of the word. The Greek verb on which 'sceptic' is based is *skeptomai* (σκεπτομαι), 'I watch out, look about carefully, examine, consider', while *skeptikos* (σκεπτικος) meant 'thoughtful, reflective'. In Homer's *Iliad*, the Trojan hero Hector retreated from battle, '*watching out* for the whistle of arrows and thud of spears'. When some Athenian representatives in Sparta heard the Corinthians (allies of Sparta) denouncing Athens and saying Sparta should attack at once, the Athenians defended themselves, 'because the matter needed to be *considered further* and not decided on the spot'. In other words, it had active connotations: the matter was up for serious debate.

The change came about with the invention of the philosophy known as 'Scepticism' by the Greek Pyrrho (*c.* 360–270 BC). In it, he suggested that it was impossible to understand the real nature of things, either because the world itself was shifting and indeterminate, or because we were just not able to understand it, however much we might try. So there was not much point in bothering, and we might as well live as untroubled a life as we can, unconcerned about all these matters. His biographer said: 'He led a life consistent with this belief, taking no precautions against anything – dogs, carts, precipices – and was kept out of harm's way by his friends.' He was happy to take things to market, and do the cleaning in the house. He once washed a pig.

Rather surprisingly, because Romans were very interested in this philosophy, the word *scepticus* does not appear in classical Latin. Romans talked instead of *Pyrrhonei*, followers of Pyrrho.

COSMOPOLITAN CYNIC

Acting like a dog: that was the accusation made against the Greek thinker Diogenes (*c.* 400–323 BC), who came from a Greek colony in Sinope on the Black Sea coast. Greek *kuôn* (κυων) meant 'dog' and *kunikos* (κυνικος) meant 'dog-like, canine'; Romans turned it into *cynicus*, from which we derive 'cynic'.

The reason for the accusation was that Diogenes appeared wholly unconcerned about behaving in accordance with normal human standards. Uninterested in theoretical or philosophical problems, he believed humans were basically primitive beings with an overlay of civilized sophistication that was quite inappropriate to their real nature or interests. Abandoning all commitment to family, state or convention, he declared himself a citizen of the world (*kosmopolitês*, κοσμοπολιτης). He lived in a large earthenware container and believed in self-sufficiency, freedom of speech and indifference to hardship. He had no interest in worldly goods and thought money the *mêtropolis* (μητροπολις, 'mother-city') of all evils.

DIATRIBES AND QUOTATIONS

All of these philosophers are better called lifestyle gurus. They were in competition with each other, and all of them churned out treatises to argue their cases. But those treatises, being composed on papyrus – a vegetable substance which lasts only about eighty years – would survive only if they were copied and recopied down the ages (see p. 147). Many were not. The Greek for 'treatise' was *diatribê* (διατριβη), whence our 'diatribe'. That word has competitive overtones. Many an ancient *diatribê* certainly felt like that too.

But although much is lost, we often know something about these people because quotations from lost works frequently appear in works that do survive, such as encyclopedias, dictionaries and accounts of ancient lives. To take an example: Diogenes Laertius (third century AD) wrote the lives of eighty-two philosophers, of whom only five today survive in whole books; make that four if you discount Socrates, who wrote nothing but whose dialogues were 'written up' by Plato. Diogenes refers in all to 365 books by a total of 250 named authors, as well as 350 anonymous ones.

'Quotation' is not a Latin word, though it is based on one: *quotus*, meaning 'having what position in a numerical series?', 'bearing what proportion?' (compare our 'quota'). From the sixteenth century 'quote' was used to mean 'mark with numbers in the margin' and so 'cite, refer to'.

WRITING AND LITERATURE

INTRODUCTION

I t is traditional to divide Latin literature into three periods:

The Early Republic (third to second centuries BC): this featured Greek-based Roman comedies (Plautus and Terence), the Romans' first shot at prose history, the development of a rhetorical style, Ennius' poetic history of Rome in epic Homeric style, and Lucilius, the inventor of satire.

The Golden Age (100 BC–AD 14): this brought into the world the great names – the love poetry of Catullus and Ovid, Lucretius' poetic account of the making of the world, Livy's gigantic history of Rome, Cicero's speeches and treatises on philosophy and government, Virgil's epic *Aeneid*, the arch and elegant poems of Horace.

The Silver Age (AD 14–180): this period too is notable for some outstanding authors – Tacitus, biting, incisive, not a word wasted, the most brilliant historian of all; one of the world's finest epigrammatists, Martial; the satirist Juvenal; and the epic poet Lucan.

But who read them? What were they trying to achieve? A metrical graffito (see p. 162 on elegiacs) on a wall in Pompeii reads:

I'm amazed, wall, that you have not collapsed in ruins,
Under the weight of so many scribblers' dreadful stuff.

We do not know how literate the average Roman in the street was, though we do know that after the collapse of the Roman Empire in the West in the fifth century AD, there were no more walls covered in graffiti as there were in Pompeii. The existence of libraries – including twenty-nine in Rome alone and the huge library of about 1,800 scrolls buried in a private villa in Herculaneum after the eruption of Vesuvius in AD 79 – tells us little about the man in the street.

That said, writers of Latin literature (like emperors) came from all over the Roman Empire – Africa, Spain, Gaul – as well as from all over Italy. Interestingly, we do not know of a single poet who actually came from Rome itself. While books were published (i.e. copied out by hand) and sold in booksellers' shops – it seems they were pretty expensive – literature was most usually conveyed by the author's live recitation (*recitatio*) to interested parties. The poet Martial constantly mocked poets like Ligurinus, who put on dinner parties solely to recite their own stuff, each course delayed while another book, and then another, was being read. But being an author was a hard slog.

In the absence of contracts, advances, royalties and copyright, a fledgling writer had either to be wealthy in his own right (we hear of few female writers) or to find a patron. Martial, who came from Spain and was indeed wealthy, still needed patrons to sustain his career.

Romans were practical people, and usefulness was a key criterion of successful literature. This was fine if one was writing an encyclopedia or treatise on battle strategy, geography, farming or language, or a history, which would be full of useful examples from the past to guide the present (on *exempla*, see p. 75). But what about poetry? The poet Horace talked of combining pleasure and utility, the latter consisting in the moral and instructional content of the poetry.

But for Romans there was always an *elephas* (ἐλεφας) in the room – the Greeks. Romans drew endlessly on Greek literature for inspiration, and they knew it. Among the earliest works of Latin literature were comedies by Plautus and Terence (second century BC) – and they were all based closely on Greek comedies, retaining the Greek names, settings and customs, though frequently adapted to the Roman world (*praetors* and *aediles* were mentioned, for example). Virgil in his *Aeneid* took a Trojan hero, Aeneas, from Homer's *Iliad* and not only turned him into the heroic founder of the Roman race but also adapted him to the political situation of the time in Rome. In many ways Aeneas was a sort of Augustus figure (the first Roman emperor), aligned with pure Roman values (*pietas*, *virtus*, etc.; see p. 185). The Roman poet Propertius said of the *Aeneid*, while it was still being composed, 'Surrender, you Greek and Roman writers, surrender: something greater than the *Iliad* is being born.'

Latin literature inevitably reflected the education that the writers had themselves received. This was devoted to producing orators skilled in argument and persuasion, with an enviable store of rhetorical tricks of the trade to draw on (see the list of figures of speech on p. 163ff) and a rich store of parallels from both Greek and Roman myth, history and literature to adapt to the special circumstances of any case they were supporting. Style was of high importance: that is, the style appropriate to any particular class or genre of writing. Epics must be written like epics, history like history (this was called *imitatio*). But at the same time, the writer must not be afraid to bring something different to the literary table, to show himself a master of the genre and not enslaved to it, by adding variety and even novelty to his presentation (this was called *variatio*).* Finally, the writer had to show that he really did know his stuff: that he was acquainted with what earlier masters, both Greek and Roman, had written and that, using his wide reading and learning, he could allude to them and do better than they. 'Spot the allusion' is a favourite game that modern scholars play: ancient writers challenged their rival authors and readers/listeners to do it all the time.

To give a simple example: Homer begins his *Iliad* with an appeal to a Muse (the Muses were goddesses of memory) to sing of the anger of Achilles, which caused mass slaughter of heroes, fulfilling the will of Zeus. He begins his *Odyssey* with an appeal to the Muse to sing of a man (Odysseus) who travelled far and wide, endured much anguish at sea in his efforts to return home, and lost all his companions.

Virgil, 700 years later, begins his epic *Aeneid*, composing in the

---

Varius, 'having two contrasting colours', possibly from *varus*, 'pimple'! Do not confuse with *vârus*, 'bandy-legged' (see p. 257).

same epic metre as Homer (hexameters), with the words 'Arms [= battles] and the man [= Aeneas] I sing' – a clear nod to both the *Iliad* and the *Odyssey*. He describes the dreadful buffeting Aeneas took at sea (*Odyssey*) because of the will of the goddess Juno (*Iliad*), before he reached his new home (*Odyssey*). He then calls on the Muse (*Iliad* and *Odyssey*) to explain why the goddess was angry.

The allusions are obvious, but note also the *variatio*. Virgil begins '*I* sing', and only later asks the Muse to help him. Why? Because Virgil knows the story of Aeneas (that was simple history), but no man can know why the gods are angry: for that, he needs divine assistance and information.

Ancient authors were first and foremost highly skilled, technically gifted craftsmen. Virgil composed at the rate of three lines a day. The idea that anyone had a poem or history in him would have struck them as absurd.

THE ROMAN ALPHABET

We use the Roman version of the alphabet. Unlike the Roman numerical system, the Roman alphabet makes things very easy. Note:

(i) We added 'w' and 'u', for which the Romans used 'v' throughout, and 'j', for which Roman used 'i'.

(ii) Since Romans pronounced 'c' hard as in 'cat', they barely used 'k' at all.

(iii) It was only in the third century BC that Romans introduced 'g', for which up till then they had also used 'c'. In the process, Caius became Gaius, and Cnaeus became Gnaeus.

Interestingly, they still used 'C.' and 'Cn.' to represent the short form of the word, e.g. C. Octavius = Gaius Octavius.

It is important to remember that both Latin and Greek were originally written in capital letters alone (think of all those inscriptions), with no gaps between the words or punctuation.

'Cursive' writing derives from Latin *cursivus*, 'running' (*curro*, 'I run', → 'current'). In the third century BC, Romans developed a form of cursive in capitals – it was not joined up but quicker and easier to write. Joined-up writing in minuscule (Latin *minusculus*, 'rather small') started developing from the third century AD, as did gaps between words and punctuation.

ELEMENTS AND BASICS

The word 'alphabet' derives from Greek *alpha beta*, the first two letters of the Greek alphabet. One term which the Romans used for the letters of their alphabet was *elementa*. In the singular, *elementum* meant 'basic substance' out of which the world was made, 'atom, particle' (on Lucretius, see p. 135). This term from physics was transferred to the arts and education, referring both to the alphabet (the basic substance out of which language is made) and education in the rudiments.

Julius Caesar invented a secret code for writing to friends on matters he wished to keep secret: the correct letter was replaced by the one three letters on in the alphabet, so 'A' became 'D', 'B' became 'E', and so on.

BARKING

Given that ancient paper was made from the inner pith of the papyrus plant, it may seem strange that the Latin for 'book written for publication', *liber* (*libr-*), meant 'inner bark of a tree', 'rind'. Pliny the Elder, in his magnificent thirty-eight-book encyclopedia *Natural History*, explained that people began to write first on palm leaves, then on bark and sheets of lead, linen or wax tablets (he could have added pottery and clay). He claimed that papyrus was not used till Alexander the Great (who died in 323 BC) came across it in Egypt; but Egyptians had been using it from the fourth millennium BC, Greeks from the seventh century BC.

The Egyptians had three words for papyrus – *wadj*, *tjufy* and *djet*. None bore any resemblance to Greek *papuros* (παπυρος), which may derive from the Egyptian for 'belonging to the Pharaoh' (was it a royal monopoly?). This became *papyrus* in Latin, giving us our 'paper'. The Greek word for the actual papyrus plant, however, was *bublos* (βυβλος), which over time became *biblos* (βιβλος), Greek for a 'book', whence our 'bible'.

A small piece of writing paper was Latin *schida*, possibly from the Greek *skheda* (σχεδα), 'page'. In its diminutive form in Late Latin it became *schedula*, which from the fourteenth century was used to mean 'ticket, label'. In 1863 'schedule' was first used of a railway timetable.

ROLL OUT THE WORDS

Sheets of papyrus were formed by extracting the pith of the plants in strips, laying them on top of each other, one layer at right angles to the other, beating them flat and smoothing them off to form a surface on which to write. These sheets were then glued together, making a strip ten to twenty-two feet long (Pliny says twenty sheets were the maximum). This was then rolled up into a *volumen* (Latin *volvo*, 'I roll', whence our 'volume'), the technical term for a roll of papyrus.

GLUE AND GLUTEN

Pliny the Elder wrote that flour reduced to a fine powder and mixed with water was used to glue together the sheets that made up a papyrus roll. The verb *glutino* was also used as a medical metaphor to describe the effect of certain substances in closing up, or glueing together, wounds. Celsus gave a long list of substances which could be smeared on for this purpose, including myrrh, frankincense, linseed, white of egg, snails crushed with their shells, 'even cobwebs'. Skin glue, used to close wounds, is a relatively recent invention.

Gluten (*glutin-*), the Latin for 'glue', is the modern name given to the protein found in wheat that gives it its elasticity and helps it to rise. That is why bread is chewy and why bread rolls retain their shape.

FROM BLOCKHEADS TO CODES

The papyrus roll was not exactly high-tech. Quite apart from its limited lifespan, you could write only on one side. Imagine unrolling in the right hand, while rolling up in the left, a roll twenty-two feet long, re-rolling it when you had finished it so that you were back at the beginning, then trying to find a reference in the middle. Seneca ended a letter: 'But I must not exceed what a letter can take. It ought not to fill up the reader's left hand.'

The scroll had been in use for thousands of years, until the first century AD, when Romans invented the book, the *caudex* or *codex*. This meant a trunk or stem of a tree, and also a blockhead, presumably thick as a plank. But it was also used to mean a number of wooden writing tablets (see below) tied together down one side to form a tablet 'book'. The name *codex* stuck when papyrus was used to replace the wooden tablets. It gives us 'code', 'codify', etc. We are told that Augustus' will was written both on bound wooden tablets and on papyrus rolls.

A roll was made of sheets of papyrus, but a *codex* of pages. Latin *pagina*, from which our 'page' derives, was originally nothing but a column of writing, or the space a column would occupy, in particular a column or page of poetry.

LABELS AND SYLLABUS

A roll clearly does not have a spine on which the title of the book can be written. So the roll had a label attached to identify it: Greek *sillubos* (σιλλυβος). The church latinized this term to *syllabus*, meaning a 'list', whence our 'syllabus', a list of school subjects. The Greek plural would be *silluboi* (σιλλυβοι), the Latin *syllabi*, the English – whatever we want to make it.

STYLISH TABLETS

Papyrus was expensive, and writing tablets were the cheap option for quick communications. They were made from two small, oblong, flat wood boards, inlaid with coated wax and threaded together to open like a book. Scratch your message in the wax with a metal *stilus* (a pointed writing implement);* fold the two tablets together so the message cannot be seen; wrap string around it and seal it; and give it to a slave to deliver. The recipient will untie it, open it, read the message, smooth over the wax, write a reply, fold it up, reseal and send it back. These *tabellae* in Latin are small *tabulae*, a *tabula* being a flat piece of wood, board or plank. *Tabula* gives us 'table', while *tabellae*, via French *tablette*, gives us 'tablet'. 'Tabloid' is also derived from this stem, used originally by a drugs company of a small, condensed tablet, and so of small-sized, condensed newspapers. (See also *tabula*, p. 233.)

LETTERS

Tablets were fine for instant messages. The letter was a quite different matter.

The Latin for a letter of the alphabet was *littera* (→ 'letter'). It may have its origin in the Latin stem *lit-*, meaning 'cover', i.e. papyrus covered with letters. From 'letter' it expanded into meaning 'line, text', and in the plural *litterae*, 'writings, literature, scholarship, learning'. While 'letter' preserves the 'tt' of Latin, the alternative Latin spelling with one 't' survives in 'literature', 'literal', etc. Romans also took over the Greek for 'letter', *epistolê* (ἐπιστολη), as *epistula* (→ 'epistle'). This derived from *epistellô* (ἐπιστελλω), 'I send (a message), command'.

The most famous collection of letters to survive from the ancient world is that of the first-century BC statesman Cicero, some of them day-by-day records of behind-the-scenes events in Roman politics.

---

* *Stilus* was Latin for 'style, literary "pen"': 'pen' derives from Latin *penna*, 'feather', i.e. a quill pen.

But one very remarkable and little-known survival is a letter written by a mother, Cornelia, to her son – the earliest prose known to us from any language to have been composed by a woman.

Cornelia had twelve children, only three surviving. The son in question was Gaius Gracchus. His brother Tiberius, a controversial political reformer, had been murdered in 133 BC in a riot stirred up by senators opposed to his reforms, and Gaius was set on committing himself to equally controversial reforms. Cornelia, who clearly did not agree with what her son was planning, attempted to persuade Gaius not to follow Tiberius' example and stand for the tribunate (see p. 39) in order to pass his legislation. Gaius ignored his mother and did stand in 122 BC, so this letter must date from around that time.

> I would take a solemn oath that, apart from those who killed
> Tiberius Gracchus, no one has given me so much trouble and so
> much pain as you in this matter, who ought to undertake the part
> of all the children I have ever had, and to make sure that I should
> have as little worry as possible in my old age; that, whatever your
> schemes might be, you should wish them to be agreeable to me;
> and that you should count it a sin to take any major step against
> my wishes, especially considering I have only a little part of life
> left. Is it quite impossible to cooperate for even that short space
> of time without your opposing me and ruining our country?
> Where will it all end? Will our family ever cease from madness?
> Can a bound ever be put to it? Shall we ever cease to dwell on

affronts, both causing and suffering them? Shall we ever begin to
feel true shame for confounding and destroying the constitution?

And so on. Cornelia failed: Gaius died in the senatorial riot that
greeted his legislation.

FROM PARCHMENT TO VELLUM

The relative fragility of papyrus resulted in the invention of a
fabulously expensive alternative which could last up to 5,000 years. It
was parchment: processed animal skin – calf, sheep or goat – soaked,
dried, stretched, cleaned and smoothed for writing on. The word
'parchment' derives from Pergamum (via French *parchemin*), the
Greek city on the coast of West Turkey where it was said to have been
invented in the third century BC (in fact the use of skins for writing
goes back to Egypt of the third millennium BC). The alternative
term 'vellum' technically refers to the most expensive parchment –
calfskin. It ultimately derives from *vitellus*, 'little calf ', as does 'veal'.

Because of its cost, parchment containing texts that were deemed
no longer useful was scoured or rubbed clean and used again. Such
a parchment is called a 'palimpsest', from the Greek *palimpsêstos*
(παλιμψηστος), 'scraped again'. It was common for Christians to
overwrite pagan Greek and Latin texts with gospels, creeds and so
on. Many of these pagan texts can now be recovered by use of infra-
red technology.

TEXT AND CONTEXT

The alphabet, parchment, *codex* and minuscule were all technical developments of the very highest importance. In 1439 Johannes Gutenberg introduced perhaps the most important of all, printing with movable type. This ushered in an era of widespread literacy and the beginnings of mass communication. For literary purposes at any rate, computerization represents a radical change only in terms of the ease with which text can now be produced and searched.

Linguistically, however, the production of texts has for thousands of years been thought of as a technical business. The Latin *textus*, from which 'text' derives, meant a pattern or style of weaving; a method of putting things together, a structure; and so the 'fabric' made by joining words together. The Latin *textum* meant 'woven fabric'. The verb *texo*, from which both words came, meant 'I weave, embroider, plait', and was related to the Greek *tektôn* (τεκτων), 'carpenter, craftsman', and *tekhnê* (τεχνη), 'skill, craft'.

Writing, in other words, is not a matter of banging down anything that comes into our heads any way we like, but a technical skill requiring the same sort of training and dedication as a craftsman – and one liable to be judged on the same sort of criteria, at least in the ancient world, where literary shoddiness at any level was wholly unacceptable.

Meanwhile, Latin *contextus*, our 'context', meant 'a whole woven together from numerous parts'. Seneca described the *codex* (see above) as a *contextus* of many *tabulae*; Quintilian said that one way of praising a man was to go into chronological detail, covering 'the *contextus* of all his words and deeds'.

AUTHOR, AUTHOR

Romans usually called an author a *scriptor*, 'writer', but they also used another term: *auctor*. In Latin, it derived from *augeo* (*auct*-), 'I increase, enlarge', and meant someone who <u>author</u>ized action, an expert, an originator, and especially a writer regarded as the final <u>author</u>ity on any subject. Historians constantly referred to their sources as such. Tacitus, typically, had it both ways: 'Following the majority of the *auctores*, I put the withdrawal of the emperor Tiberius to Capri down to Sejanus' intrigues back in Rome, but I wonder if his real purpose was to hide his cruelty and perverted habits...'

Auctor is the source of our 'author' (→ 'authoritative', etc.). One can see why this flattering title appeals so much to today's scribblers.

CELEBRITY

Ancient writers longed for celebrity status as much as their modern counterparts do. When Pliny the Elder was describing Africa, he began by wondering at the unpronounceable (*ineffabilia*, as in 'ineffable') names of its people and towns and the many miraculous stories which Greeks put out about it. He said of Mount Atlas (Ἄτλας), named after the god who supported the world on his shoulders:

> At night, they say, it gleams with fires innumerable lighted up; it is then the scene of the gambols of the Goat Pans and the Satyr crew, while it re-echoes with the notes of various pipes, and the clash of drums and cymbals. All this is what *celebrati* authors have

stated, in addition to the labours which Hercules and Perseus there experienced.

There is a degree of irony to that *celebrati*, 'celebrated': Pliny clearly does not believe a word of what they say! But that is 'celebrity' for you. The word derives from Latin *celeber* (*celebr-*), which basically meant 'busy, crowded' and so 'extensive, common, much talked of'.

RHETORIC

The writer was one thing; the speaker quite another. But you had to be master of both, since recitation of texts (*recitatio*) was the standard means of delivery of your crisp masterpieces.

Rhetoric was also the route to power. The Greek *rhêtôr* (ῥήτωρ) meant 'speaker', and *rhêtorikê* (ῥητορικη) 'the art of persuasion'. The Romans used *rhetor* for a person who taught professional speaking, reserving *orator* for the public speaker: the verb *oro* (*orat-*) meant 'I beseech, pray to, plead a case'.

Today, thanks to papers, radio, TV, and electronic and satellite communications, there are myriad means of connecting with people all over the globe (Latin *globus*, 'round cake, heavenly sphere, clique, band'). In the ancient world, there were only two: by the written word and by the spoken word, including rumour (Latin *rumor*, 'cheering, shouts; gossip').

Given the levels of literacy, the absence of printing and the sheer labour of book production (see p. 146ff), the written word was largely confined to the wealthy educated classes. So it is difficult to overstate the importance of the spoken word, the sole means of communicating verbally with the masses (and with no microphones either). It was the main route to power in the ancient world and at the heart of Roman education.

Aristotle wrote the definitive text on the art of rhetoric; Cicero wrote no fewer than six treatises on the subject. Roman education was in this sense almost wholly pragmatic, devoted to producing men who could sway political and legal gatherings in the Senate, assemblies and the courts. The art of persuasion these days seems to be wholly in the hands of frequently illiterate speech-writers, advertisers, advisers and wonks.

PROSE AND VERSE

The first Roman literature we hear of (bar laws and edicts) is, as it was in the Greek world, verse: a translation of Homer's *Odyssey* by one Livius Andronicus (third century BC). The Latin *versus*, from which our word derives, meant 'furrow, row, line', whether a line of writing or a line of poetry. It derives from Latin *verto*, 'I turn', and referred to the plough turning from one line to the next.

Latin prose seems to have developed in the second century BC as a means of political and moral persuasion, and was used subsequently as a medium for facts, arguments, instructions, propaganda and so on, especially technical matters. The law, history, agriculture, the art of war and so on were always subjects of considerable interest to practical-minded Romans. Our 'prose' derives from Latin *pro(r)sus*, 'following a straight line, moving straight ahead', i.e. without any 'turning', ornamentation or metrical structure of verse.*

---

* English 'versus', as in 'A v. B', means 'turned *against*'.

HISTORY

One of the Romans' most popular prose mediums was *historia*.*
Ancient Greeks had invented it, if by 'history' we mean giving an
account of the past which is comprehensible in purely *human* terms
and so excludes supernatural beings from playing any part (which,
for example, discounts most of the Bible). In the fifth century BC,
Herodotus in his history of the Persian Wars (490–479 BC) all but
reached this requirement; Thucydides in his history of the great
conflict between Athens and Sparta (431–404 BC) did reach it.

Historia (ἰστορια) meant basically 'enquiry, investigation; account;
information'. It could cover any topic. Roman historical writing was
especially marked by its interest in how the present had been formed
by the past, and the lessons it had to offer (see *exempla*, p. 75). The
most usual format was annalistic (*annalis*), i.e. year by year (Latin
annus, 'year', as in our 'annual'). Foundation stories *ab urbe condita*
(literally 'from the city having-been-founded', traditionally in 753
BC) were a big feature, and *utilitas*, 'usefulness' (→ 'utility'), was the
key. Moral lessons were eagerly sought.

POETRY

The Greek philosopher Gorgias defined poetry as 'words in metre'
and assigned a mysterious power to it. Presumably thinking of tragedy,
he described its overwhelming emotional effects: 'fearful shuddering,

---

* The Latin adjective *medius* meant 'central, middle; non-committal, neutral', and
the neuter form *medium* was a noun meaning 'intermediary'. In the sixteenth century
it was used to mean 'channel of communication'. In 1927 'media', the Latin plural
of *medium* – still neuter if not exactly neutral – was used of newspapers, radio, etc.

tearful pity and sorrowful longing'. Incantations likewise, he went on, could enchant and persuade, like magic.

Yet the Greek root of our 'poem' (and so 'poet', 'poetry') is the common-or-garden verb *poieô* (ποιεω), 'I make, do, create'. That verb was used for the creation of anything, whether of wood, stone, metal and so on; and the result was 'something created, work, product' – a *poiêma* (ποιημα) – by a 'creator', a *poiêtês* (ποιητης).

In these senses there is the notion of a skilled craftsman at work; and such craft also applied to people working not with materials but with words. Not, however, everyday words – anyone could do that – but with words built into complex, repeating, metrical systems, i.e. verse. That required real skill. So a *poiêma*, 'something made', could, in the right context, mean a 'poem', and *poiêtês* 'a poet'. Romans took these words over purely in that poetic sense, producing *poêta*, 'poet'; *poêma*, 'poem'; *poêticus*, 'poetic', and so on.

WHAT'S AFOOT?

In Greek, Latin and English, verse is made up 'feet': Greek *pous* (πους) (*pod*-), 'foot', as in podiatrist, a foot doctor; Latin *pes* (*ped*-), 'foot' (→ pedal, pedestrian, etc.). But there is a big difference between Greek/Latin and English poetic feet. In English, stress is all. To take an example: in the famous line 'The cúrfew tólls the knéll of párting dáy', the stress falls where the accent is marked, so the rhythm goes: ti-túm, ti-túm, ti-túm, ti-túm, ti-túm.

Technical note: the foot 'ti-tum' is called an 'iambus' (Greek *iambos*, ἰαμβος). There are five of them in the quoted line. The Greek for five is *pente* (πεντε), so the metre is called an iambic pentameter:

five x ti-tum = ten syllables, the metre of Shakespeare, Milton, Pope and many other English poets. Or rather, it *should* be ten syllables. Shakespeare and all the poets play fast and loose with this. Count the syllables in 'To bé or nót to bé, that ís the quéstion'.

In Greek and Latin, by contrast, it is not stress but the length of each syllable that is crucial. The Greek *metron* (μετρον, Latin *metrum*), from which we get 'metre', had nothing at all to do with stress. It meant anything by which something was measured, whether by content (a <u>litre</u> of milk), space (three <u>miles</u>) or time (an <u>hour</u>); and in poetry it referred strictly to the measured length of each syllable, about which there were hard and fast rules that could not be broken.

Take, for example, King Oedipus. In Greek he is *Oidipous* (Οἰδιπους): long-short-long. In Greek poetry, you cannot muck about with his name to make it scan in any other way. Take Socrates. In Greek he is *Sôkratês* (Σωκρατης): long-short-long. No change possible. Take Euripides. In Greek he is *Euripidês* (Εὐριπιδης): long (the diphthong *Eu*)-short-short-long. That's it. And so on.

Conclusion: Greek and Latin verse was difficult to compose. There were strict rules: you did not have the flexibility of stress-based English to stress as you felt like. The rules had to be followed.

SOME MERRY METRICS

As we have seen, a pentameter has five feet, each one ti-tum. A hexameter has six feet (*hex* [ἑξ], 'six'), and is a combination of dactyls (tum-ti-ti) and spondees (tum-tum), both Greek words. Here is an English example. The *tum* syllables are stressed – as that is what we do in English – but think of them as long syllables, and all the rest as short syllables, as if they were Greek:

> Géntlemen / áre not al/lówed tó/ wálk on the / gráss of the / cól/lége

Can you hear the metre?

> Tum-ti-ti / tum-ti-ti / tum-tum / tum-ti-ti / tum-ti-ti / tum-tum

DACTYLS AND SPONDEES

(i)   Tum-ti-ti, long-short-short, is a foot called a dactyl (*daktulos*, δακτυλος). What is that? It is a finger, which has one long and two short bits. (A <u>ptero</u>-dactyl has <u>wings</u> for fingers – *pteron* [πτερον], 'wing'.)

(ii) Tum-tum, long-long, is a foot called a spondee (*spondeios*, σπονδειος). It was used in melodies played while a libation (*spondê*, σπονδη) was poured to the gods (nobody knows why).

A verse so scanned is called a dactylic hexameter. It was the metre of epics, from Homer's *Iliad* and *Odyssey* to Virgil's *Aeneid* and beyond.

If we ask 'How come spondee does not feature in the name "dactylic hexameter"?', the answer lies in terms of the *metron*, the measurement of time: for long-long was designed to take the *same time* to say as the dactyl's long-short-short. So the spondee is an alternative form of the dactyl.

As you can see, the ancients (unlike modern poets) were very strict indeed about feet. Quite right too: if ancient poets wanted to climb Helicon, the mount of inspiration where the Muses lived, they needed feet to do so.

FAMOUS, FABULOUS NOVELS

Novel-style, fictional narratives in prose were written in Latin. Petronius' *Satyricôn* and Apuleius' *The Golden Ass* are good examples. In this latter tale, the narrator Lucius gets mixed up with a witch and is accidentally turned into an ass. He is stolen by thieves, as is a young woman, and in their cave he hears the story of Cupid and Psyche. The woman is rescued, the thieves are killed and Lucius is found a new home. He is moved on from there, and various adventures follow as – still an ass – he is sold to a priest, a baker, a farmer, a soldier and a cook. All the time he is hearing about and observing low life. A woman then falls for him, and Lucius is set up to have sex with her at a carnival, but full of shame at the thought he runs away. He falls asleep and the goddess Isis appears to him and shows him how to resume his human form. This he does, becoming a priest of Isis in gratitude.

These tales were not, however, classified as 'novels'. They were *fabulae*, 'gossip, fiction, entertaining tales' (as in 'fable'), based on the *fa*- root, 'say, speak'. This is also the root of *fama*, 'news, report, rumour, hearsay, reputation, renown', as in 'fame, famous'.

'Novel' derives from the Latin *novus*. This meant 'new, unheard of, surprising', and *novellus* was the diminutive form, used of young, tender plants and animals. The term 'novella' was first used in the sixteenth century to describe a short story. *Fingo* (*fict*-), 'I fashion, invent, devise, fabricate', is the source of our 'fiction'.

SATIRE

Ancient Greeks were credited with inventing the three main literary genres, each neatly divided into three subdivisions, as follows: *poetry* (epic, lyric, pastoral); *prose* (history, philosophy, rhetoric); and *drama* (tragedy, comedy, satyr/burlesque). Romans took on the poetry and prose options and, of the dramatic options, mainly comedy.

The Romans' one claim to invention was satire. The Latin *satura* meant basically 'a dish of mixed ingredients'. The satirist Juvenal (*c.* AD 100) described his work as follows: 'Whatever humans get up to, their prayers, fears, rages, desires, pleasures, distractions – that is the *farrago* of my little volume.' *Farrago* meant 'mixed animal feed, made from inferior grains', i.e. a cheap medley, mishmash, hotchpotch.

Most interestingly, the metre chosen by poetic satirists was the hexameter – the metre of grand epic! But that is satire for you – it hit out, and still does, at all targets, fairly and unfairly: pretentions, hypocrisies, cant, snobberies, sexual perversions; individuals great and small, male and female, good and bad, rich and poor, weak and powerful; by parody, mockery, exaggeration, caricature and so on. The solemn, sonorous metre in which it is composed makes the trivial subject matter all the more amusing.

Our grand epics (such as Milton's *Paradise Lost*) are composed not in hexameters but in pentameters (see above). Like Juvenal, Alexander Pope used this heroic form in his *Dunciad*, a devastating satire on literary critics, to the same effect.

ELEGY

The epithet 'elegiac' suggests mournful, wistful reflection on life and death. Thomas Gray's magnificent 'Elegy Written in a Country Churchyard' perfectly fits the bill ('the paths of glory lead but to the grave... full many a flower is born to blush unseen...'). The Greek *elegeion* (ἐλεγειον), Latin *elegeum*, was in fact a metrical term. It had nothing to do with subject matter, but simply referred to a poem made up of alternating hexameter (six-foot) and pentameter (five-foot) lines. However, it later became associated with the poetry of lament.

Interestingly, Romans associated the metre especially with love poetry. Perhaps they thought it would always end badly. The witty Roman poet Ovid wrote of walking alone one day in an ancient grove and being approached by Elegy and Tragedy. Elegy wore long, perfumed hair and limped, rather fetchingly, one foot being shorter than the other (ho ho), delightful to look at and wearing a see-through dress. Tragedy came in stormy and scowling, taking huge strides, a king's sceptre in one hand, feet encased in laced, theatrical boots. Each argued her case for what Ovid should write next. Elegy naturally won Ovid's approval: 'You [Tragedy] are eternal toil; what Elegy wants is the work of a moment.'

SOME LITERARY TERMS

Allegory: Greek *allêgoria* (ἀλληγορια), 'veiled language'. In 59 BC Cicero was fearful of his personal future. He wrote to his friend Atticus: 'From now on, if I need to write more to you, I shall obscure my meaning with *allêgoria*.'

Caricature: Latin *carrus* meant a wagon, and *carrico* (*carricat-*) 'I load up a wagon', with the suggestion of overloading it. Via Italian *caricatura*, it came to mean an overloaded or exaggerated description of someone

Chiasmus: the Greek letter *khi* looks like a diagonal cross: X. It described a phrase or clause shaped in the order ABBA (imagine A and B at the top of the X, and B and A at the bottom). The Greek was *khiasma* (χιασμα), the Latin *chiasmus*. For example: 'He punched (A) quickly (B) and slowly (B) his opponent fell (A).'

Climax: Greek *klimax* (κλιμαξ), 'ladder', from *klima* (κλιμα), 'a slant'. One climbs and climbs and climbs till one reaches the top...

Critic: Greek *kritês* (κριτης), the juryman in a court case; Latin *criticus* meant 'literary critic'.

Drama: Greek *drama* (δραμα), 'something done, an action'. Aristotle defined tragedy as 'the representation of an action which is serious, complete and of a certain magnitude'.

Elision: running words or letters together, Latin *elido* (*elis-*), 'I smash, crush'.

Ellipse: Greek *elleipsis* (ἐλλειψις), 'omission' (of a word or letter).

Exaggerate: Latin *exaggero*, 'I pile up, heap'; *agger* meant 'mound, earthwork, bank'.

Hiatus: Latin *hiatus*, 'yawning, opening' – a gap in a text.

Hybris: Greek *hubris* (ὑβρις), 'physical violence', turning into a determination to stay on top and humiliate others. The meaning 'pride' is not classical.

Nemesis: Greek *nemesis* (νεμεσις), 'indignation felt at another's conduct'. The meaning 'retributive justice' is not classical.

Hysteron proteron: directly from the Greek (ὑστερον προτερον) 'later earlier', getting a sequence in the wrong order ('bred and born'). The Latin form was *praeposterus: prae-*, 'before' + *posterus*, 'later'. Preposterous!

Hyperbole: Greek *huperbolê* (ὑπερβολη), 'over (*huper-*) shooting (*bol-*)' a target, 'excess', 'going too far'.

Irony: Greek *eirôneia* (εἰρωνεια), 'purposeful ignorance', of the sort Socrates used to baffle opponents.

Metamorphosis: 'shape-changing', direct from the Greek μεταμορφωσις, 'change' (μετα-) + 'shape' (μορφη).

Metaphor: Greek *metaphora* (μεταφορα), 'transferring a word to a new sense'.

Onomatopoeia: Greek *onomatopoeia* (ὀνοματοποιια), 'coining a word in imitation of a sound'.

Oxymoron: Greek *oxumôros* (ὀξυμωρος), 'pointedly foolish' ('bitter-sweet').

Paradox: Greek *paradoxos* (παραδοξος), 'contrary to expectation'.

Parody: Greek *parôidia* (παρῳδια), 'contrary to a song, burlesque'.

Pastoral: Latin *pastor*, 'shepherd'; to do with the countryside.

Personification: Latin *persona*, 'person' + *-fico*, expressing the idea of 'making', 'turning [a thing] into a person, endowing it with life'.

Rhetoric: the art of the Greek *rhêtôr* (ῥητωρ), 'public speaker'; Latin *orator*.

Sarcasm: Greek *sarkazô* (σαρκαζω), 'I rip/tear flesh'.

Simile: Latin *similis*, 'same, like, resembling'.

Stanza: Italian, literally 'stopping place', i.e. the marked end of a unit of verse. From Latin *stans*, 'standing still'.

Syllable: *sullabê* (συλλαβη), literally 'held (*lab*-) together (*su*-)'; 'letters held together to make a single sound', Latin *syllaba*.

RELIGION

INTRODUCTION

In the late second century AD, one Celsus (about whom we otherwise know nothing) published in Greek *The True Word* (*Ho Alêthês Logos*, Ὁ Ἀληθης Λογος). His aim was to refute Christian doctrine. It does not survive in full, but quotations from it survive in Origen, a Christian writer who in his *Against Celsus* set out to destroy his argument. Celsus' work gives a fascinating insight into how a pagan saw Christianity and at the same time what paganism meant to a pagan. The sorts of problems Celsus raised were:

- A mortal would obviously want to become a god, but why should a god want to become a mortal?
- Why would a god be interested in the 'sinners and the refuse' of society?
- Why would a god choose a poor woman of no royal ancestry as a mother?
- Why would a god allow humans to mock and crucify him?
- How could a dead human become an immortal god?

- Why should anyone accept transparently absurd tales of death and resurrection? (There was nothing irreverent about asking serious questions about gods.)
- Since Christians worshipped two gods (Jesus and his father), why object to polytheism?
- Why worship a corpse while attacking those of us who make grand statues of our deities?

And so on, in similar vein.

For a pagan it is clear that a god had no need of humans: the world was designed for the gods' benefit, not ours. Gods likewise were of an aristocratic frame of mind, having no interest in the lower orders. In fact, no human could expect anything as a matter of right from the deities. All error-prone man could do was acknowledge the deity through ritual, keep his fingers crossed and be prepared to endure whatever life threw at him. Something like justice might be seen to be done at some stage, but one could never tell. No one was guaranteed anything like lasting happiness in this fragile, uncertain life, let alone after it. It is no surprise, then, that a far more hopeful religion such as Christianity should prove so appealing.

Nevertheless, pagans still had hope (expressed in the myth of Pandora's box), and there were fellow human beings, all in the same boat, to whom one could turn for consolation. And at least worship of the gods, through state and local festivals, promised a good time for all: gladiatorial fights, theatrical and musical performances and chariot races at one level, sacrifices, food, drink and sex at the other.

A good example is the festival of the ancient Roman goddess Anna Perenna. It fell on the Ides of March, the first full moon of the year (reckoned by the old Roman calendar). Ovid described it as follows in his *Fasti*, celebrating the Roman year:

> On the Ides, the merry festival of Anna Perenna is held
> Not far from your banks, river Tiber.
> The plebs come and, scattered about on the grass,
> Lie down, every man, with his girl.
> Some take their luck in the open, others pitch tents,
> Some use branches to make leafy huts,
> While others stake out reeds to make rigid pillars,
> And stretch out their togas over the top.
> The sun and wine warm them up, and they pray
> To live as many years as the cups they drink, keeping count.
> You will find there a man who drinks up Nestor's years,
> A woman as old as the Sibyl – in her cups.
> There they sing the songs they've heard in the theatres,
> Their ready hands beating time with the words;
> Then they put down the bowl, and do a rough dance,
> The trim girl cavorting with her hair loose.
> Home they come, staggering, a sight for the crowd to see,
> Who call them 'blessed' when they come across them.

Nestor and the Sibyl were renowned for their age; 'blessed' was a word reserved for gods!

One of the ways Romans made sense of their religion was to regard contemporary rituals as practices that had been developed from time immemorial. Their very age gave them their authority. When Ovid began his *Fasti*, he said he was celebrating 'Times and their reasons' (*tempora cum causis*), i.e. what festivals happened at what times and why this was the case. This was, of course, to align the ritual calendar with history, which also dealt with times and reasons; and Ovid found the reasons buried deep in Rome's past. So whatever one made of the gods, no one could deny their ancient historical standing; and in the light of that, and Rome's obvious success as a state, perhaps it might be a good idea to continue worshipping them in the good old way.

None of this prevented fierce philosophical debate about the nature of divinity. The poet Lucretius thought the gods were simply atoms, having little interest in us; Cicero had severe doubts about the value of the auspices and of prophecy in general. In a long discussion he pointed out, among much else, that if divination was the foreknowledge and foretelling of events that happened by chance, it could not, by definition, be predicted: otherwise it could not be said to have happened 'by chance'. If an event were truly to happen 'by chance', Cicero went on, even the gods would not be able to predict it: so how could a diviner? *Divinatio* was therefore impossible if everything was controlled by chance. Let us then assume, Cicero argued, that everything was controlled by Fate. In that case, it was hard to see what advantages *divinatio* could bring: for if something was fated, it would happen, come what may. No amount of divination could help a person to avoid it. And so on.

But this was not to deny the importance of *religio*. Ancients did not believe that the gods made the world. Far from it: they were made by the world, as the world itself developed out of chaos. So gods were in fact part of the same material, natural world as men were. Understand nature, therefore, and you would understand the gods. For Cicero, it was superstition that was the problem and needed to be 'torn up by the roots': for superstition 'pursues you at every turn, when you listen to a prophet or an omen, offer sacrifice, watch the birds, consult an astrologer, see lightning. Since these signs are given all the time, no one who believes them can ever be at peace.'

DEUS

What do the day, a journal, Diana, Zeus, Iup(p)iter (Jupiter), Jove, and the Latin for a god (*deus*) all have in common? Answer: the same Proto-Indo-European (PIE) root.

That root is **dieus-* (the asterisk indicates that this word has been reconstructed by working back from existing words to the presumed PIE root). It seems to have meant 'light, day', very appropriate for Jupiter and Zeus, who were gods of the bright sky. We can see how 'Zeus' (who in Greek was pronounced 'Sdeus') and Latin *deus* line up with **dieus*. But what about *Iuppiter*? *Iuppiter* is in fact a combination of **dieus* + *pater* ('bright sky' + 'father'). He sometimes appears in Latin as *Diespiter*.

No surprise, then, that the Latin for 'day' was *dies*. *Diurnus* meant 'daily' and is the source of our 'journal', and *diarium* was indeed a 'diary'. Further, there is a 'v' lurking in **dieus*, which produced the stem *di(v)-*, as in *divinus* and the goddess Di(v)ana.

That 'v' appears again in the stem of *Iuppiter*, which was *Iov-*, whence our 'Jove'. In astrology, birth under the planet Jupiter bestowed a cheerful frame of mind (→ 'jovial'). The Roman god

Mercurius (Mercury) had a reputation for fickleness. Those born under his sign are 'mercurial'.

BINDING RITUAL

The derivation of the Latin *religio* is not clear to us; but some Romans associated it with *religo*, 'I bind fast, hold firmly in place'. If so, it came from the same family as *obligo*, 'I secure, assign, pledge, make morally or legally liable', the source of our 'obligation' (see p. 69). *Religio*, then, made binding demands on you. Cicero talked of it in terms of 'justice [*iustitia*] regarding the gods'. That 'justice' took the form not of faith or belief but of cult.

ANCIENT PRACTICES?

In Latin *superstitio* meant 'irrational religious awe or credulity'. It derives, bafflingly, from *sto*, 'I stand', and *super*, 'over, above'; and its adjective *superstes* meant 'survivor'. Perhaps *superstitio* implied practices of ancient times, theoretically long out of date?

The first-century BC statesman Cicero saw '*religio* as a term of respect, *superstitio* one of contempt'. He defined *superstitio* as 'pointless fear of the gods', and contrasted those who explained the world 'through the superstitions of fortune-telling hags' with those who did so 'through explanations based on natural causes'.

In other words, the gods had ordered the universe so that it was comprehensible; and *religio*, with its various cults and ritual, reflected that ordered comprehensibility. Admittedly, Cicero still had doubts about taking auspices, for example, but thought on balance they were 'harmless'. But the Roman authorities took *superstitio* very seriously if it seemed to threaten Roman order: magic books, the use of drugs for sinister ends, alternative religions (such as Christianity and Druidism) could all evoke the state's intervention.

FASCINATING STUFF

Literature tells us much about such superstitious practices: astrology, witchcraft, calling up the dead, curse tablets and voodoo dolls were all commonplace. In his *Characters*, Theophrastus (fourth century BC) described 'the superstitious man' as someone who went far beyond normal religious devotion; one, for instance, who would not walk on if a weasel crossed his path unless someone went before him, or until he had thrown three stones across the road.

The poet Tibullus (first century BC) told how a witch had given him a spell with which he could bamboozle his lover's husband:

> I've seen her bringing stars down from the sky,
> Reverse fast-flowing rivers with her song.
> Her spells can split the ground, lure up the dead,
> Summon bones from smoking pyres...

The Latin for 'casting a spell' was *fascinatio*, and a thing that cast a spell was a *fascinum*, 'evil spell, bewitchment'. *Fascinum* also meant 'penis' and 'phallic amulet, worn round the neck as a charm'. Pliny the Elder described the protective power of the god Fascinus, from whom the neuter noun *fascinum* derived:

> Infants are guarded by Fascinus, and so too are generals. Fascinus,
> dangling from under the chariot of a general celebrating a triumph,

protects him from envy. The worship of Fascinus is overseen by the Vestal Virgins.

Lucky them.

NO MATCH FOR VESTAL VIRGINS

The Roman goddess of the domestic hearth (see p. 61) was *Vesta*; and that was the term applied to her temples and any location where sacred fire was burning. Hence the match 'Swan Vestas'. The purpose of the cult of *Vesta* was to ensure Rome's permanence, and the prime responsibility of the Vestal Virgins was to keep Rome's sacred fire burning. One of the sacred objects which they worshipped was a large erect *fascinum* (see above).

The Vestals did not live the life of pagan nuns in a pagan nunnery. They were women of patrician background, often chosen as young as six, and lived in a magnificent house, with every facility at hand. Their high status ensured that they were protected by their own lictors (see p. 26) wherever they went and were regularly visited by emperors and senators alike; and they had secular as well as religious functions to perform. They were also expected to demonstrate the appropriate feminine virtues of modesty and purity as well as ritual piety. Punishment for letting the fire go out was a beating; for losing their virginity, being buried alive.

MAGIC

The *Magoi* (Μαγοι, biblical 'Magi') were priests and wise men from Persia (Iran) who, according to St Matthew, attended the birth of Jesus. Our 'magic' derives from *Magoi*, via Greek *magikos* (μαγικος) and Latin *magicus*.

Pliny the Elder, drawing on what he thought to be the earliest book on magic by the Persian Osthanes, mentioned superstitions like divination by 'water, globes, air, stars, lamps, basins, axes... as well as interviews with ghosts and those in the underworld'. He castigated the emperor Nero for being fascinated by magic: 'His main ambition was to give orders to the gods... no one supported magic arts more keenly.' But Pliny then said that Nero did in fact give it all up – which proves magic must all be nonsense, given how much time, money and effort he had dedicated to it.

A DIVINE TERMINATOR

Latin *numen* (our 'numinous') meant literally 'nod' and came to have a religious significance as a 'divine or supernatural power or influence, divine presence, deity'. When two young Trojans in Aeneas' army proposed a daring expedition against enemies in Italy, an old soldier praised the god under whose *numen* Troy had been sheltered for continuing to look after them. Ovid talked of places you saw of which you could say 'there is a *numen* here'. Objects too could be imbued with *numen*. One example was the stone used as a boundary marker, confirming who owned what. The god *Terminus* was the deity of such stones. *Terminus* came to mean 'remotest limit, furthest point', and the point at which an activity or process stopped.

CULT

Cicero defined *religio* as *cultus deorum*: 'cult/worship of the gods'. *Cultus* derived from *colo*, 'I inhabit, cultivate, adorn, look after, care for, practise, foster', and embraced knowledge about, and active caring for, everything to do with the gods, from their holy places, such as temples and shrines, to the ceremonies and rituals with which they were worshipped, including those enjoyed by early trade unions. These were professional associations of bakers and leather-workers and social clubs (for examples, funerary clubs, to pay for one's burial), which met under the *cultus* of a divinity.

Since emperors were included among the gods, they too received cult. In praising the emperor Trajan, Pliny the Younger condemned the *cultus* which attended the worship of the earlier emperor Domitian: 'Shows and riotous entertainment, the dancing and howling, effeminate screams and antics, approved by Senate, consul and actor alike.' He contrasted these 'disgusting public theatricals' with the more serious and respectful *cultus* that Trajan preferred.

CEREMONY AND RITUAL

Roman religion was deeply influenced by their neighbours the Etruscans, and Romans thought that *caerimonia* ('sanctity', 'religious rites'; our 'ceremony') derived from various rituals carried out by Etruscan priests from the town of Caere. These ceremonies had to be carried out in the right way and at the right place and time, and *ritus* ('rites') were the correct procedures that made up a ceremony.

Incidentally, *ritus* has no connection with English 'right', a word of Germanic origin related to kings (compare *Reich*, 'kingdom', 'reign', 'state'); but *ritus* is perhaps connected with 'a<u>rith</u>metic' (Greek *a<u>rith</u>mos* [ἀριθμος], 'number') in the sense of numbering, i.e. counting things off in the correct order.

TEMPLE

Templum is perhaps connected with the Greek *temnô* (τεμνω, 'I cut') and *temenos* (τεμενος, 'a place cut off, sanctuary'). When, for example, a priest examined the flight of birds to try to divine the will of the gods, the first thing he did was to use the correct procedure to 'cut' or mark out a space in the sky – the *templum* – where the relevant birds would appear. On land, a *templum* was a piece of ground marked out for the gods, and then the building constructed on it. The Roman Senate was built on one such area, and its meetings were always liable to be blocked or stopped by a divine sign of some sort. Our word 'template' – a pattern or gauge for shaping a piece of work – derives from *templum*. So does 'contemplate', as in someone watching attentively for an augury from a *templum* (see p. 182).

It was not necessary for a temple to be a grand, imposing building. It was a home for a god and could be a simple 'one-roomed house' with the god's statue inside (see p. 39). Temples were not designed to hold huge congregations: worship was usually carried on outside, often at the altar.

CULT STATUES

Our 'statue' derives from Latin *statua*, whose root was *sto* (*stat-*), 'I stand', and was something fixed in the ground to remain upright (your stature – *statura* – was and is your height in an upright position). To throw a *statua* to the ground was to deny its very nature, a tremendous insult. When Roman emperors were thrown out of office in disgrace, their statues were usually uprooted – together with their *status* (same derivation), their 'standing' in the world.

A cult statue was normally called a *simulacrum*, a simulated image (*simulo*, 'I pretend, counterfeit'), because you could not tell what a deity looked like; by contrast, the usual term for a human statue was *imago*, a 'representation', 'reflection', as in a mirror. A speciality of Roman cult statues was that they tended to act human during crises, when they had the habit of sweating, weeping or talking. But during the Empire such activity gradually ceased as intellectuals rational-ized the occurrences. Plutarch put sweating, weeping and bleeding (common in Greek cult statues) down to the effects of different sorts of mould.

SHRINES AND THEIR FANS

A 'shrine' is a receptacle for sacred objects, usually a box, chest or repository for relics or a dead body. One Latin term for it was *sacrarium*, from *sacro*, 'I set apart for the service of a god', as in *sacer* (*sacr-*), 'duly consecrated to, the property of, a deity'. The shrine was a place where objects belonging to the deity were kept, 'even in a private home', said one legal authority. Our notion of 'the sacred' is not quite the same.

Another term for 'shrine' was *fanum*, a word connected with *festus*, a day set apart for the gods (see 'festival', p. 40). The person in charge of a *fanum* was a *fanaticus*, a term also used to describe religious fanatics. It may, in shortened form, be the origin of our 'fan'.

By contrast, Latin *profanus* meant basically 'not dedicated for religious use' or 'removed from divine use'. Pliny the Elder talked of a cliff in Libya dedicated to the south wind which, if touched by human hand, became *profanus*. The angry south wind would respond by causing a sandstorm.

SANCTUARIES

Any holy place could also act as a sanctuary, that is, a place of refuge. In Greece, theoretically, any criminal could expect to be safe there; but in Rome sanctuary was confined to refugees from other states (and much later, maltreated slaves) – a tactic the first king Romulus adopted, we are told, to enlarge the population of the city. Our 'asylum' derives from the temple of the god Asylaeus, which Romulus used for the purpose.

The Latin *sanctuarium* – a place like *sacrarium* where sacred, or private, confidential things were kept – derived from *sanctus* and the verb *sancio* (*sanct-*), meaning 'I solemnly ratify, confirm, sanction, prescribe by law'. In other words, *sanctus* ('inviolate, under divine protection') had something of a legal force to it, and was particularly used of human institutions (for example, laws, oaths, special places like the treasury where Rome's war reserve was kept) and people by virtue of their office. Note *sacrosanctus* (our 'sacrosanct') – a combination of *sacer* reinforced with *sanctus*!

To disturb the sanctity of a place was to violate it (*violo* [*violat-*]), while *polluo* (*pollut-*) meant 'I make foul, infect' (whence our 'pollution').

BURNT OFFERINGS

For Romans an *altaria* was a burnt offering, or the altar itself (it seems to be connected with a Latin word 'to burn'). It was always out in the open air next to a temple and the place where the god was worshipped. Jews too made burnt offerings on altars, but when Christianity adopted the terminology, it changed its meaning: the altar became the table where the Eucharist was celebrated, and 'sacrifice' related to the life and death of Christ.

SACRIFICE

When Agamemnon 'sacri-ficed' his daughter Iphigeneia, he literally 'made her sacred' – *sacer*, 'sacred' + *ficio*, 'I make, do' (*facio* in compounds becomes -*ficio* or -*fico*). Rather as a *templum* marked out a space dedicated to the gods, sacrifice marked out some *object* dedicated to the deity. The object in question could be anything from a cake left on an altar or wine spilt on the ground, to an animal killed and burned or – in Iphigeneia's case – a human (though human sacrifice is barely heard of in the classical world, hence Lucretius' extreme disgust). Sacrifice was a complex ritual, part of which involved scattering a barley-and-salt cake (Latin *mola*) over the *victima*. The verb *immolo* meant 'I scatter *mola* over a victim' and hence 'I kill a victim', and so is the origin of English 'immolate'. A 'hecatomb' was technically a sacrifice of a hundred oxen, a massive operation, though we rarely hear of it in practice (Greek *hekaton* [ἑκατον], 'hundred' + *bous* [βους], 'ox').

CARNIVAL!

When Greeks sacrificed an animal, they burned some of it for the god and ate the rest. This was one of the occasions when they would eat meat, a special treat. Our 'carnival' is associated with meat-eating – or rather, giving it up. Latin *caro* (*carn-*) meant 'flesh, meat' (→ 'carnage', 'carnivore'); and *levare*, 'to remove'. The old Italian *carnelevare* meant 'removing meat', and that became *carnevale*, the word to describe Shrove Tuesday, the last day before Lent. The 'popular' derivation – *Carne, vale!* ('Meat, farewell!') – is mistaken.

ORACLES

Like all ancients, Romans were keen to ascertain the god's will. This could be done in any number of ways. The Latin *oro* meant 'I pray to, beseech, supplicate', and an *oraculum*, a place where prayers were said (whence 'oracle'), was also the divine utterance in response to the prayer. Such responses were always made through the agency of a priest or priestess.

But there were many other ways of contacting the gods or finding the gods contacting you, including omens, dreams, astrology, magic and the Sibylline books. These last had been bought by the Roman king Tarquin (*c.* 600 BC) from a Sibyl (a woman with prophetic powers) and were consulted when trouble threatened. They recommended carrying out rituals of one sort or another to appease the gods.

SIGNS AND PORTENTS

The ancient world was full of *signa*, 'signs'. A *signum* meant basically 'a mark written or impressed' to signify ownership, a 'distinguishing feature', or an 'indication'. It seems to be linked to *seco* (*sect-*), 'I cut' (whence 'section'), presumably in the sense 'inscribe' or 'engrave'. A *signum* might or might not be significant of divine activity. Cicero mentioned the Roman general Gaius Flaminius, who 'ignored prophetic signs and was responsible for a catastrophic disaster' when he was defeated by Hannibal at Lake Trasimene in 217 BC.

A *portentum* was what a god portended, i.e. indicated by portents. It was always something unnatural or monstrous. Pliny the Elder was most concerned about such unnatural occurrences and blamed the Greeks for even mentioning them:

> I personally do not mention abortion-inducing practices, let alone love-potions, remembering as I do that the famous general Lucullus was killed by a love-potion, nor yet any other magic *portenta*, unless it be by way of warning or denunciation, especially as I have utterly condemned all faith in such practices.

AUGURY

The behaviour of birds was seen as a particularly potent indicator of divine (dis)pleasure. The religious official who adopted this technique was called an *augur*, whose derivation is a mystery, or an *auspex* (*auis*, 'bird' + *spex*, 'watcher', from the *spec-* root, → 'inspect', etc.). An augury gained from avian behaviour was an *auspicium*, whence our 'auspices, auspicious'.

To take a bird augury, pitch a tent at dawn on a high hill, face south (Greeks faced north), hold a knotless stick in your right hand, pray to the gods, and identify landmarks to help mark off a section of the sky (see *templum*, above) into the four quarters north, south, east and west. Transfer the stick to your left hand, and wait. Birds flying left to right are propitious, right to left unpropitious. Ravens, crows, owls and hens give their augury by noise; eagles, vultures and lammergeyers by flight (very satisfactory if they come in twelves); woodpeckers and lapwings by both.

VICTIMS

Another popular method of ascertaining the will of the gods was to examine the entrails – for example, the liver, heart or lungs – of a slaughtered animal. The technical term for this animal, used only in relation to animals, not humans, was *victima*: it is connected with a Sanskrit word meaning 'holy'. The priest in charge was called a *haruspex*, 'gut-inspector', the *haru-* being associated with a Sanskrit word meaning 'guts'.

The liver of a sheep was a popular entrail for inspection, probably because a sheep was relatively cheap and has a smooth liver on which it is easy to spot defects. The ancients were also well aware that blood was vital for life, and the liver is a very blood-packed organ, so life-and-death issues hung on it. There survives a bronze model of a liver, marked with 'good' and 'bad' areas. Folds in a liver could, apparently, be good. Augustus sacrificed on the first day he came to power, and Pliny the Elder said of the outcome: 'the livers of six victims had the bottom of their tissue folded back inwards, interpreted to mean that he would double his power within the year.' A good omen!

OMENS, PRODIGIES AND EXPIATION

The derivation of *omen* is obscure, but in Latin it meant something that foreshadowed the outcome of an event, good or bad (it gives rise to 'ominous' and 'abominate', from *abominor*: 'I try to avert an *omen* or eventuality by prayer, detest'). In supporting a memorial in honour of a friend who, despite severe illness, agreed to go on an embassy that was the death of him, Cicero reported that, as he left on that fatal embassy, 'he spoke to me in a way that seemed an *omen* of his fate'; and in a marriage hymn the poet Catullus talked of conducting the bride across the threshold 'with a good *omen*'.

The Latin saying *nomen omen* ('the name [is] an *omen*') suggested that a person's name could play a part in determining some aspect of his or her character, life, etc. So if your name is (say) 'Barber' or 'Savage' or 'Peacock' or 'Craven', there is a chance your life will somehow be shaped by it.

PRODIGIES

A *prodigium* was an unnatural event, suggesting a disaster was about to strike (and so any amazing or monstrous event, or person, hence our 'child prodigy').

Expiatio (whence our 'expiation', 'expiate') meant in Latin 'performing a ceremony of purification to avert any disaster'. It was a common response to baffling events. *Expiatio* drives from the verb *pio* (stem *piat-*), 'I appease [a god], I perform rites of expiation'.

Romans kept careful records of such ominous events and how they responded to them, in order to prepare for similar occurrences in the future. Not surprisingly, words such as *prodigium* and *expiatio* occurred regularly when such events were being described. For example, in 200 BC the temple of Persephone at Locri (in south Italy) was robbed. The Senate demanded it be fully investigated and sacrifices performed. The historian Livy went on:

> The concern to *expiate* the sacrilege was inflamed by the announcement of *prodigies* that had occurred all over the country at the same time [flames in the sky... sun shining red... strange noises in temples... lamb born with pig's head... pig born with man's feet... a colt with five feet] and a child of uncertain sex was born, and a sixteen-year-old of indeterminate sex discovered. Nature seemed to be confusing the species. These hermaphrodites, *abominated* beyond all others, were ordered to be taken out to sea, as a similar *prodigy* had previously.

FROM PIETY TO A PITIFUL PITTANCE

The verb *pio*, 'I appease', is also connected with the adjective *pius* in Latin (our 'pious'), meaning 'dutiful/loyal/faithful to gods, country and family'. *Pietas* (our 'piety') is from the same stem.

Incidentally, *pietas* also gives us 'pity' and 'piteous', via French *pitié*, 'compassion' — a quite different meaning from the Latin. It gives us 'pittance', too, a pathetically small amount of money. In Old French a *pitance* was the food that pious charitable foundations gave to monks.

STAR LAWS

We make a firm distinction between astronomy and astrology. The ancients did not. For them, the scientific study of the stars, in as far as the Greeks were capable of it, was both *astronomia* (ἀστρονομια) – the *astr-* stem meaning 'star' and the *nom-* stem meaning 'law, statute' – and *astrologia* (ἀστρολογια), of which the *log-* stem meant 'reason, rational account'. The Romans took over both words, and again used both to refer to a 'scientific' study. At the same time, however, like the Greeks, the Romans gave an *additional*, unique meaning to *astrologia*: the observation and study of the stars to predict human affairs – what we mean by 'astrology'.

HEAVENLY FIRE

Meteors, comets and other flashing lights in the sky were of special interest to the ancients, since they were taken to portend some momentous event, often a disaster.* Meteors, derived from the Greek *meteôros* (μετεωρος), simply meant things 'up in the air' (as in the monasteries of the Meteora in Greece). Comets leave a trail and so were 'long-haired', which is what Greek *komêtês* (κομητης), and Latin *cometes*, meant. In this category Pliny the Elder records a 'spark seen to fall from the sky, increasing in size till it became as large as the moon, diffusing a sort of cloudy daylight, and then changing into a torch and returning to the sky'.

The Latin for 'spark' was *scintilla*, whence 'scintillate', but also

---

* Our word 'Elysium', taken directly from Latin, derives from the ancient Greek [ἐν]ηλυσιος ([*en*]*êlusios*), meaning 'struck by lightning' and therefore removed from worldly use.

(via French *estincelle*) sparkly 'tinsel' and 'stencil', which originally involved decorating with bright colours.

CLOAKING THE HEAVENS

The Greek word for 'eclipse', *ekleipsis* (ἔκλειψις), meant 'failure, cessation'; in the case of the sun, a failure of light. The Romans took their word *eclipsis* directly from it. Pliny the Elder cited the Greek thinker Thales from Miletus (seventh century BC) as the first man to predict an eclipse, and credited Sulpicius Gallus with being the first Roman to predict solar and lunar eclipses – he predicted an eclipse on the day before the battle of Pydna (168 BC) against the Greek king Perseus.

Eclipses generally caused panic. The essayist Plutarch (second century AD) told a lovely story about the fifth-century BC Athenian statesman Pericles. He was about to set off with his navy when a solar eclipse occurred. In the ensuing panic, Pericles immediately took off his cloak and wrapped it around his helmsman's eyes, asking whether he thought that was an omen. 'Don't be daft', replied the helmsman. 'Same difference', said Pericles. 'The eclipse has just been caused by something bigger than this cloak.'

Pericles drew this information from his friend, the philosopher Anaxagoras, who correctly explained solar eclipses as the result of the moon crossing the face of the sun. He also argued that the stars were fiery stones and the moon shone by light reflected from the sun, which was a mass of red-hot metal.

WHIRLING GALAXIES

At one level the heavenly bodies were felt to be divine (though not by Epicureans, p. 135) – hence the names of the planets – and so given characteristics: some were male, some female, some friendly to humans, others not, and so on. But that did not prevent thinkers speculating about their part in creation. Simple observation of the sun, moon and stars suggested the idea of a rotating universe. The thinker Anaxagoras thought that originally the universe was a mixture of all its ingredients (that is, everything that made it up), which, at some stage, started to rotate. This motion expanded the ingredients, separated them out and caused them to recombine, and the result was our universe in all its variety. Not, then, a big bang, but a big whirl of stars and galaxies.

Our 'galaxy' derives from the Greek for 'milk' – *gala* (*galakt-*) [γαλα, γαλακτ–] – because Greeks so named the Milky Way. For them it was a *galaxias kuklos* [γαλαξιας κυκλος], the 'Milky Circle', *galaxias* for short; it was the Romans who called it the Milky Way (*lactea via*, → 'lactation', etc.). Once it was thought that the Milky Way made up the whole universe. Now, thanks to modern astronomy, we know it is but one of billions upon billions of such galaxies, though how milky they are is another question.

NEBULAS

Claudius Ptolemy (*c.* AD 150) saw in space what he thought were clouds of some sort and gave them the Latin name for 'cloud' – *nebula*. Collecting such clouds became a favourite sport of astronomers from the eighteenth century onwards. Some were indeed clouds of dust and gases, but others were in fact distant galaxies of stars – for instance, what was called the Andromeda Nebula. It now appears that nebulas and stars are very closely associated.

TIME AND PLACE

In the ancient world it was vital that ritual be carried out at the right time and place. Consequently, the calendar was of great importance. The poet Ovid composed his *Fasti* ('days that were *fastus*; list of festival days', p. 190) to record the seasonal dates on the Roman calendar and explain why they were there and how they had come about (see p. 169).

But more than that: as well as feasts, rituals, foundations of temples and so on, Ovid recorded important moments in the history of Rome. He included not only its great military triumphs but also significant dates and moments in the rise to power of the emperor Augustus and in the lives of his family. Ovid thought it convenient to confirm that Roman history, and the first Roman emperor's history, were stamped firmly on the annual round of ritual celebrations.

This sense of the importance of dates survived into the church calendar. Arguments still exist between different branches of Christianity on the dates of Christmas and Easter, for example.

DAYS OF THE WEEK

Our 'calendar' derives from Latin *Kalendae*, the word for the first day of the Roman month. Romans had an eight-day week, labelled A B C D E F G H. They marked each day of each month with an indication of the religious festivals, banquets, games, holidays and so on that took place, and whether official state business could or could not be done on it. To give an idea of how it worked, here is a reconstruction of one week in one such calendar, painted on plaster in a house in Antium and dating to the first century BC:

A	**K**[alendae]	**APR**[ilis]	**F**[astus]
B	**F**		
C	**C**[omitialis]		
D	**C**		
E	**NON**[es]	**N**[efastus]	**To Public Fortune**
F	**N**		
G	**N**		
H	**N**		

Key:

Kalendae: first day of the month.

Fastus: a day, ordained by priests, on which the courts could sit. Latin *fas* meant 'that which was permitted by divine law'.

Comitialis: a day on which public assemblies (*comitia*) could meet, and courts could sit. Our 'committee' derives from Latin *committo* (*commiss-*), 'I bring/join together' (see p. 303).

NONes: fifth day of the month.

Nefastus: a day, ordained by priests, on which no public assemblies could meet nor courts sit.

To Public Fortune: there were three temples to Fortune on the Roman hill called the Quirinal. This day would see the ceremonial re-dedication of one of them.

Incidentally, our 'red-letter' days are so called because special days were marked with red in the Roman calendar.

HOLIDAYS, FEASTS AND FESTIVALS

A 'holiday' is a 'holy day', a religious festival, and all holidays in Rome were connected with a religious cult. Feasting together was typical of such Roman holiday celebrations, usually paid for by a member of the wealthy local elite. His generosity raised his status in the community and gave the plebs a brief taste of the aristocratic life. Such 'perks' were called *commoda* ('benefits', as in our 'commodities', from *commodus*, 'advantageous, convenient'). Our 'feast' derives from Latin *festus*, a word also related to Latin *feriae*, 'holiday', and means 'keeping a festival day or holiday', so 'festive', 'merry'. Holy days, feasting and merriment are part of our culture too (see Anna Perenna, p. 169).

THE LUNATIC CALENDAR

The ancients were farmers, and farming is season-dependent. Respecting the power of the gods, they tied the farming year closely in with religious ritual, which demanded that all ritual take place at the right time.

Now, the ancients knew that the seasons coincided with the time it took the sun to complete its annual course (the 'solar' cycle of 365.25 days – Latin *sol*, 'sun'). The problem was that they counted time by the moon, and the average 'lunar' month lasts 29.53 days (*luna*, 'moon'). Twelve of these make only 354 days, so the full lunar cycle left a shortfall of eleven days on the solar year. So every three years, the calendar was a month 'late', and spring festivals were soon being celebrated in mid-winter. Lunacy!

ADDING MONTHS

Those who stayed with lunar months, therefore, needed to adjust. As early as 2400 BC we hear of Babylonians (in modern-day Iraq) occasionally 'intercalating' a month (i.e. adding it within the year) to keep the calendar in time with the seasons (Latin *intercalo*, 'I summon in between'). Greeks intercalated seven months over a nineteen-year cycle. It was in fact the Egyptians who made the breakthrough: they abandoned the link between the twelve-month lunar cycle and the year, and in its place created twelve thirty-day months, plus five days, giving 365 days – a very close shot indeed.

Julius Caesar copied the Egyptians to produce the 'Julian' calendar of 365 days, plus one day every fourth year – nearly right, but now superseded by the 'Gregorian' calendar introduced by Pope Gregory XIII in 1582.

CALENDAR MONTHS OF THE YEAR

In early times, the Roman calendar functioned only during the working year – that is, March to December. So it originally had only ten months. The twelve-month year, common elsewhere, was perhaps introduced in 153 BC. January was named after Janus, the god who looked both ways, forward and back;* February, from *Februa*, month of 'expiation'; March, after the god Mars, start of the fighting season; April (not

---

* From Janus came *ianua*, 'door', which does roughly the same; the leaf of a door was *valva*, source of our 'valve', which also opens and shuts.

known); May, after Maius, some ancient unknown deity; June, after the goddess Juno; July, after Julius Caesar (previously *Quintilis*, 'fifth', counting from March); August, after the emperor Augustus (previously *Sextilis*, 'sixth'); and then *Septem-ber*, *Octo-ber*, *Novem-ber*, *Decem-ber*, from the Latin for 'seven', 'eight', 'nine' and 'ten'.

CALENDAR DAYS OF THE MONTH

Or, as the Romans spelled it, *Kalendarium* – one of only ten words in Latin beginning with 'k', all also spelled with 'c'. The days of each month were determined by three fixed points in that month:

1. *Kalendae* (the Kalends), the first day of the month;
2. *Nonae* (the Nones), the fifth day of the month (in March, May, July and October, the seventh);
3. *Idus* (the Ides), the thirteenth day of the month (in March, May, July and October, the fifteenth).

Unless the day fell on a named date (such as 1 October: Kal. Oct.), all dates were expressed as follows: the xth day *before* the next fixed date – for example, the third day before the Kalends of August. The exception was the day *before* a fixed day, expressed by *pridie*, e.g. *prid. Kal. Mai.*, 'the day before the first of May'.

MODERN RELIGIOUS TERMINOLOGY

As we have seen (p. 180), Christians regularly took over Roman (and Greek) religious words and reused them in Christian terms (for example, 'sacrifice', 'sacrament'), giving them quite different significance. Another example is D.O.M., often seen on Roman inscriptions: *Deo Optimo Maximo*, '[dedicated to] God Greatest Best', i.e. Jupiter, a very ancient form of address. Christians happily took it over, referring to the Christian deity.

But Christians also took over many wholly *secular* Greek and Latin words which had nothing to do with pagan religion at all. As you will see from the following examples, the Greek words were usually transliterated by the Roman church straight into Latin and entered our language either via Old English (after England was Christianized) or via French. Here are some examples:

Acolyte: derived from Greek *akolouthos* (ἀκολουθος), literally a 'follower', it became *acolythus* in Late Latin and in ecclesiastical parlance, a minor assistant in religious ceremonies.

Angel: Greek *aggelos* (ἀγγελος) meant simply 'messenger'. It had nothing to do with divine beings. Latin transliterated it directly as *angelus*. Add the Greek prefix *eu-* (εὐ), 'good, well', to yield Greek *euangelistês* (εὐαγγελιστης), Latin *euangelista*, 'evangelist', originally a preacher of the gospel, i.e. bringer of good news.*

Apostle: the Greek *apostolos* (ἀποστολος) meant 'one sent out' and was used to mean 'envoy' or 'commander' (Latin *apostolus*).

Bishop: Greek *episkopos* (ἐπισκοπος) meant 'overseer', of slaves or builders, for example; 'watchman, look-out, guardian, tutor, supervisor'. It became Latin *episcopus*, and via early English *[e] biscop*, 'bishop'. The Spanish is *obispo* and the French *évêque* (!) – Greek p softened to *v*, while *ê* = *es*.

---

* It is worth noting here that the Greek suffix *-istês* (-ιστης), Latin *-ista*, English '-ist' means 'someone who acts in some capacity' – for example, flautist, jurist, florist.

Blaspheme: Greek *blasphêmeô* (βλασφημεω) meant 'I speak irreverently, slander', especially of gods; *blas-* may derive from a word meaning 'hurtful', the *phêm-* root means 'say, speak', → Latin *fama* (p. 161). Our 'blame' derives from it, via Late Latin *blasphemo*.

Calvary: the Aramaic name for the mount where Christ was crucified was *Gulgalta*. In the Greek of the New Testament this became *Golgothas* (Γολγοθας) and was then immediately glossed as meaning 'place of the skull' (*kranion*, κρανιον, → 'cranium'). This may be because it was a place of execution or a cemetery or (in some traditions) where Adam's skull was buried. When translating the text, St Jerome saw the gloss, ignored the real name, and turned *Golgothas* into *Calvaria*, the Latin for 'skull', a word derived from Latin *calvus*, 'bald'!

Cardinal: derives from Latin *cardo*, 'hinge', 'pivot', 'axis', from which came *cardinalis*, 'serving as a hinge' (architecturally).

Church: Greek *kurios* (κυριος) meant 'in authority over'. It was used of, for example, a husband over a wife. As a noun it meant 'lord, master', especially of the household. Applying *kurios* to the Lord Jesus, Christians created [*dôma*] *kuriakon* ([δωμα] κυριακον), '[house of] the Lord'. This became in Old English *cirice* (German *Kirche*), from which came our 'church'. Note, incidentally, *Kurie, eleison* (Κυριε, ἐλεισον) – 'Lord, have mercy'. *Kurie* was used when addressing someone.

In fact the most common word for 'church' was the Greek *ekklêsia* (ἐκκλησια), Latin *ecclesia* (whence French *église* and our 'ecclesiastical'). In Greek that meant a 'summoned assembly'.

It was the technical term for the democratic assembly of all Athenian male citizens over eighteen. Between them, they made every decision about how Athens should be run. *Ekklêsia* derives from the Greek *ekkaleô* (ἐκκαλεω), 'I call out, summon'.

The clergy: the Latin for 'priest' is *sacerdos* (→ 'sacerdotal') – someone 'made sacred'. Our 'priest' probably derives, perhaps via Old English *preost*, from the Late Latin *presbyter*, 'elder' (Greek *presbuteros*, πρεσβυτερος). Another suggestion is that it derives from Latin *praepositus*, 'placed in front, at the head' – source of our 'preposition'!

Our 'clergyman', 'cleric' and 'clerk' all derive via Late Latin *clericus* from the Greek *klêros* (κληρος). This meant 'lot, voting token'; then 'an allotment, piece of land'. It is not precisely clear how these became associated with clerics.

Devil: the Greek *diabolos* (διαβολος, Latin *diabolus*) comes from *diaballô* (διαβαλλω), meaning 'I slander, accuse, misrepresent'. It became deofol in Old English, whence 'devil'.

Grace: our 'grace', in the sense of God's unmerited goodwill or favour, derives from Latin *gratia*. Its Greek equivalent was *kharis* (χαρις).* Both words had meanings rooted in the idea of reciprocity, i.e. the voluntary, unforced returning of benefits (or injuries) tit-for-tat. This was a key feature of ancient social values. Christianity put a quite different gloss on the idea: God's favours, freely given, were impossible to reciprocate.

---

* Our 'charity' derives from Latin *caritas* 'high price; love, affection'. The 'charity' of St Paul's 'faith, hope and charity' is in Greek *agapê* (ἀγαπη), 'Christian love', translated as *caritas* by St Jerome in his *Vulgate*; the church also interpreted *caritas* as 'compassion', especially for the poor.

Incarnation: the Latin *caro* (stem *carn-*) meant 'flesh, meat'. The church invented the word *incarnatio* ('the act of being *in-fleshed*') to describe Christ being made man. The word does not appear in the Bible; it was first used around 1300. See 'carnival' (p. 181).

Pagan: this derives from Latin *paganus*, 'countryman, peasant'. But it also meant 'civilian' as opposed to 'soldier'. Apparently, when Christians began calling themselves 'soldiers for Christ', *paganus* was applied to those who were not such soldiers, and therefore must be 'heathens'. It might be thought that pagans got their own back by calling Christians 'cretins', for that is the derivation of the word. But (apparently) it was first used in the eighteenth century to refer to mentally disabled people, not to abuse them but to remind people that they were humans after all.

Redemption: *redemptio* in Latin basically meant 'purchase, the act of buying'; but it also meant the 'act of ransoming/buying back', 'procuring the release of', the root of the Christian usage.

Renunciation: *nuntio* meant 'I announce', and *renuntio*, 'I report back'. But the prefix *re-* had another force – that of withdrawal or reversal. So it also meant 'I send a message cancelling a previous engagement' and so 'I call off, withdraw from' a friendship or alliance, 'I give up, renounce'.

Sacrament: in Latin a *sacramentum* was an oath, particularly an oath of military allegiance, or solemn duty. Christians first used it to refer to a ceremony such as baptism which bound man and God together in an unbreakable bond.

Vicars, dioceses (and dukes): in the late third century AD, the
emperor Diocletian faced a major financial crisis. In order to
increase the tax take, he greatly enlarged bureaucracy across the
Roman Empire. He replaced the original forty-two provinces
with 120 areas, grouped into twelve 'dioceses' (*dioikêsis*
[διοικησις], 'administration'). Each diocese was overseen by a
vicarius, 'deputy, substitute', an official taking over the role of
a praetorian prefect (a vicar is Christ's 'substitute' on earth).
Military command of these new regions was handed to *duces*,
'leaders, generals', whence our 'dukes'.

ARCHITECTURE
AND TECHNOLOGY

INTRODUCTION

Vitruvius (*c.* 75–*c.* 15 BC) composed *On Architecture*, the only ancient work on the subject to survive into the modern world. It was based mainly on Greek architectural practice, from which the Romans were gradually departing, and did not go into the detail of topics like proportion and the 'orders'. In ten books, it covered first principles, the layout of cities, building materials, temples, public and private buildings, finishing off (flooring, plasterwork, etc.), water supply, sundials, clocks and machines (see p. 77). His central thesis was that buildings must be solid, useful and beautiful.

All our manuscripts of Vitruvius derive from a copy probably brought from Britain to Charlemagne's court by Alcuin in the ninth century AD (see p. 117). From the eleventh to the twelfth century, it was used as a practical guide to building, and much of the detail was altered to fit contemporary practice. During the Renaissance, his work, whose language is difficult and interpretation controversial, was used by Alberti and Raphael among others to form the basis of a humanistic and aesthetically pleasing architectural conception built around the idea of the orders and the precise proportional relationship of each element of them.

Our 'architect' derives from the Greek *arkhitektôn* (ἀρχιτέκτων). That meant a master-builder, the *arkh-* stem meaning 'rule, sovereignty, mastery' and *tektôn*, 'carpenter, craftsman'. Romans took the word over, giving it a Roman ending – *architectus*. But a master builder was not necessarily the same as our architect. According to Vitruvius, an *architectus* (in our sense) needed to be educated to a high standard over a forbiddingly wide range of disciplines. Among these were draughtsmanship, geometry, optics (to get windows right), arithmetic (so that he could cost his work properly and measure accurately), history (to understand the significance of various architectural features), philosophy (to make him honest and trustworthy), physics (to control water flow in aqueducts, for example), medicine and climates (to ensure buildings were conducive to health), law, astronomy (he must know his north from his south), and mathematics and music, to have a good grasp of proportion and tuning (for example, getting the tension of catapults right). The consequences of the abandonment of Vitruvius' architectural curriculum can be seen all around us.

Pliny the Elder (born *c.* AD 22), who was killed investigating the explosion of Vesuvius in AD 79, composed a thirty-seven-book encyclopedia of all contemporary knowledge, the *Historiae Naturalis* ('On Natural History'), which survives in full. It covers astronomy, meteorology, geography, ethnography, anthropology, human physiognomy, zoology (mammals, snakes, birds, marine life, insects), botany (agriculture, horticulture – especially vine and olive – and medicine), pharmacology, magic, water, aquatic life, mining and mineralogy, especially in relation to art, gold and silver, statuary, painting, modelling, sculpture and precious stones. Enormously influential down the millennia – it was one of the first books to be printed in the Gutenberg revolution (1469) – it was a masterclass in collecting, cataloguing and arranging, as he said, '20,000 facts from more than 2,000 volumes' (a serious underestimate).

After the Preface, Pliny provided in Book 1 a list of contents. It runs to seventy pages of Latin. To give some idea of the coverage, here is just *one* page of the contents from Book 9, on the 'nature of animals arranged by parts of the body':

(lvii–lx) Cheek-bones; nostrils; cheeks, lips, chin, jaws. (lxi–iv) Teeth – kinds of; species with teeth in one jaw only; with hollow teeth; snakes' teeth, snakes' poison; which bird has teeth; remarkable facts as to teeth; age of ruminants indicated by teeth. (lxv) Tongue – tongueless species; croaking of frogs; palate. (lxvi–viii) Tonsils; uvula, epiglottis, windpipe, gullet, nape, neck, backbone, throat, jaws, stomach. (lxix–lxxi) Heart, blood, life; which species has largest heart, which smallest, which two hearts; when inspection of heart of victims began. (lxxii) Lungs – which species has largest, which smallest, which no internal organ besides lungs; cause of speed in animals. (lxxiii–vi) Liver – head of internal organs; its inspection by augurs; species with two livers, and their habitats; gall – what species have two, and where; what animals have none, which have gall elsewhere than in liver; its function; species whose gall grows and shrinks in size with moon; observation of these species by augurs, and marvellous portents. (lxxvii) Diaphragm; nature of laughter. (lxxviii) Stomach; species that have none; the only species that vomit. (lxxix) Smaller intestines, entrails, stomach, great gut; why some animals have voracious appetites. (lxxx–iii) Caul, spleen – species without spleen. Kidneys; habitat of species with four kidneys – with none; chest; ribs; bladder – animals without bladder; entrails; membranes. (lxxxiv–viii) Belly – the 'parts,' the womb, sows' womb, paps; what species have suet, what tallow; nature of each; what species have no fat; marrow; species that have none; bones; prickles; species that have neither bones nor prickles; cartilages; sinews; species without sinews.

One feature stands out above all: Pliny's interests in human needs and aspirations. Nature was there, he thought, to serve us, but needed to be respected in turn. Indeed, so respected that the more Pliny observed it, 'the more difficult I found it to believe that any statement about it was impossible'.

He also composed six other works, all lost, amounting to another sixty-five volumes, while pursuing a political and military career across the Roman Empire in Europe and North Africa, before winding up as admiral of the fleet in the Bay of Naples. That was how he came to be present when Vesuvius went up. His first thought was to investigate it; then he received a letter begging for help from a friend and launched his warships to try to help. He managed to land at Stabiae, four miles south of Pompeii, and stayed most of the night, but when the courtyard started filling with pumice and ash and earthquakes shook the building, he was woken and went down to the shore to investigate the chance of escape by sea. Overcome by fumes, he collapsed there and died.

HELPING HAND

Imagine what it would have taken to build the Colosseum: forty-foot foundations covering six acres, the building 615 feet long, 510 feet wide, seating around 50,000 spectators in four tiers, 185 feet high in all, and about 100,000 cubic metres of marble (around 250,000 tons). Don't even think about the supporting stonework, infill, the tiles, bricks, cement; the tens of thousands who must have worked on it, from the quarries in Tivoli twenty miles away to the workshops that produced the standardized stairs and seats, and the engineers, artists and decorators in the Colosseum itself. Imagine the wagons trundling through Roman streets night after night for ten years delivering the basic materials.

Human hands surely needed some help, and they got it. Greek *mêkhanê* (μηχανη) derived from *mêkhos* (μηχος), 'remedy, expedient, means', i.e. a clever way of dealing with otherwise very difficult problems. In Latin, it became *machina*. It did not wholly remove the need for the human hand but enabled humans to do certain things far more easily. Typical *machinae* (plural) – all made by hand, of course – included cranes, derricks, windlasses, revolving stages, mills, siege engines, stone-throwing ballistas and catapults, scaffolding, platforms, cages (to confine people, or cattle for treatment) and so on.

The architect Vitruvius devoted a whole book to *machinae*. He defined a *machina* as 'a continuous piece of joinery oustandingly well suited to moving loads'. He mentioned devices for raising water (such as Archimedes' screw and Ctesibius' water pump), a water organ and a hodometer ('road-measurer': Greek *hodos* [ὁδός], 'road' + *metron* [μετρον], 'measure'). This was a cogged device recording the distance it travelled. It calibrated the wheel diameter with a series of cogs such that every time the wheel and lower cog had turned 400 times, the upper cog turned once, releasing a pebble into a tin wth a loud rattle, announcing 'one mile'.

But machines that worked automatically existed only in fantasy worlds. The Greek *automatos* (αὐτοματος) meant 'acting of one's own free will', and of things 'self-acting', like the gates of Mount Olympus. Latin *automatum* (*-on*) meant what it means in English. The *auto-* root is the Greek for 'self' – for example, 'autopsy', seeing (as in 'optics') for oneself; 'automobile', 'moving by itself, self-propelling'. Compare 'auto' + '-crat' ('ruling'), + '-nomous' ('laws'), + '-graph' ('writing').

CEMENT

It is not known exactly when Romans started using a form of cement made out of wet lime and volcanic ash, but by the first century AD it was widely used across the Empire. The ash is called 'pozzolana', or 'pozzolan', from Latin *puteolanus*, 'from Puteoli', a town near Vesuvius. This 'volcanic' cement was light compared with stone, had great strength and endurance (thousands of years, unlike modern concrete), could be poured into preformed shapes and would set underwater. Most commonly it was mixed with small stones or rubble and used as infill, to be finished off externally with a facing of materials such as bricks or marble. That, in fact, is where our term 'cement' comes from: Latin *caementum*, 'rubble', from *caedo*, 'I crack, smash, break'. Such was the importance of this volcanic ash that it was transported all over the Mediterranean, for example to Caesarea Maritima in Israel and Alexandria.

RANDOM NETWORKS

There were various styles of Roman masonry. One was called 'network' masonry (*reticulatum*, from *rete*, 'net', the facing bricks angled against each other to produce a diamond-like pattern). Vitruvius commented that, while it was very popular because it looked so pretty, it tended to fall apart because there were so many seams in it. 'Random' masonry (*incertum*), however, was different: the courses of rubble filled in with lime and sand were so strong that they needed no brick facing at all and were simply 'tidied up' to look neat. This, said Vitruvius, lasted far longer. Its strength was partly down to the crystal structure of the volcanic ash that prevented tiny cracks from spreading.

ARCHES

The Latin *arcus* meant a 'bow' (as in bow and arrows), and so a rainbow, and then an arch or a vault. The arch was a key feature of Roman architecture. It had been known around the Mediterranean for a very long time, but Romans used it to revolutionize building. The point is that, because the arch is immensely strong, it can span very wide spaces indeed. Think of a Roman aqueduct: you could not build one of those with columns and a stone or wooden beam across the top! The result was huge self-standing buildings like the Colosseum, quite impossible with Greek column-and-crossbeam technology. Domes and barrel vaults (a single passageway formed out of a series of arches) are extensions of the same principle, equally exploited by Roman engineers. (For *fornix*, 'arch', see p. 217.)

'Arcade', via seventeenth-century Italian, is a passageway formed out of a series of arches. It has nothing to do with Arcadia, a scrubby, mountainous region of southern Greece turned by the sixteenth-century Italian poet Jacopo Sannazaro into a rural paradise where, while happy shepherds enjoyed their innocent pleasures, he could vent his frustrations at his lost loves.

WORM-RIDDEN MOSAICS

Floors were regularly decorated with mosaics, both black-and-white and coloured. The pictures depicted by them often gave a clue to what the room was for, and in the Roman harbour town of Ostia acted as guides to the shops. Everyday mosaics were made of *tesserae*, small squares or cubes of stone or coloured glass, which were laid on site (whence our 'tessellated'). They may be named after the Greek for 'four', *tessares* (see p. 125), for having four corners.

Very small mosaic pieces, no more than four millimetres square, were constructed in frames in workshops, to be placed ready-made in walls. These tiny-cubed mosaics allowed for very fine, delicate work, almost resembling painting. Such work was called *vermiculatum*, 'producing a wavy-line effect', from *vermiculus*, 'larva of a grub or maggot' (from which we get 'vermin').

The Greek for 'mosaic' was *lithostrôtos* (λιθόστρωτος), 'paved with stones', especially of mosaic pavements. Pliny the Elder says that *lithostrôta* were first introduced into Italy by the famous luxury-loving dictator Sulla (*c.* 80 BC), but were then, as it were, unnaturally driven up out of the ground into vaulted ceilings (*camara*, see p. 222). Pliny liked things to be in their 'correct' place.

Our 'mosaic' comes, via Italian, from *Musa*, the work of the Muse (see p. 230).

LENTIL LENSES

Working with minute mosaics or precious stones with which to make jewellery was a severe strain on the eyes. The ancients did not grind lenses but used glass and crystal to focus light rays in order to start fires and magnify images. Pliny the Elder said that doctors used crystal balls to focus the sun's rays and cauterize wounds. For magnification Romans used crystal, while Seneca commented that 'even small and indistinct letters can be enlarged and seen more clearly through a glass or globe filled with water'. It is said (Pliny again) that Nero used a glass called *smaragdus* (source of our 'emerald') to watch gladiator fights. But it is highly unlikely that he is talking about sunglasses. Pliny may have been describing a green glass with good reflective qualities like a mirror, and Nero was experimenting with it.

Our 'lens', however, a shape convex on both sides, derives from Latin for a 'lentil, lentil seed': *lens* (*lent-*), a crop domesticated perhaps as long as 13,000 years ago. Pliny the Elder, talking about the 'concave or convex' shapes of precious stones, commented: 'An elongated shape is most valuable; then what is called "like a lentil"; and then a flat, round shape.' So the shape of the lentil is halfway between a long, thin stone and a round stone – convex on both sides. Nowadays, lenses of various shapes make possible spectacles and contact lenses, telescopes, cameras, projectors, photovoltaic cells, radio astronomy, radar and much more.

A VILLA'S CRUSTY WALL PANELS

Latin *crusta* had nothing to do with pies. It was applied to the hard covering of a shellfish (→ 'crustacea' such as crabs, lobsters, krill, barnacles, etc.) or insect or scab, and then to the thin marble panels that the wealthy used to cover floors or overlay walls in their villas. The marble was carefully cut with a saw, using fine sand to help its cutting edge. If one could not afford marble, the walls would be painted to look like marble.

Crusta also gives us 'custard', via French *c(r)oustade*. Lumpy custard we know, but crusty...! Meanwhile, *villa*, the Roman's luxury country house complete with estate and farm, gives us 'villain'. Late Latin produced *villanus*, a worker in a villa, i.e. a serf, a term which (via French) degraded into a scoundrel or villain.

GAPS IN CEILINGS

A particular luxury feature of Roman halls, basilicas and temples was ceilings inlaid with panels of wood that were decorated with gold leaf. Romans called such a panel a *lacunar*, literally 'covering gaps' (in the wooden beams of the roof structure). A *lacuna* in Latin meant 'gap', as it does in English.* Such ceilings added a luxurious eastern touch to Roman buildings, bringing to mind Greek temples or the Temple in Jerusalem. St Basil said that in death no gold-panelled ceilings would cover us, but the heavens, picked out with the indescribable brightness of stars.

'Coffered' is our technical term for such an inlaid ceiling, from the Greek *kophinos* (κοφινος), Latin *cophinus*, meaning originally a 'basket' (whence 'coffin'). Our 'ceiling' is related to Latin *celo*, 'I cover, hide', though it may have been influenced by Latin *caelum*, 'sky, heavens' (whence our 'celestial').

IRON SUSPENDERS

The Greek for 'magnet' was *magnêtis lithos* (μαγνητις λιθος), 'Magnesian stone'. These stones were pieces of iron ore that were naturally magnetized, and were so named because they were thought to have come from a town called Magnesia, either the one in Greece or the one in Asia Minor. Pliny the Elder tells us that the architect Timochares had begun to use such stone to build the vaulting of a temple in Alexandria. His aim was to suspend an iron statue within the vaulting so that it looked as if it was hanging in mid-air. Had he done so, he would have also found that it stayed in that position for only a very brief time indeed. Perhaps fortunately, he died before the work could be completed. Greeks also knew that the mineral amber had such properties: if rubbed by wool or fur, for example, it could attract light objects to stick to it.

---

* Our 'lake' derives from *lacus*, a gap or hollow filled with water; Greek *lakkos* [λακκος] meant 'pond, pit, reservoir'.

The ancients were fascinated by magnetism: what hidden force was it that caused this attraction between two objects? The natural scientist Thales (sixth century BC) thought it was because there was some life force in the iron ore. The Roman poet-philosopher Lucretius (first century BC) thought the force in the iron ore sucked the air away between it and the object, creating a vacuum which drew the object towards it. We now know that electricity is at the heart of it.

The term 'electricity' was coined by Dr William Gilbert in AD 1600. He was working on the problem with amber and iron ore, and named this new force after the Greek for 'amber' – *êlektron* (ἠλεκτρον), Latin *electrum*. The magnetic compass, pointing north, was a Chinese invention (fourth or second century BC); such compasses were used in Europe from the thirteenth century AD.

LINTEL

A lintel stone is the one that makes up the threshold you step over to enter a building. It derives, via French, from Latin *limitaris*, which was all about setting limits: it also referred to the boundary between plots of lands. The German version of Hadrian's Wall was called the *limes Germanicus* ('the German boundary') and it ran alongside the Rhine–Danube. It consisted simply of a ditch and a mound of earth, with a line of wooden stakes on top. It was designed to help protect the Romans from German invasion.

The Latin for 'threshold' was *limen* (*limin*-), which is the source of our 'eliminate' via the Latin *elimino* (*eliminat*-), 'I turn out of doors'.

FORUM

Every town has, or had, a marketplace, a central point where shops, businesses, banks, courts and town administrations were located. In Latin, this was a *forum*. Its derivation is dubious (some try to associate it with Latin *foris/foras*, 'out of doors', source of 'foreign' and 'forest').

The Roman forum was low-lying and liable to flooding. This problem was solved by turning a river running through that area into a drain (the *Cloaca Maxima*), first by adding ditches and then by engineering it into a closed drain, complete with sewerage facilities. The geographer Strabo said of it in the first century AD:

> The sewers, covered with a vault of tightly fitted stones, have room in some places for hay wagons to drive through them. And the quantity of water brought into the city by aqueducts is so great that rivers, as it were, flow through the city and the sewers; almost every house has water tanks, and service pipes, and plentiful streams of water... In short, the ancient Romans gave little thought to the beauty of Rome because they were occupied with other, greater and more necessary matters.

Cloaca, 'drain, sewer', derived from *cluo*, 'I purify'. Our 'sewer' derives ultimately from Latin *ex*, 'out of, away' + *aqua*, 'water'.

TWO-EDGED EXCREMENT

Our 'excrement', incidentally, derives from Latin *excrementum*, 'bodily waste products' (including urine and spit and giving our 'excreta'); but *excrementum* also derived from a quite different Latin root, meaning 'outgrowth' – for instance, a beard! We can imagine the endless hilarity that wordplay evoked among Roman schoolchildren.

INSULA

Rome in the first century BC was a warren of winding streets and tenement blocks, six to eight storeys high, mostly built of mud-brick and timber, with cantilevered balconies, which were regularly subject to collapse and fire. Vitruvius recommended locating such blocks not head on to the prevailing winds but at an angle to them, thus breaking their force. At a time when experiments in fired brick were just beginning – a development of which Vitruvius strongly approved – he urged that mud-brick buildings should get proper protection by having tiled roofs with cornices to throw off the water.

Such tenements were called *insulae* (singular *insula*), 'islands', because they were free-standing, unattached to other buildings. Our 'insulation' isolates cables from their surroundings – and 'isolate', too, derives from *insula*. A 'peninsula' is an 'almost [Latin *paene*] island'. Juvenal described life in one such tenement and in the winding, crowded, brawling streets below:

> Think now about all those other perils
> Of the night: how high it is to the roof up there
> From which a tile falls and smashes your brains;
> How many times broken, leaky jars
> Fall from windows; how hard they strike and break
> The pavement. You could be thought lazy and careless
> If you go to dinner without writing a will.

There are as many deaths waiting for you
As there are open windows above your head.
Therefore you should hope and fervently pray
That they only dump their sewage on you...
Someone below is already shouting for water
and shifting his stuff; smoke is pouring out
of the third-floor attic, but you know
nothing of it; for if the alarm begins in the ground-floor,
the last to burn will be the man who has nothing
to shelter him from the rain but the tiles,
where the gentle doves lay their eggs.

TILES

A flat tile was a *tegula*, from *tego* (*tect-*), 'I cover, shield, protect'; a semicircular tile, placed over the gaps between the flat tiles, was an *imbrex* (*imbric-*), from *imber*, 'rain shower, storm'. Pliny the Elder tells us that one Butades was the first person to fix gargoyles on the end of the *imbrices* nearest the gutters.

On the matter of weather, 'climate' derives from Greek *klima* (κλιμα), 'slope' (of the earth), 'region, latitude, astrological zone'. There were seven of these zones, related to the slope of the sun, each thought to govern a regional climate. See also on 'climax' (p. 164) and 'clinic' (p. 279).

AQUEDUCTS

Latin *duco* (*duct-*) meant 'I lead, guide, conduct'; combined with *aqua*, 'water', it produced *aquaeductus*, a water conductor. On the same principle, a *viaduct* is a road (*via*) conductor. We tend to associate the word 'aqueduct' with dramatic and beautiful arches bestriding a valley, but it refers to the whole length of the conduit, from source to outflow, much of which would be along channels or underground.

Romans did not invent aqueducts, but thanks to their building techniques (see p. 205), they used them far more extensively than anyone else. Until quite recently, it was reckoned that aqueducts serving Rome, Cologne and Carthage were the longest, each of those great cities making use of aqueducts about fifty-five miles long. Now it seems that an aqueduct serving Constantinople far outstrips them – seventy-five miles as the crow flies, but 155 miles in all when the various twists and turns needed to negotiate difficult terrain are taken into account. Rome alone was served by eleven aqueducts (total mileage – 300), delivering well over 250 million gallons of water a day to its one million inhabitants. The largest aqueduct bridge is the Pont du Gard in France, which is some 300 yards long and 53 yards high. Tunnels ran to a mile and half long.

REMARKABLE WATERWORKS

The Romans were intensely proud of their capacity to deliver water over such distances. Pliny the Elder said:

> If we take into careful consideration the abundant supplies of water in public buildings, baths, pools, open channels, private houses, gardens and country estates near the city; if we consider the distances traversed by the water before it arrives, the raising of arches, the tunnelling of mountains and the building of level routes

across deep valleys, we shall readily admit that there has never
been anything more remarkable in the whole world.

The Latin for Pliny's 'remarkable' was *mirandus*, 'worthy to be admired'. Our 'mirror' ultimately derives from its associated verb *miror*, 'I am amazed, wonder at': a means of admiring yourself.

The Roman senator Frontinus (*c.* AD 40–103) was put in charge of aqueducts (see *curator*, p. 41) and wrote a treatise on the subject. Having described the aqueducts of Rome in detail, he said: 'With such an array of indispensable structures carrying so many waters, compare, if you will, the idle pyramids or the useless, though much celebrated, works of the Greeks.' (On 'celebrity', see p. 154.)

GRADIENT

The point about a 'gradient', steep or shallow, is that it is measurable and in theory controllable. Latin *gradior* (*gress-*) reflects this: it meant 'I walk, proceed' but especially in a stately or deliberate manner (whence our 'progress' – proceeding forward). Cicero argued that men of reputation, 'won not by popular acclaim but by the approval of good men, will *proceed steadily* towards death in confident spirit'.

In the absence of pumps, Romans relied on deliberately controlling the gradient to deliver the water safely to its destination without it bursting out of the fountains in the middle of towns at a million miles an hour. The main Carthage aqueduct has a very steep (28 per cent) slope over a four-mile stretch, superbly graded; by contrast, an exquisitely engineered six-mile stretch from the Pont du Gard has a slope of just 0.07 per cent.

HOT STUFF

The main purpose of such vast quantities of water being delivered into town centres was not to provide drinking water (no town could be founded without that being available in the first place); it was to supply Romans' leisure needs. These were the huge public baths, one of Rome's most important inventions: Latin (plural) *balnea*, derived from Greek *balaneia* (βαλανεια), or *thermae*, derived from Greek *thermos* (θερμος), 'hot'. The baths had hot (*calidus*) rooms, cold (*frigidus*) and warm (*tepidus*) rooms, gymnasia, shops, brothels, even libraries. Once the water was available, it could of course be used for other things, such as supplying (at a cost) private homes.

GYMNASIA

Greeks and Romans exercised naked – Greek *gumnos* (γυμνος) – and Latin *gymnasium* derived from Greek *gumnasion* (γυμνασιον). Romans had a perfectly good word for 'naked', *nudus*, but being partial to most things Greek, chose to imitate Greek cultural practice and language. The cultural cringe, as some Romans saw it, is nothing new; but many Romans were proud of their absorption of Greek culture.

LATRINES

The function of what we call a lavatory is not well described by its derivation from *lavo*, 'I wash', but since the Romans used the same circumlocution ('roundabout speak') as well, it must obviously be OK: *lavatrina* (the *-ina* suffix indicating 'place for an activity'), which was shortened to *latrina*.

On which theme: 'laundry' derives from *lavandaria* (plural), literally 'things needing to be washed'. The *-nd-* infix in verbs indicated 'needing to be' – so *agenda*, '[things] needing to be discussed', *propaganda*, '... to be propagated', and so on.

FORNICATIO

Many inscriptions recorded the successful completion of facilities in a town. Here Lucius Betilienus Varus was thanked for constructing in his home town of Aletrium:

> all the street-paths; the *porticus* (colonnade, portico) along
> which people walk to the stronghold; a playing-field; a sun-dial
> (*horologium*); a meat-market; the stucco-ing of the *basilica*; seats; a
> bathing-pool; a reservoir by the gate; an aqueduct about 340 feet
> long leading into the city and to the height, with arches (*fornices*)
> and good sound water-pipes.

The arches (singular *fornix*) are of interest. The story has it that prostitutes in Rome plied their trade underneath the arches, where (presumably) the lights were low, and thus – via *fornicatio*, 'vaulting, arch' – supplied us with 'fornication'. But *fornix* also meant a 'cell' or 'brothel'.

BASILICA

Named after the Greek for 'king' (*basileus* [βασιλευς]), a basilica was a large, oblong hall with internal colonnades or aisles on either side. The basilica was used as a law court and business centre. It was usually located next to the forum. The nave of the Basilica of

Maxentius (AD 313), situated in the forum at Rome, was nearly 300 feet long and some 115 feet high. Its arches (*arcus*, 'bow') were 80 feet high and 76 feet wide.

In structure a basilica looks rather like a church. That is because early churches were designed like basilicas, to hold large congregations of the faithful in a location with good acoustics – quite unlike pagan temples (see p. 177). The nave was the central space between the aisles, so called after Latin *navis*, 'ship', because the ceiling looked like an inverted hull. 'Aisle' derives from Latin *ala*, 'wing', used of a bird or an army. The semicircular apse at the end derives from Latin *apsis*, 'arc described by a planet; segment of a circle'.

CIRCUS

'Circuit training' should mean going round and round in circles, and on a bad day it may feel like that. It derives from *circumeo* (*circu(m)it*), 'I go round, surround'. The Latin 'circus' referred to the shape of the performing area: it meant 'orbit in the sky; circular or oval space'. It referred in particular to the Circus Maximus, where the hugely popular chariot races were held in Rome.

Some did not approve. Tacitus in his *Histories* described the varying reactions in Rome to the death of Nero in AD 68, commenting that the senators and *equites* (p. 35) were delighted; decent people – those connected to the great houses, and clients (p. 71) and freedmen of those exiled by Nero – were hopeful; but 'the *plebs sordida*, addicted to the circus and theatre, the worst slaves, and those who had lost all their property, shamelessly dependent as they were on Nero's handouts, were very dejected'. One reason was that Nero was passionate about theatre and races and staged lots of events, some (to many people's disgust) featuring himself. Latin *sordida*, derived from *sordes*, 'dirt, filth', was used of character, conduct and language too.

CROWD CONTROL

At racecourses, courts and theatres, Romans put up the barriers in order to control crowds. These often took the form of grilles or gratings in a lattice or criss-cross pattern. The poet Ovid wrote a poem about going to the races to try to win the favour of his girl. They sat down in the front row, but her legs were too short to reach the ground. So, gentleman that he was at least pretending to be, he suggested she inserts her toes into the grating.

The Latin word for this grille/grating was *cancellus*, also used of the criss-cross lines on an elephant's hide, and is the source of our 'cancel' – which you do by using a pen to *cross* things out. It also gives us 'chancellor' – these days a powerful governmental or university official, originally a *cancellarius*, the doorkeeper guarding the emperor's palace behind a grill, or a legal scribe sitting behind a grating separate from the crowds. The 'chancel' in a church was originally the lattice barrier that divided the choir and altar from the nave, and then became used of that protected space around the altar.

WATCHING OR HEARING?

The Latin for one who watched or observed was *spectator*, from *specto* (*spectat-*), 'I see, watch, observe', and was used in exactly the same sense as we use it, for those watching a play or game. Our 'spectacle' (*spectaculum*) usually has overtones of something special or 'spectacular' about it, as the Latin does. The Seven Wonders of the World were the *septem spectacula*. An 'audience' should, if English imitated Latin, mean something different, since it derives from Latin *audio* (*audit-*), 'I hear, listen'. But rather like our 'audition', an 'audience' often involves more than simple listening.

MONUMENT

Those who study Latin will know that *moneo* (*monit-*) meant 'I advise, warn' (whence 'admonition', etc.), but they may be surprised to learn that *moneo* is at the root of *monumentum*. In fact, *moneo* is linked to *memini*, 'I remember', and the basic meaning is 'I bring to the notice of, remind, tell of'. And that is exactly what a *monumentum* does. Horace said, hopefully, of his poetry: 'I have put up a *monumentum* more lasting than bronze.'

In AD 9 the Roman general Varus had lost three legions to the Germans. The then Roman emperor Augustus was devastated at the loss. In AD 16 Germanicus, the highly popular nephew of his unpopular and jealous uncle, the new emperor Tiberius, launched a successful revenge attack and erected a vast pile of enemy weapons under the tactful notice:

AFTER SUBDUING THE NATIONS BETWEEN THE RHINE AND
THE ELBE, THE ARMY OF TIBERIUS CAESAR CONSECRATED
THE MONUMENT TO MARS, JUPITER AND AUGUSTUS

The German leader was Arminius; in the sixteenth century, Luther (possibly) claimed that the name 'Hermann' derived from him.

STONE MONUMENTS

Latin *lapis* (*lapid-*) meant 'stone', and our 'lapidary' derives from *lapidarius*, which meant 'concerned with stonecutting or quarrying'. 'Lapidary', however, also refers to a particular brief and pointed literary style – the sort of clipped, precise, elegant sentiments we find on inscriptions, where space is at a premium.

Eventually monuments and houses fall down (see 'decrepit', p. 38). Cicero mentioned in a letter that 'two of my shops have collapsed and the others are showing cracks, so that even the mice have moved elsewhere, to say nothing of the tenants'. Latin *lapido* meant 'I shower with stones', and the prefix *di(s)-* indicates separation (for instance, dismembering); so *dilapido*, a reinforced form of *lapido*, suggests a dilapidated house falling down, scattering stones over helpless passers-by.

CARPENTERS ON WHEELS

What job does the Latin *carpentarius* do? Not what you might think. The word derives from Latin *carpentum*, which meant a horse-drawn two-wheeled carriage, used especially by women in Rome. So a *carpentarius* was a carriage-maker, or cartwright. The historian Livy told the story that when the Romans were unable to raise the money to pay a vow to Apollo, the women came to the rescue by handing over all their gold ornaments. The Senate promptly gave them the right to be driven about in four-wheeled carriages during festivals and games days, and in *carpenta* during sacred and working days.

The *carpentum* had an arched covering to protect against rain and sun and guard female modesty. This covering was a *camara* or *camera*

(Greek *kamara* [καμαρα]). Over time it came to mean an arched or vaulted room, source of our 'chamber', 'comrade' (one who shares the same room, → 'camaraderie') and of 'camera' in the sense of a chamber where private meetings are held – *in camera*, as we say.

The 'camera obscura' is a dark box or room with a hole, or more often a lens, in it. Light passes through the hole/lens and reproduces on a surface inside the box/room an image of the scene outside. The origins of photography are to be found here.

CANOPIES, GNATS AND HORS D'OEUVRES

What have canopies got to do with gnats? Greek for a 'gnat' was *kônôps* (κωνωψ), and a *kônôpion* (κωνωπιον) was a mosquito net. Romans turned this into *conopium*, meaning a bed provided with a mosquito net, whence (via French *canapé*) our 'canopy'. In a brilliant satire on women, the Roman satirist Juvenal said that all women liked a bit of rough, and when a posh family sported its latest baby in its tortoiseshell cot and *conopium*, it often looked strangely like some thug from the gladiatorial ring.

Second question: what has a *canapé* (French 'bed, couch') got to do with canopies? A *canapé* was apparently so called because the garnish on top of the base resembled people sitting on a couch – a sort of up-market couch potato.

ARTS, DRAMA
AND MUSIC

INTRODUCTION

The poet Horace gives us an account of early Roman literature. It was a story of faithful old Roman farmers, when the harvest is over, making a sacrifice and enjoying a drink or two, and then watching boisterous, rollicking entertainments featuring lots of genial abuse. The abuse then turned nasty and laws were passed to control it. But, says Horace, 'many traces have been left of our uncouth past'. Then come the famous lines 'Captive Greece made her savage conqueror captive, and brought the arts to rustic Latium' – Horace's acknowledgement of the radical changes that knowledge of the ancient Greeks' cultural achievement wrought in Rome.

Our first surviving complete works of Roman literature are the comedies of Plautus and Terence from the second century BC. These were in fact Greek comedies translated into Latin, Greek names and all, suitably adapted for the Roman audience. They were put on at festival times in the temporary wooden theatres typical of the day

(Rome had no permanent stone-built theatres till the first century BC). Filled with tricky slaves, tyrannical fathers, young lovers, pimps and prostitutes, boastful soldiers and so on, these plays were boisterous affairs in more ways than one: Terence (born in Africa) made an actor complain in the prologue of one comedy that the first production had been called off because of all the shouting and women screaming at the rumours of a boxing match and a tightrope walker. The second attempt was aborted because of word about a gladiatorial show. Now he expressed the hope that the third performance would finally take place. So Roman drama was not acted with all the solemnity of a nativity play at a convent. Certainly the audience, to judge by the way they are addressed in the prologues, was very mixed: men and women, free and slaves, socially high and low, rich and poor, old and young, and so on.

There were writers of tragedy, too, in the second century BC – Ennius, Pacuvius, Accius to name some names – though none of their works survive. Perhaps they lived too much in the shadow of their Greek rivals 250 years earlier – Aeschylus, Sophocles and Euripides. But though neither comedy nor tragedy as a creative medium outlived the second century BC, the comedies in particular remained very popular and were regularly restaged well into the imperial period.

Farces were already being played alongside comedies in the second century BC – knock-about stuff with much horseplay, slapstick and general buffoonery – and this format continued alongside the newly developing mimes and pantomimes. Mime was a formless, varied entertainment featuring acrobats, conjuring, naked women, dancing and song, and other lewd material. Storylines were simple: kidnaps, shipwrecks, love affairs, and so on. There could be veiled political references. They were hugely popular.

Pantomime was essentially a dance medium. The dancers did not sing or speak but worked entirely by bodily movement. They were backed up by music and a chorus. Greek myth was a popular theme. Here the Greek satirical writer Lucian described how a performance should be:

> In general, the dancer undertakes to present and enact characters and emotions, introducing now a lover and now an angry person, one man afflicted with madness, another with grief, and all this within fixed bounds... within the selfsame day at one moment we are shown Athamas in a frenzy, at another Ino in terror; presently the same person is Atreus, and after a little, Thyestes; then Aegisthus, or Aerope; yet they all are but a single man... The dancer should be perfect in every point, so as to be wholly rhythmical, graceful, symmetrical, consistent, unexceptionable, impeccable, not wanting in any way, blended of the highest qualities, keen in his ideas, profound in his culture, and above all, human in his sentiments.

The most famous, or perhaps rather notorious, actor was the emperor Nero. Nero regarded himself primarily as a great supporter and performer of the arts. He put on an immense variety of entertainments, compelling the great and good to take part as well (one rode an elephant down a sloping tightrope, others fought in the arena). He staged a naval battle complete with sea monsters, and a ballet of Daedalus and Icarus in which Icarus fell rather too realistically, spattering Nero with blood. His Great Play Festival once featured a burning house, from which the actors were allowed to keep the furniture they rescued. Throughout the festival, gifts were distributed to the populace, including vouchers for corn, clothes, gold, silver, paintings, slaves, wild beasts, and even ships, tenements and farms. No wonder the populace adored him.

Nero was passionate about music, took lyre and singing lessons, and kept his weight down with enemas and emetics. His singing debut was in Naples, where he disregarded an earthquake to complete the performance (the theatre collapsed soon afterwards). In another competition, he performed the whole of the opera *Niobe*. This took till nearly dusk and left no time for anyone else to perform. He regularly toured musical competitions in Greek cities (they sent him in advance every prize they could lay their hands on, which convinced him Greeks really understood about music), and protected his vocal chords by getting others to read out his speeches. He kept a voice trainer constantly by his side. He performed in tragedies, taking the roles of gods and heroes, and even goddesses and heroines, wearing masks modelled on his own face or that of his current mistress. One story is that he fiddled while Rome burned (during the Great Fire of Rome in AD 64). But the fiddle had not been invented then. Another story had him returning from his palace in Antium to Rome to co-ordinate action against the blaze; another had him watching Rome burn while he played the lyre and sang of the destruction of Troy.

All these entertainments were accompanied by music and song, which was a staple of Roman life – from theatre (song and dance during the intervals in comedies) and buskers in the streets to the military (the brass sounded retreat, advance, etc.) and the games (chariot-racing and gladiatorial combat, the latter started and accompanied by a range of instruments); and from religious rituals and all civic celebrations to the warbling Nero.

But 'cultured' it was not. Most Romans, unlike Greeks, did not regard music as a means of shaping the soul or elevating the mind: it was good, honest noise to march to, sing with and generally enjoy at a very basic level. That said, to be taught to sing or play an instrument was expected of the children of the elite, probably as a nod to Greek ways of doings thing. Poetry was not automatically accompanied by the lyre, as Greek poetry seems to have been, though it was enjoyed on private occasions. Pliny the Younger talked of lyre- or pipe-playing or even a comedy after dinner.

But fancy singing always carried the risk of the accusation of degeneracy or mockery. Horace said of the famous singer Tigellius that he was one of those who 'among friends can never bring themselves to sing when requested; but fail to make a request, and they'll never stop'; and went on to describe him as a real prima donna, whose next move or demand one could never hope to anticipate.

Musical instruments were of three varieties: wind (pipes, pan-pipes, bagpipes, trumpets, horns); string (plucked or struck with a plectrum; lyres and harps were the only two basic types); and percussion (drums, cymbals, clappers, and the *sistrum*, which was shaken). One oddity was the *hydraulis*, a form of organ whose air supply was powered by a water pump, and later by a bellows. Famed for its loudness, the *hydraulis* became even louder with this development. It was very popular indeed in Rome. One, we are told, had a wind chest made of two elephant hides, fed by twelve bellows, and could be heard a mile away. It was the forerunner of the modern organ.

However that may be, of all the cultural achievements of the ancient Greeks and Romans that have been so influential down the millennia in the West, their music is the one exception. Though Greek musical theory was keenly studied in the Middle Ages and during the Renaissance, ancient music was not harmonized in the way we understand harmony, and it was impossible to relate it to contemporary developments in polyphony. As a result, ancient musical practice has had no influence on Western music.

As for art, the Greek satirist Lucian talked amusingly of his efforts to find a trade. His uncle suggested sculptor. His initial efforts were not a success, but that night he was visited by a dream in the shape of Sculpture herself, taking the form not of a beautiful, elegant Muse but of a blokeish, calloused workman, covered in dust. She was followed in the dream by Education, and the two tried to persuade Lucian to take their option. Education offered this account of the sculptor's lot:

> This woman has told you what profit you will get from becoming a sculptor: you will be nothing but a workman, putting all your hopes of a livelihood in hard physical labour. You will be personally insignificant, getting meagre and demeaning returns, feeble-minded, a figure of no importance in public life. No friends will court you; no enemies fear you; no citizens envy you. You will be nothing but a labourer, just one of the mob, always cringing before your superiors and sucking up to the well-educated, leading a dog's

[the Greek says 'hare's'!] life, and a pawn in the hand of anyone stronger. Even if you became a Phidias or a Polycleitus and created many marvellous works, everyone would certainly praise your craftsmanship, but no sensible man would ever pray to be like you. For whatever sort of person you actually might be, you will be regarded simply as a mechanic, a handyman, a manual worker.

The interest of the passage is that there is no mention of aesthetics (*aisthêtika* [αἰσθητικα], 'things perceived by the senses', rather than the mind), let alone inspiration with respect to this (to us) creative art. The word translated as 'mechanic' here sums it up: *banausos* (βαναυσος), our 'banausic', also meaning in Greek 'vulgar, in low taste'.

That did not mean that the ancients had no feeling about their art. They made judgements about quality and value, as we do, but did not write about what art 'was' or agonize about 'artistry' or in what sense it engaged the emotions (all essentially eighteenth-century concerns). Those stories that were told about ancient artists (in Pliny the Elder, for example) often concentrated on the extent to which art did or did not imitate real life. Zeuxis, Pliny tells us, painted a picture of grapes so realistic that birds flew up at them. His rival Parrhasius then painted a picture of a curtain so realistic that Zeuxis asked for it to be drawn aside so that he could see the picture. When he saw how he had been deceived, he confessed that Parrhasius was the better painter. Realism was the artist's priority.

Romans were as committed to realism (or 'naturalism') as the Greeks were, and always held Greek art and sculpture in high regard.

One aspect of this, perhaps encouraged by their habit of making death-masks, was the Roman portrait, which regularly showed creases, wrinkles and warts in abundance. Romans ruthlessly plundered statues from Greece during their military forays there in the second century BC, and Greek artists flooded into Rome to meet the demand from Roman collectors. Greek work in precious metals, bronze and marble was very highly valued; decorated garden furniture became popular. Copying Greek statues became common (which is why most of the surviving 'Greek' statues are Roman copies), as did designing buildings to show off collections of statues and busts. Luxury interior decorations, featuring elegant wall-painting of the sort found in wealthy Greek homes, became all the rage. In all this, Romans were doing what they did across their culture: taking what Greeks did and adapting it to their own tastes.

MUSES AND MUSEUMS

Ancient gods were invented to cover every aspect of life, including the arts, especially poetry, music and dance, and all were regularly co-ordinated: Greek poetry was sung; dance was performed to music; and the chorus in a Greek tragedy sang and danced to music during the choral passages.

The goddesses of the arts were called by the Greeks *Mousai* (Μουσαι, singular Μουσα); the Romans took them over directly as *Musai* (*Musa*). Traditionally there were nine of them, covering epic poetry, lyric poetry, pipe-playing, dancing, tragedy, comedy, hymns/pantomime (all these with strong musical elements), and history and astronomy. The *Mous-* stem seems to be connected with a root meaning 'think, remember' in Greek. The arts require thought and memory; and if one was going to sing of the deep past, especially about the deeds of the gods, one needed secure *information* about it, to which only the Muses could give access.

The Muses lived on Mounts Olympus and Helicon, and a shrine to the Muses was called in Greek *Mouseion* (Μουσειον), in Latin *museum*. In both cultures the word also came to embrace a place set apart for intellectual and cultural study, whence our 'museum'.*

ARTS AND CRAFTS

Today, 'artists' are treated by many with an almost awed reverence. But the Latin *ars* (*art-*) meant basically 'craftsmanship' – a learned skill, developed by practice, applied to anything requiring technical ability (see p. 145). Inspiration did not come into it. Sweat did. Virgil composed his *Aeneid* at a rate of three lines a day, 'like a bear licking its cubs into shape'.

Cicero, talking of statesmanship and making a comparison with navigation, said that 'it is good *ars* to run before the gale, even if the ship cannot make harbour'; Ovid encouraged the lover to sing *arte* ('expertly'), if he sings, and to drink *arte*, if he drinks. Dentists, surgeons, plumbers and car mechanics are today's true artists.

Ars comes from a root meaning 'fit together, join' and also provides Latin with *artus*, 'limb'.

---

* 'To muse' is a word of Germanic origin meaning 'muzzle, snout', and via French *muser* meant 'dream, waste time', perhaps 'sniff about' like a dog. For English-speakers, 'muse' may have shifted its meaning through the influence of the classical usage.

SCULPTURE

Latin *scalpo* meant 'I draw the nails across, scratch'. Possibly because no Great Sculptor would want to be known as a scratcher, *sculpo* (*sculpt-*) was formed as if it were a completely unconnected verb. *Sculpo* meant 'I work on any material by carving or engraving', whether a statue, ornament or inscription. The educationalist Quintilian even used it as an image of literary production, advising a would-be orator to 'deliver only what he has written and, if circumstances permit, what he has carved into shape, as Demosthenes [the great Greek orator] said'.

PAINTING

'Paint' (via French), 'picture', 'pigment' and 'Pict' all derive from one Latin word: *pingo* (*pict-*), 'I adorn with colours', and 'I paint, decorate, draw'. The Latin probably derives from a root meaning 'cut'. Cicero wrote to his wealthy friend Atticus to say how pleased he was with the way his men had *painted* his library and bookshelves; Lucretius reflected on the life of early man, with the weather 'smiling upon them, and the seasons *painting* the green grass with flowers'; Cicero again had no time for poetry or prose which, however brilliantly *coloured*, just banged on, lacking variety or relief.

Pigmentum was Latin for 'colouring matter, dye' – Pliny the Elder commented how useful dyed wax was 'for the innumerable purposes of mankind'. A Pict was, of course, a painted barbarian living in northern Scotland with the short-sighted habit of attacking the Romans down south.

DYEING FOR ARSENIC

Arsenic derives from the Greek *arsenikon* (ἀρσενικον). It refers to arsenic trisulphide. In its mineral form, it had a golden tinge and was used as a dye in the ancient world by artists and cosmeticians. Pliny the Elder said that it was

> dug up in Syria for use by painters. It is found on the surface, and easily broken. The emperor Caligula, with his unbounded passion for gold, gave orders for vast quantities to be smelted. It did indeed produce excellent gold,* but in such small quantities that he found himself the loser from an experiment prompted by avarice... no one else has repeated it.

This was seen as a very precious and powerful substance, so naturally the Greeks derived it from the Greek *arrh/ars-*, 'male, manly'. The Greeks were wrong. As Pliny showed, the substance came from Syria, where its name was *al ẓarniqa*, the *ẓarn-* stem meaning 'golden'.

TABULA

While modern artists tend to paint on canvas, ancients painted on wooden panels (see below). The Latin for 'panel' was *tabula* (whence our 'table', etc.), a word which had many uses. It covered a games board, a noticeboard, a public tablet of metal or stone for laws and inscriptions, a writing tablet (see p. 150), account books (p. 114) and a document, especially a will.

A *tabula rasa* is not a classical idea. It means (literally) 'scraped

---

* This is obvious nonsense. It may have produced a sort of golden powder. One thing is certain: the smelting process would not have done the workmen any good at all.

tablet' (Latin *rado* [*ras-*], 'I shave, scrape', → 'razor'), alluding to the ease with which a wax tablet can have its writing smoothed out. It is the equivalent of our image of a 'blank slate' (slates used to be used in schools for pupils to write on), and psychologically refers to the theory that everyone is born with a mind entirely free of content. As Aristotle said:

> The intellect is in a sense potentially whatever is thinkable, though it is actually nothing until it has thought. What it thinks must be in it, just as characters may be said potentially to be on a writing tablet, on which as yet nothing stands written.

EASEL

Artists traditionally prop their paintings up on an easel. Romans propped them up on a *machina*, a multipurpose word for 'platform', 'scaffolding', 'crane' and much else (see p. 203).

Pliny the Elder – is there anything he did not write about? – told a wonderful story about the famous fourth-century BC Greek painter Apelles. He wanted to see the paintings of one Protogenes, who lived on Rhodes, but did not find him in his studio. He did, however, find there an old woman 'guarding a very large *tabula* already set up on the *machina*'. Apelles drew a fine line on the panel and told the old woman to say that that was the 'signature' of the caller. When Protogenes returned, he knew at once who had drawn the line and drew an even finer one on top. He then left, and when Apelles came back and saw what Protogenes had done, he drew an even finer line on top of that one. Protogenes admitted he had met his match, and the abstract painting with its increasingly fine lines became a much acclaimed masterpiece.

Modern artists do not use 'machines' – at least not for propping up their canvasses – but rather easels. 'Easel' derives (via Dutch) from Latin *asinus*, 'ass, beast of burden', also used for carrying heavy, unwieldy objects to market.

ICONIC

The Greek *eikón* (εἰκων) meant 'likeness, image; statue; phantom'. Romans produced an adjective based on the Greek, *iconicus*. It meant 'giving an exact image', used of a work of art. Pliny the Elder, for example, praised Panaenus, brother of the Athenian sculptor Phidias, for painting the battle of Marathon between the Athenians and Persians (490 BC) in colour, with such perfection that he produced exact portraits of the generals involved on both the Athenian and the Persian sides. Statues that gave exact representations of personal likenesses were called *iconicae*.

To a Greek or Roman, therefore, 'an iconic building' would be a building that looked exactly like another building. Today it seems to mean 'famous, popular, very significant'.

PERSPECTIVE

Used today of drawing an object to give an appearance of distance and depth, the term 'perspective' derives from Latin *perspicio* (*perspect-*), 'I inspect, see through, become aware of' (hence the see-through plastic 'Perspex'). But this is surely the wrong verb. The Latin *prospicio* (*prospect-*) – whence 'prospect' – meant 'I see before me, look ahead', and of tall buildings 'I give a view of' as from a vantage point. The poet Horace mocked the man who built in the city, but filled his courtyard with trees to make it feel like the country and so could (absurdly) 'praise the house which gives *a prospect* over fields far into the distance'.* But nature would get him in the end: 'You can drive out nature with a pitchfork, but it will soon be back, breaking through everything you in your stupidity have built.' So it should be 'prospective', not 'perspective'. The Italians got it right: *prospettiva*.

CANON

Not to be confused with a cannon (the weapon),† Greek *kanôn* (κανων, Latin *canon*) originally meant a rod or bar, to keep a thing straight (see p. 36), and then a straight edge of a ruler. The word developed over time to mean both 'rule, standard', and 'model, standard' for the artist.

Pliny the Elder tells us that the Greek artist Polykleitos 'made what artists call a *canon*; they draw their outlines from it as from a sort of standard'. Pliny was referring here to Polykleitos' treatise on art, which he called *Kanôn*, and the statue he made to illustrate its principles, the *Doruphoros* ('Spear-carrier'). He called that *Kanôn* too.

Church clerics known as 'canons' are so called because they are supposed to live according to rules; 'canon law' is a decree of

---

* 'Absurd' derives from Latin *surdus*, 'deaf, unhearing', which, combined with *ab-* to produce *absurdus*, meant 'completely deaf'. It signified 'discordant' with reference to music, then in general 'preposterous, inappropriate'.

† 'Cannon' – a large tube through which cannonballs are delivered – derives from Greek *kanna* (καννα), Latin *canna*, 'reed, pipe'. The medical 'cannula', direct from Latin *cannula*, is a small tube inserted into the body to feed in or extract fluid.

the church. Today the term is also used to mean 'official status as a model or standard'. So we might argue about who should make up a contemporary poetic canon: W. H. Auden, T. S. Eliot, Seamus Heaney, E. J. Thribb...?

PORNOGRAPHY

In Athenaeus' account of a lengthy feast entitled *The Learned Banqueters*,* one of the diners was accused of being mad about prostitutes, and his accuser went on: 'One wouldn't go wrong in calling you a *pornographos* (πορνογραφος), like the painters Aristides, Pausias and Nicophanes.' The root meaning of *porn-* is 'sell', and was used of the male *pornos* (πορνος, 'catamite, sodomite') as well as the female *pornê* (πορνη, 'whore'), all for sale. So a *pornographos* was 'one who paints pictures of prostitutes'. It is the only time the word appears in ancient literature. It entered the English language via French in the nineteenth century meaning a depiction or (less often) description of sexual subject matter aimed at arousing the user.

How far the average Roman was 'aroused' by the acres of pornography spread across the walls of inns, brothels and private homes of a town such as Pompeii is difficult to say. Male nudity was normal in the public baths, in gymnasia and at athletic competitions; nude statues of heroic figures, mythical or otherwise (for instance, emperors), were commonplace; nude images of Aphrodites (Greek) and Venuses (Roman) survive in their thousands. On the other hand, males in particular have been genetically designed to be aroused

---

* *Deipnosophistai* (Δειπνοσοφισται), literally 'Dinner-sophists'.

by what they see, and in the absence of photography and film, the ancients may well have appreciated the sensuality of art and sculpture more than their modern counterparts.

THEATRE

Our word 'theatre' derives from the Greek *theatron* (θεατρον), Latin *theatrum*. It meant literally 'viewing place', and because of its acoustic properties, was used in the Greek world both for dramatic performances and for meetings of political assemblies.

'Scene' derives from the Greek *skênê* (σκηνη), Latin *scaena*, the stage building on, or in front of which, the action took place. Dancing and singing played a large part in such performances. The derivation of 'obscene' (Latin *obscenus*, meaning much the same as the English) is unknown. Some try to connect it with the stage. What is the case is that Graeco-Latin obscenities did not feature in exclamations, as they do so tediously in English today. The ancients sensibly preferred to exclaim in the name of gods, who might actually do something about the problem, rather than of the sexual or excretory organs, whose potential for problem-solving has always been limited.

Our 'chorus' derives from Greek *khoros* (χορος), Latin *chorus*, 'dance', especially to music. Greek tragedies, for example, featured a 'chorus' that was twelve strong. The *khoros* danced and sang as well as spoke. Its function in relation to the individual actors was to act as an alternative, group voice of the less empowered.

Our 'orchestra' derives from Greek *orhkêstra* (ὀρχηστρα), Latin *orchestra*. This was the circular area in front of the stage where in

Greek drama the chorus danced and sang – nothing to do with the musical unit that we think of as an orchestra.

Romans never quite took to Greek tragedy or the conventions of Greek theatre. They much preferred broad humour – comedy and slapstick (see pp. 224, 242).

ODEON CINEMA

See the sign 'Odeon' on a high street today and it will be a cinema. The modern name strikes a neat balance between the Greek and the Latin version. The Greek *Óideion* ('Ωιδειον, based on *óidê*, ᾠδη, 'song'→ 'ode') became Latin *Odeum*. It was a small theatre for musical performances, usually looking like a small version of an ancient Greek theatre, the 'platform' facing a semicircle of seats rising up a slope. It could be used as a law court, lecture hall, distribution centre, and so on.

The original *Óideion* was built in Athens by Pericles in 435 BC; it was probably square, with a roof supported by ninety internal pillars. Pericles, who fancied himself as an impresario, made himself manager of the musical contests there and drew up the rules for singing and pipe- and lyre-playing.

'Cinema' comes from Greek *kinêma* (κινημα) meaning 'movement' – hence 'the movies'.

ECHO CHAMBERS

In order to amplify and clarify the actors' speech or song, some architects placed bronze vessels called 'echoes' (named after the nymph Echo of Greek myth) at certain points around theatres. One reason why Vitruvius wanted architects to understand mathematics and music was so that they could accurately position these vessels to best effect. Whether they made the slightest difference is open to debate.

According to myth, Zeus was always trying to cheat on his wife Hera, and the nymph Echo (Greek *Êkhô*, Ἠχω) aided and abetted him. Every time Zeus' wife Hera was about to catch him out, Echo distracted her with long conversations, enabling Zeus to leap out of the relevant bedroom window. When Hera worked out what was going on, she placed a curse on Echo which meant that she could speak only by 'echoing' the last words she had heard. As a result, when Echo fell madly in love with the handsome young Narcissus, all she could do was secretly follow him. When he heard a noise and said 'Anyone here?', she replied 'Here!'. When finally he said 'Let's get it on!', she took the word for the deed and leapt out on him. He was not impressed and bolted.

AGONIZING ACTORS

The Latin *actor* derives from *ago* (*act-*), 'I drive, perform, do, act' (whence 'action', 'activity' and so on). So it meant everything from a herdsman driving his cattle, to an agent, an advocate, an imperial official and, indeed, an actor in a play. The Greek word for 'actor' had gone down a quite different route: *hupokritês* (ὑποκριτης), whence our 'hypocrite'! What was going on?

The Greek for debate between competing parties to a dispute was *agón* (ἀγων), whence our 'agony'. Indeed, that is essentially what Greek drama (δραμα, 'something done') was: not so much physical as verbal action in the form of intense arguments between antagonists on stage. Debate was at the heart of Greek drama.

Hupokritês meant in fact 'a responder, one who answers'. It derived from a verb meaning 'I reply'; and the noun *hupokrisis* meant 'a reply', 'playing a part', and 'verbal delivery', whether on the stage or (for example) in political debate.

The great orator Demosthenes (fourth century BC) once performed so badly in a debate that he was hissed off the platform. The actor Andronikos told him that, while the content of his speech was good, his *hupokrisis* was rubbish, and illustrated it by repeating his speech, with appropriate action, intonation and so on, from memory. Demosthenes was convinced and asked Andronikos to teach him how to deliver or act out a speech persuasively. When someone much later asked Demosthenes what was the essence of successful oratory, he replied, 'Delivery'; and what next? 'Delivery'; and what finally? 'Delivery'.

In the light of these meanings – everything from simply 'replying' to 'acting' and 'playing a part' – it is no surprise that *hupokritês* also came to mean 'pretender, sham', and that is the meaning of the Greek that English has taken on board.

PERSONAL OVERACTING

We are used to footballers throwing themselves histrionically about like pantomime dames in efforts to win penalties. Little do they know that they *are* pantomime dames – or rather were.

The Roman historian Livy tells us that in 364 BC Rome was wracked by a plague. Among other measures to try to ward it off, they invented 'play-acting entertainments' ('a novel departure for a warlike people', Livy commented drily), getting the idea came from the Etruscans, a people living just over the Tiber.

The Etruscan for 'actor' was *hister*, which Romans turned into *histrio*, whence 'histrionics'. At the same time, the Etruscans seem to have provided the Romans with the word *persona*, source of our 'person'. In Latin it originally meant 'theatrical mask', 'character in a play' (as in our 'dramatis personae'); then 'part played by someone in real life', 'individual', etc.

These early entertainments developed from dances to the pipe and exchanges of insults in verse, to musical medleys and farces with plots and songs and plenty of abuse. Just like football, in fact.*

MIME, PANTOMIME AND DILDO

Some Greek forms of entertainment may also have played a part in early Latin theatre. Pantomime (Greek *pantomimos* [παντομιμος], Latin *pantomimus*) consisted of a dancer acting in a dumbshow, supported by a chorus and music; mime, from the Greek *mimos* (μιμος), Latin *mimus*, was a licentious type of farce. The plots were parodies of myths, adventure stories in historical settings, romances and tales of everyday life. In one, a woman discusses the dildo she has bought from a man pretending to be a shoemaker:

> As for his work, what work it is! You could be looking at something
> Athena herself had made... He came with two, and when I saw

---

* 'Farce' is from Latin *farcio*, 'I stuff, cram', used in Latin of fattening birds for table and from the fourteenth century of force-meat (stuffing) and low comedy (see *farrago*, p. 162).

them, well, my eyes almost popped out of my head. No man has a
prick *that* straight! And so soft, as soft as sleep, and its little straps
were made of wool!

This is the sort of thing Romans enjoyed. The *mim-* root is the source
of our 'mimic'. As for dildo (*c.* 1590), it may be derived from Italian
deletto, 'delight', Latin *diligo* (*dilect-*), 'I adore'.

EXPLOSIVE APPLAUSE

Our 'plaudit', a round of applause, derives from Latin *plaudite!*,
'Applaud!', the instruction with which Roman actors finished their
plays. The verb is *plaudo* (*plaus-*), 'I strike with the flat of the hand,
beat (with wings)'. 'Plausible' once meant 'worthy of applause', but
now it means only 'possible to applaud', while 'implausible' means
'impossible to applaud'.*

'Explode' comes from the same source, though differently spelled:
Latin *explodo*, 'I drive off the stage by making a noise, including a
clapping noise, reject'. Cicero told of the hapless comedian Eros
'*driven off the stage* with hisses [*sibilus*, whence our 'sibilant'] and
abuse, and having to take refuge at an altar [in someone's house]'.

There is a wider point to be made here. In the ancient world, in
the absence of polls, Twitter, Facebook, TV audience numbers (etc.),

---

* Latin *speciosus* and English 'specious' underwent the same sort of change: originally
meaning 'attractive, spectacular', they both edged into meaning 'showy, fine-
sounding', with suggestions of bogusness. The noun, too, from which it derives,
species, meaning 'spectacle, sight', also morphed into 'splendour, pomp', and then
mere 'outward appearance'; its meaning 'subdivision of any class or kind' is the sense
in which English uses it. Latin *specialis* meant 'individual, particular' – as opposed to
the general class or kind – and hence 'special'.

how did you determine your (un)popularity? Only by coming face to face with audiences or crowds, or by rumour. So for politicians, big public occasions were an important form of crude opinion poll. An emperor attending the games that he had staged would soon find out if he was doing a good job or not. The following happened to the emperor Claudius:

> When there was a scarcity of grain because of long-continued droughts, he was once stopped in the middle of the forum by a mob and so pelted with abuse and pieces of bread, that he was barely able to make his escape to the *Palatium* [his abode: whence our 'palace'] by a back door; and after this experience he resorted to every possible means to bring grain to Rome, even in the winter season.

But such mob behaviour was not intended to foment revolution (see p. 113). The people rioted in the certainty that the emperor would respond. And he did. He had little option.

GREEK V. ROMAN MUSIC

Lucius Anicius (second century BC) had just been celebrating a triumph over the Illyrians. Hiring four of Greece's finest pipe-players, he put them on stage with a chorus (singing and dancing). But it was all far too graceful, balletic and polite for the bored Roman military. So Anicius told the performers to jazz it up a bit, bringing in lots of action and preferably violence. So the pipe-players and chorus split off into teams and enacted mock attacks on each other, charging and retreating, then pretending to box. Four prizefighters came on stage with trumpet and bugle (good Roman instruments) and complete chaos descended.* The audience absolutely adored it.

This story is telling, because it contrasts the exquisite high musical attainments of the Greek world, which Romans were just coming into contact with in the second century BC, and the general tastes of the Roman public at big civic displays. They preferred good old-fashioned Roman music, all drums and trumpets and a hell of a racket, to this rather refined stuff from Greece.

PLASMA

It may not be absolutely clear what a 'plasma TV screen' actually is, but in Latin *plasma*, from the same stem as *plasticus*, 'to do with modelling', meant 'fancy, affected singing'. What?

Plasma (πλασμα) in Greek meant 'anything formed or moulded', and is used today (from 1928) as a general term for anything that is not gas, solid or liquid. The sun and stars are forms of plasma. So too are neon lights: the pressure of the neon gas in the tube is lowered to a level at which it will accept an electric current; this changes its nature and it lights up.† Plasma TV screens too use electrically charge gases. But Greeks associated the word with anything made up or invented; so it came to mean 'counterfeit, forgery', and in music 'fancy, affected singing', with trills, falsetto and so on.

---

* 'Bugle' derives from Latin *buculus*, 'young ox, bull' (Greek *bous* [βους], 'bull'). A *bucina* was a curved trumpet or horn, and a *bucinus* a trumpeter.

† The noble gas neon takes its name from Greek *neos* [νεος], 'new'.

'Stereo', incidentally, derives from ancient Greek. The Roman surveyor Balbus defined Latin *solidus* (see. p. 254) as 'what the Greeks call *stereos* (στερεος) and we call "cubic feet" whose length, breadth and width we can measure'. We would call it 'three-dimensional'.

HARMONY

Pythagoras is credited with discovering the relationship between music and mathematics. Stretch a string tight over a bridge. Move the bridge so that the two segments produce notes in the basic relation of an octave; then a fifth; and finally a fourth. Measure where the bridge is for each, and the ratio of lengths either side of the bridge comes out at 2 to 1, 3 to 2, and 4 to 3. Pythagoras concluded that all music could be understood on clear mathematical principles.

Our 'harmony' derives from Greek (and Latin) *harmonia* (ἁρμονια), whose basic sense was a 'means of joining or fastening'. Note that 'harmony' was not used in our sense of simultaneous interacting pitches and chords, or counterpoint. Ancient music was melodic – made up of a single tune – and *harmonia* referred to the structure of the tune.

THEORETICAL MUSIC OF THE SPHERES

The Pythagoreans extended the notion of mathematical and musical harmony across the whole ordered universe (the *kosmos* [κοσμος], 'order', the very opposite of its earliest form, thought to be 'chaos' [χαος]). Plato imagined the spheres (*sphaira* [σφαιρα]) producing their own perfect harmony across the universe.

This is well in line with Professor Stephen Hawking. He theorizes that 'strings' of minute particles (a 'string' particle is to an atom as an atom is to the universe) create the world's energy by *vibrating*. And what happens when a string vibrates? Why, it creates music – no other music, surely, than the music of the spheres.*

SOME MUSICAL TERMS

Chord: *khordê* (χορδη), 'guts; string; musical note'.

Chromatic: *khrôma* (χρωμα), 'colour, chromatic scale'.

Diapason: the full range of an instrument or voice. Greek *dia pasôn* (δια πασων), 'through all' – but all what? Chords? Notes? We do not know.

Dirge: from the Latin command *Dirige*, 'Direct (O Lord, my way...)', the opening of a funeral service.

Hydraulis: *hudraulis* (ὑδραυλις), 'water organ' – *hudr-*, 'water' + *aulos*, 'pipe'. Compare 'hydraulics', the mechanics of liquids being drawn through pipes.

Hyphen: *huphen* (ὑφ᾽ ἑν), literally 'in one', a sign linking two notes as one.

Lyre: *lura* (λυρα), 'stringed instrument', with four to seven strings. All such instruments were plucked or struck with a *plêktron* (πληκτρον), Latin *plectrum*. Bows were a later invention.

Melody: *melôidia* (μελῳδια), 'singing, chanting, choral song'.

Paean: *paian* (παιαν), 'chant, song, song of triumph', usually in honour of Apollo or Artemis.

---

* 'Theory' derives from Greek *theôria* (θεωρια), 'spectacle, contemplation'. 'Cosmetic' derives from *kosmos*. Cosmetics too create order out of chaos.

Rhythm: *rhuthmos* (ῥυθμος), 'any regular, measured motion or time'.

Threnody: *thrênôidia* (θρηνῳδια), 'lamentation'.

Tonic, tone: *tonos* (τονος), 'key; tone, pitch'.

Tympany: *tumpanon* (τυμπανον), 'shallow frame drum'.

WARFARE

INTRODUCTION

Homer's *Iliad*, the West's first work of literature (*c.* 700 BC), had war at its heart. Even then, there were procedures and issues with which we are familiar today: the justice of going to war, parleys, treaties, treatment of the dead and setting up of monuments to them. Classical Greeks made peace under treaty by means of sacred oaths and exchange of hostages, vowing 'to have the same friends and enemies'. Romans instituted their own official procedure of surrender – handing oneself over into Roman good faith (*fides*, whence our 'fidelity', 'confide', etc.).

Cicero (first century BC) defined the two big questions as *ius ad bellum* (rightful conduct to declare war) – retaliation and self-defence, under the appropriate authority, were the key; and *ius in bello* (rightful conduct on the battlefield). St Augustine thought war should punish wrongdoing – vengeance was not permitted and the defeated should be converted to Christianity. Machiavelli argued that all war was just. Others argued that war could be pre-emptive: fear alone could justify it. The seventeenth-century Dutch jurist Hugo Grotius was most influential in arguing for a true 'law of nations' and the concept of international intervention.

Writing about war began with Homer and became a staple diet of ancient Greek and Roman poets and historians. Xenophon left a memoir of his expedition to help the Persian Cyrus, and Julius Caesar left diaries of his wars in Gaul and the civil war against Pompey – the personal account was born and flourishes today. One of the most important books on Roman battle tactics was written by Vegetius, and was used widely up to the seventeenth century.

Depictions of war on pottery were commonplace in the Greek world, while decorated marble monuments were put up to soldiers, both living and dead. Romans followed suit. Trajan's column celebrated that emperor's victories in Dacia, depicting the army in all its various activities; the arch of Titus celebrated a victory parade after the capture of Jerusalem. The tradition continues today, expanded into film, photography, cartoons and so on.

DULCE ET DECORUM EST PRO PATRIA MORI

'Sweet and honourable it is for one's fatherland to die' (*morior* [*mort*-], 'I die', → 'mortal', etc.), began a poem by Horace. The poet Wilfred Owen called this the 'old lie'. He could see nothing glorious about warfare.

The ancients could (see p. 259). For them, it was a simple matter of survival – survival of the whole race. If their men could not fight a successful defensive battle, it was potentially the end of their family, people, tribe, past and future. The past was an unforgiving place.

The Latin *virtus*, source of our 'virtue', meant 'moral excellence' at one end of the scale, but its stem meaning derived from *vir*, 'man' (whence our 'virile'), and what it meant to be a man, and that was 'manliness', 'valour', 'steadfastness', especially in battle. The Horace poem continued:

> Death hunts down even the man who runs away,
> And does not spare the back or hamstrings
>> Of young cowards.
>>> (trans. David West)

There was no escape in battle: death would get you one way or another, but you could at least die with honour. The only alternative was to run like a coward and lose everything. Our 'coward' seems to derive from Latin *cauda*, 'tail' + '-*ard*', a suffix which can indicate something discreditable, for example, 'drunkard', 'sluggard'.

LEADING THE ARMY

The word *imperator* meant literally 'one with the supreme authority to give orders', and was used to mean both 'commander-in-chief' of the army and also 'emperor' (see pp. 26–7). The word derives from *impero*, 'I order, command' (→ 'imperative'), and is also the source of *imperium* (our 'empire'), the power vested in emperors and top officials such as consuls and provincial governors to give orders in the sure knowledge that they would be obeyed (or else).

STRATAGEMS

The Greek for 'military commander', both on land and sea, was *stratêgos* (στρατηγος), literally one who led (*-êg-*) the fighting force (*strat-*); and *stratêgêma* (στρατηγημα) referred to the action that general should take in any situation, especially a ruse or trick. Latin took the term over directly.

Practical treatises on fighting and farming were probably the Roman toff's favourite reading. Frontinus (see p. 215) wrote a book of *strategemata* (plural) in twelve main sections, covering such topics as concealing one's plans, finding out the enemy's, escaping tricky situations, distracting the enemy's attention, and other wizard wheezes and top tips (Julius Caesar: 'Conquer the foe by hunger rather than steel'; Hannibal: 'Throw jars full of vipers onto enemy ships'; Scipio Africanus: 'Give the enemy a road to escape by, and pave it too').

ENEMIES

Latin had two words for 'enemy': one was the public, military sort, *hostis*. This gives us 'hostile', etc., but its basic meaning was 'stranger, foreigner', and it is linguistically related to 'guest'! The other was the private sort, *inimicus*. This was the negative of Latin *amicus*, 'friend' (→ 'amicable', etc.) – literally 'not-friend'. Our 'enemy' derives from *inimicus*.

HOSPITAL HOSTS

The word 'host' was once regularly used to mean 'army'. To us it is someone who entertains a guest. 'Host' in that sense derives from

Latin *hospes* (*hospit-*), which meant both guest and host, and is at the root of 'hospital', originally a shelter for the poor and outcast. On the battlefield, a mobile hospital was needed, and this was called in French an *hopitâl ambulant*, literally 'walking hospital' (1798), from Latin *ambulo*, 'I walk' (→ 'ambulance', 'amble'). Latin *perambulo* meant 'I walk about, tour, make the rounds of a place', as every mother of a young baby knows; it is the source of 'perambulator' (1881), or 'pram'. A 'funambulist' is a tightrope walker, from Latin *funis*, 'rope' + *ambulo*. Romans called him a *funambulus*.

ARMS AND ARMIES

Our word 'army' derives from Latin *arma* (found only in the plural), 'implements, weapons, troops'; the *ar-* root meant 'fitted on/into', e.g. the hand. Our 'military' derives from Latin *miles* (*milit-*), 'soldier' (the derivation of the Latin is unknown); the Latin *militaris* meant 'someone qualified for, engaged in, military service'.

The Latin for 'army' was *exercitus* (→ 'exercise'). Why? Latin *arca* meant 'box', where something was enclosed or shut in (→ 'arcane'), and *arceo* meant 'I contain'. Get things out of (*ex-*) the box, and they keep moving. Hence *exerceo*, 'I keep moving' and so 'I train, exercise'.

At its peak, the Roman army was perhaps as near perfection as any human institution could be. As the Jewish historian Josephus said of it in the first century AD:

> It will be seen that this vast empire [of the Romans] has come to them as the prize of valour, and not as a gift of fortune. For their

nation does not wait for the outbreak of war to give men their first
lesson in arms; they do not sit with folded hands in peace time,
only to put them in motion in the hour of need.

On the contrary, as though they had been born with weapons
in hand, they never have a truce from training, never wait for
emergencies to arise. Moreover, their peace manoeuvres are
no less strenuous than actual warfare; each soldier daily throws
all his energy into his drill, as though he were in action. Hence
that perfect ease with which they sustain the shock of battle: no
confusion breaks their customary formation, no panic paralyses, no
fatigue exhausts them; and as their opponents cannot match these
qualities, victory is the invariable and certain consequence. Indeed,
it would not be wrong to describe their manoeuvres as bloodless
combats, and their combats as bloody manoeuvres.

We may not know the derivation of *miles*, but we do of 'soldier', and
rather unheroic it is too. The Latin *solidus* referred to a gold coin
introduced by the emperor Constantine in the fourth century AD. Via
Old French, a soldier was someone *paid* to do soldiering. 'Solder',
however, derives from the more heroic sense of *solidus*: 'rigid,
unyielding, complete'.

SOME WEAPONS

The spear, *pilum*, probably got its name from *pilum*, 'pestle, grinding/
pounding instrument', such as was used to break up parched earth.
The sword, *gladius*, was also used of the swordfish and the plant
gladiolus ('little sword'); the *gladius* was the main weapon of the

gladiator. The sword was kept in a sheath — *vagina*. This technical term is at the root of the popular ice-cream flavour 'vanilla', from Spanish *vainilla*, 'a little *va(g)ina*', so called from the shape of the vanilla pod. The shield, *scutum*, came from a root meaning 'cover, protect'. The dagger, *pugio*, derived from *pungo* (*punct-*), 'I puncture, pierce', which is probably related to *pugnus* 'fist' and *pugna* 'battle' (whence our 'pugnacious').

TIROS AND VETERANS

The first two lines of the Roman legions were filled by those learning the business, wielding a short throwing spear and stabbing sword; the third line was made up of those who had already learned it. These were the *veterani*, with long thrusting spears. The first two lines would normally see the enemy off; if they fell back and it came to the third line, it meant things had become serious. The term *veteranus* did not mean 'old'; it meant 'experienced, mature', especially of soldiers. Manning the third line, they could be relied upon to ensure victory.

Seneca told of the young Scipio, in battle against Hannibal in 218 BC: even though a *tiro* (a novice, especially a newly enlisted soldier), he galloped through the ranks to save his *veteranus* father when matters had indeed come to the third line, and the situation was desperate.

CAMPS

A *castrum* was a fortified settlement; in the plural, *castra*, it meant a collection of fortified structures, i.e. a 'camp' (whence, for example, Doncaster, a camp by the river — since 'don' in Celtic meant 'river'). Is the word connected with *castro* (*castrat-*), 'I cut' and all its unmanly implications? It is possible: a *castrum* may have been a piece of land 'cut off' for military use. Or it may refer to the tents that were the original 'buildings' inside a camp, all cut out of material. Or, from its Proto-Indo-European associations, it may simply be a tract of enclosed land. Or it may be none of these.

CAVALRY

Owning a horse in the ancient world was a bit like owning a helicopter or luxury yacht in the modern world: it cost a very great deal both to purchase and to manage. *Equus* was the Latin for 'horse', and *eques* (plural *equites*) for 'horseman' or 'cavalryman'. The *equites* were the wealthiest men in Rome (see p. 35), and as such are also translated as 'knights'.

Our term 'cavalry' has a different origin, from the Latin *caballus*, 'riding-horse, packhorse, nag', the everyday 'vulgar' word for 'horse'. The Italian *cavalliere*, 'a lady's mounted escort', derives from it, as does the French for 'horse', *cheval* (→ Spanish *caballo*, 'horse'; *caballero*, 'knight', 'gentleman').

This is a good example of a word in *everyday* use in Latin providing the source of words in romance languages. Another example is French *tête*, 'head'. It derives from Latin *testa*, 'brick, tile', also used of an outer shell.

ARMY DISCIPLINE

Exercise and practice were one thing; discipline (*disciplina*), derived from Latin *disco*, 'I learn', was something else. With its overtones of orderly conduct, obeying orders, knowing where you fitted in and why, and general organization on a small and large scale, *disciplina* did not come naturally; it was a matter of education and experience.

When Caesar was expecting trouble in Gaul in 53 BC, he needed to raise troops quickly 'to impress public opinion in Gaul not only for the present but for the future too'. Within a short time he had raised three legions. Caesar commented that 'the size of the reinforcements and the speed of their assembly showed the natives what Roman resources and *disciplina* could achieve'. Such a reinforcement was called a *supplementum*, from *suppleo*, meaning 'I fill up with additional liquid'.

NO PREVARICATION

Many were the stories told of men, young men in particular, keen to impress, who resisted *disciplina* and paid for it. One such was Manlius. In 340 BC, in a battle against a powerful local force, the army was instructed by Manlius' father, the consul, to hold its position. But Manlius advanced into single combat, killed his opponent and presented his father with the spoils. His father at once ordered him to be decapitated. No prevarication there – Latin *vârus*, 'bandy-legged', *praevaricor* (*praevaricat-*), 'I straddle, have my feet in both camps' and 'I act or speak evasively'. Not to be confused with 'procrastinate', Latin *procrastino*, 'I put off till tomorrow (*cras*)'.

SUBJUGATING THE ENEMY

Latin *sub*, 'under' + *iugum*, 'yoke' gives the key to the origin of 'subjugation'. When a Roman army was defeated, one way of humiliating it was to form a 'yoke' of three crossed spears and force the soldiers to stoop under it. Hence *subiugo*, 'I subjugate'.

At the battle of the Caudine Forks (321 BC), the Roman army was trapped in a narrow pass by Samnite forces. There was no escape and they surrendered. The Samnite general Pontius did not know whether to let them go and win Rome's favour, or execute them all and win undying hostility. In the end he forced them all to walk under the yoke of spears and let them go. Rome soon had its revenge for this humiliation.

INFANTRY DRILL

Training and experience were the major reasons for the Roman army's success. In 209 BC, in the war against Hannibal, Scipio Africanus had taken the battle to Cartagena, Hannibal's main outpost in Spain. After capturing it, he spent many months training his men up for the battles to come:

> He devised the following scheme for the training of the infantry. He ordered them on the first day to do a run of nearly four miles in full kit, on the second to rub down, clean and generally make a close examination of their equipment; on the next day to rest and do nothing; and on the following, some men to fight with wooden swords sheathed in leather with a button at the end, and others to throw javelins similarly fitted with buttons; on the fifth day to revert to the marching they had done on the first, and so on.

But why 'infantry'? An *infans* in Latin meant, literally, one who could not speak (*in*, 'not' + *fans*, 'speaking'), i.e. a baby. But in time it came to mean 'young man', and from that, via Italian and French, 'foot soldier'.

Julius Caesar was always keen to keep his infantry on the go:

He often did this where there was no need at all, especially when it was raining and on public holidays. Sometimes he would warn them to watch him closely and then quite suddenly steal away from the camp at any hour of the day or night, expecting them to follow. The march was made longer than usual to wear out those who straggled.

We are also told that on one occasion a gladiator trainer was hired to sharpen up the army's skills in weapon-handling – basically, hitting and avoiding being hit.

CAMPAIGN

'Campaign' and 'champagne' derive from Latin *campus*, 'a flat expanse of open land', for whatever use. In Rome, for example, the *Campus Martius*, the field of the war god Mars, was used for assemblies and elections as well as sport and recreation.

Campus also meant the field of battle. Indeed, given Roman battle tactics, an open field was exactly what they wanted, where armies could meet head-on and battle it out. In AD 69, the infamous year of the four emperors, Antonius, general of the ultimately victorious Vespasian, led his army against the ruling emperor Vitellius at Bedriacum. In the run-up to the battle, he urged on troops who had been humiliated there previously, saying that 'these were the very *battlefields* which offered them the chance to wash away the stain of past humiliation and regain their glory in men's eyes'.

In the Second Punic War (218–204 BC), when the Romans met the great Carthaginian general Hannibal, who cheated by waging battles in different locations and with very different tactics, they were in serious trouble. But a bad defeat, far from inducing Romans to surrender, guaranteed no surrender. They looked and learned from Hannibal and eventually beat him at his own game.

FROM PRESSING TO PRINTING AND THE PRESS

The Latin *premo* (*press-*) was the term used to describe the relentless pressurizing, driving and harassing that was at the heart of all ancient battle, the aim being to turn the enemy to flight and slaughter them as they fled. Here Caesar described the climax of the battle in 58 BC that ended the interest of the Germanic leader Ariovistus in supporting the Gauls against Caesar's invasion:

> Although the army of the enemy was routed on the left wing and put to flight, their advantage in numbers enabled them to put our men on the right wing under considerable pressure. Publius Crassus, a young man who commanded the cavalry, noticed this, and because he had more of an overview than those doing the fighting, sent in the third line to relieve the desperate soldiers. Battle was immediately rejoined, at which the enemy ran for it, and did not stop running until they reached the river Rhine about fifty miles away.

It was this word, via Old French *preinte*, 'impression', that gave us 'printing' – Caxton uses 'emprint' in 1474 – to describe the pressure exerted by the printing press. 'Press' originally referred to a throng of people (*c.* 1300) but, after the Gutenberg printing revolution, became used of printing and publishing houses; hence 'freedom of the press'. This was extended to journalism, and in 1921 'the press' became a term for journalists.

VINDICATING VIOLENCE

Romans have a reputation for ruthless aggression on the field of battle. The Latin for such aggression was *vis* (*vir-*), a word presumably related to 'violence' (but do not confuse it with *virtus* and 'virility', see p. 251).

In fact, they were no more aggressive than anyone else at that time. Every tribe they came up against would willingly have done to the Romans what the Romans did to them. When Germanic tribes under Arminius ambushed three Roman legions in the Teutoberg Forest in Germany (AD 9), the slaughter was as brutal as any inflicted by a Roman army.* Five years later, the Romans came to seek revenge, and found human heads still fastened to tree trunks and remains of the altars at which commanders had been ritually massacred. The Latin for 'revenge' was *vindicta*, 'force asserted' (*vis* + *dicta*, 'spoken') – which indeed it was when Romans asserted it.

TERRITORIAL ARMY

The Roman state was said to have been founded in 753 BC. The very earliest warfare – if we can trust the accounts written by the historian Livy some 700 years after the event – was little more than a one-day scrap for territory between neighbouring bands, led by a local bigwig

---

* Arminius was later said to have been the latinized name of Hermann ('the German', see p. 220).

and his followers – basically, his retainers and farm tenants taking a day off work. 'Territory' derives from *terra*, 'dry land, ground', which may be related to *torridus*, 'dry' (→ 'torrid'). An interesting, but unlikely, alternative derivation is from *terreo*, 'I terrify'; 'territory' would then be a place from which fear warns you off.

THE EARLY ARMY

Traditionally, Rome was said to have been divided into three artificial tribes (*tribus*) – Tities, Rhamnes and Luceres – and it was these that were thought to form the basis of the first proper army. Each *tribus* was said to have supplied 100 cavalry and 1,000 infantry. The word for levying or raising the infantry was *legio*, from *lego* (*lect-*), 'I pick' ('se*lect*' derives from it).

That word *tribus* is teasing. It is clearly the origin of *tribunus* ('tribune', a tribal officer, military leader, see p. 39), but does it derive from the Latin for 'three' (*tres, tria*)? Is it also the source of our 'tribe'? Perhaps, but 'tribe' could also be of Germanic origin.

ROLLOVER

This first Roman army, built up from the seventh century BC, imitated the Greek *phalanx* (φαλαγξ: note that our 'nx' represents the sound made by the Greek '*gx*'). *Phalanx* was connected with the Greek for 'roller', and that is what it was designed to do: a line of heavily armed men, up to sixteen rows deep, each armed with jabbing spears and shields overlapping, shoved, stabbed and generally pressurized its way relentlessly forward, 'rolling over' the enemy in front of it.

These fighters were called 'hoplites' from the Greek *hoplon* (ὅπλον, the circular shield which hoplites carried), and were made up of men who could afford the very expensive full suite of bronze body-armour and weapons.

PANOPLY

Armour was expensive stuff because metal was expensive. Only the well-off could afford it. That is why in the Greek world it was the well-off who fought in the front line. Our 'panoply' comes from the Greek *panoplia* (πανοπλια), which meant the full suit of armour of a hoplite (*pan* [παν], 'all' + *hopla* [ὅπλα], 'arms and armour') – shield, breastplate, helmet, greaves, sword and spear.

TYRANTS

The Greek historian Herodotus told of a trick played by Peisistratos, the son of Hippocrates, to persuade the Athenians to make him tyrant (Greek *turannos* [τυραννος]). He dressed a very tall woman called Phye in full armour and drove with her in a chariot into Athens, sending messengers ahead to say that Athena herself (who was a goddess of war) was accompanying him. Herodotus commented that Athenians had a reputation for high intelligence, but they fell for it like simpletons.

Turannos (Latin *tyrannus*) in its original usage meant nothing much worse than 'prime minster'. It was only later that it gathered tyrannical associations.

COHORTS

In time, the Roman legion came to be subdivided into ten units called cohorts. A *cohors* (*cohort-*) originally seems to have meant a farmyard, i.e. a space surrounded by buildings, and is connected with Greek *khortos* (χορτος), 'enclosed space, farm', and Latin *hortus*, 'garden' (→ horticulture). This sense can be seen in other derivations from *cohors*, e.g. 'court' as in 'courtyard' and even (such is the complexity of etymology) 'yard' itself. Somehow it came to mean an armed force, especially a contingent from a particular place, and was then applied to the legionary unit.

OBSESSION WITH SIEGES

In 133 BC, Scipio Aemilianus was preparing his troops for the siege of Numantia in Spain:

> Scipio did not dare to engage in active warfare before he had trained his men by hard exertion. He went over all the low-lying ground in the vicinity, and had one new camp after another fortified and then demolished each day, very deep trenches dug and then filled up again, high walls built up and then pulled down, while he himself watched the work from dawn until dusk.

They needed the training. Scipio encircled Numantia with a stone wall with a ditch, eight feet wide, ten feet high and six miles in length. There were wooden towers every thirty yards, and seven forts. Every Roman soldier had the skills of a builder as well as a killer. Look at Hadrian's Wall (AD 122).

The Latin for 'siege' was *obsidio*. It derived from *ob*, 'against' + *sedeo* (*sess-*), 'I sit' (→ 'sedentary'), which means 'I plant myself, take up a position, blockade'. It gives us our 'obsession' – something that lays siege to the mind. Our word 'siege', literally 'seat', also derives (via French) from *sedeo*. The 'Siege Perilous' was the empty chair in King Arthur's court, waiting to be filled by the knight who would discover the Holy Grail.

PAYING FOR BATTLE

In 406 BC, Rome began a lengthy conflict with its bitter Etruscan rival, the wealthy town of Veii (ten miles north-west of Rome, sharing a border along the Tiber with Rome), which it brought to heel under Camillus in 395 BC.

This was an important moment. First, Rome had needed more soldiers to win this protracted war, and therefore enlisted men outside the hoplite group. Secondly, never having launched a campaign lasting so long, Rome needed to pay their soldiers a daily allowance. This was the *stipendium* (our 'stipend'), from *pendo*, 'I pay', and *stips*, 'alms, small sum of money'. Thirdly, to raise the money, the state imposed a property tax on the wealthiest: *tributum* (our 'tribute') was the term used; a war tax paid through the tribes (*tribus*; see above). Finally, in 394 BC, after another lengthy siege, Camillus imposed an indemnity on the town of Falerii to pay for his army's costs. 'Indemnity' derives from Latin *damnum*, 'loss', from which come *indemnis*, 'suffering no loss', and *indemnitas*, 'security from financial loss' – in this case, no loss for the Romans.

SALARIES

The standard Latin word for 'pay for holders of military or civil posts' was *salarium*. Pliny the Younger described a situation in which his friend Egnatius Marcellinus, serving as a quaestor in a province (p. 40), wondered what to do with the *salarium* of his secretary who died the day before it was due to be paid:

> He felt strongly that he ought not to keep the money which had been paid over to him to give to the secretary. So when he returned to Rome, he consulted first the emperor and then the Senate, on the emperor's recommendation, as to what was to be done with it. It was a trifling question, but, after all, it was a question.

The case was brought to court, and it was decided to return the *salarium* to the treasury and not to give it to the man's heirs.

It is regularly claimed that, because *salarium* is associated with *sal*, the Latin for 'salt', Roman soldiers were paid in salt. As the above story makes clear, that is a myth. It was invented by Pliny the Elder, to try to explain why a *salarium* was so called.

MAKING PEACE

The Latin for peace, *pax* (*pac-*), meant basically 'settlement'. It derived from *paciscor* (*pact-*), 'I negotiate, arrange an agreement; I secure by bargaining; come to terms'. Its final meaning was 'I become engaged to'. Romans would have thoroughly approved of prenuptials.

In 193 BC, the Romans were trying to conclude a peace treaty with the Greeks. The Greek negotiator Menippus explained how he thought an agreement might be reached. The Romans rejected it, but it gives a good idea of some of the principles behind the making of ancient treaties. Menippus said:

> There were three kinds of treaties by means of which states and monarchs came to terms with one another.
>
> In one case, the conditions were imposed upon those conquered in battle. For when everything had been surrendered to the winning general, he had the absolute right to determine what the enemy might keep and what give up.
>
> In the second case, states equally matched in war formed a treaty of peace and friendship on equal terms: they reached a mutual understanding in respect of claims for indemnity; and where ownership of property had been disturbed by the war, matters were settled either with reference to established principles or the convenience of both parties.
>
> The third class of treaties came into play when states which had never been enemies united in forming a league of friendship; no conditions were either imposed or accepted, for these existed only between victors and vanquished.

The Latin for 'treaty', *foedus* (*foeder-*), was based on Latin *fides*, 'good faith, trust'. 'Federal' states are those bound together in a 'confederation' ('all-together treaty').

GENERAL

In what sense is a general general? General in relation to what? Latin *genus* (whence 'genes', etc.) meant 'birth, origin', 'race, kind', and then 'type, class, variety' of humans, species and so on. The adjective derived from it was *generalis*, 'of universal application'. Our 'general' was originally a 'captain general' (from the French). 'Captain' indicated an officer of rank; the epithet 'general' then extended the scope of his authority.

PRIVATE

From the same root as our 'deprive', a *privatus* in Latin was someone who did not hold public office. In other contexts it referred to one's subject status.

In 105 BC Rome was in conflict with Jugurtha, king of Numidia in North Africa, and Jugurtha attempted to persuade his son-in-law Bocchus, king of the Moors, to join him. Bocchus agreed and was beaten in battle. The Roman general Marius then sent his guileful quaestor Sulla to persuade Bocchus to come over to the Romans. Bocchus began his speech to him as follows: 'I would not have believed it possible that I, the greatest king in Africa, and indeed of all the kings that I know, should now find myself indebted to a *private individual*.' A quaestor (see p. 40) was hardly a private individual, but in terms of rank, that is what Sulla must have seemed to the great king.

REGIMENT

We all know about rules and regulations. *Rego* (*rect-*) in Latin meant 'I rule, control', and *regimen* originally meant 'ship's rudder' (actually, more of an oar), then 'control, management, guidance'. Of Rome's might, Valerius Maximus said: 'Fiercely imposed military discipline gave Rome authority over Italy, and then *regimen* over many cities, great kings and powerful nations.' 'Regiment' took the meaning 'army unit' in the sixteenth century, referring to a body under strict discipline and organization.

Ranks that derive from Latin include cadet (little *caput*, 'head'), sergeant (Latin *servio*, 'I serve'), corporal (either *corpus* [*corpor*-], 'body', of which he was in charge, or *caput*), captain (*caput*), major (*maior*, 'greater'), colonel (*columna*, 'column', because he was in charge of a column of soldiers: what one might call a pillar of the army).

BOMBS AWAY!

Whatever the damage a bomb may wreak, it is initially its noise that is so terrifying. That is in fact the origin of its name. Greek *bombos* (βομβος), Latin *bombus*, meant a deep, rumbling, booming sound, anything from (in Greek) the roar of the sea and the roll of thunder to (in Latin) the buzzing of bees and even applause.

Nero, we are told, was greatly impressed by the applause his operatic performance was granted by some Egyptian visitors to Naples. So he ordered over 5,000 young men to learn how to do it. The applause came in three varieties: the *bombus* (buzzing like bees), 'roof tiles' (clapping with hollowed hands) and 'bricks' (clapping with flat hands). See p. 243 for 'explosive' applause.

MEDICINE

INTRODUCTION

As far as the West is concerned, Hippocrates invented the language of medicine – from prognosis to diagnosis, from phlegm to haemorrhoids. He was a Greek from the island of Cos and lived in the fifth century BC. He was enormously famous in the ancient world and is regarded as the father of 'rational' medicine. All that means is that he attempted as best he could to use reason and experience to analyse and explain illnesses, rather than regarding them as incomprehensible divine visitations. Other than that, we know nothing about him: he is 'a name without a work'.

Or rather, with hundreds of works. It was only in the age of the Roman emperor Hadrian (second century AD) that any agreement was reached about what he had and had not written, and that agreement was not all well founded. It is clear that many medical treatises written well after the fifth century BC were included in the collection, such was the enthusiasm of later medical practitioners to be associated with the great man. His name is always associated with the doctors' 'Hippocratic Oath'. Wrongly: that oath was composed later than the fifth century BC.

When Romans made Greece a province in the second century BC, they were captivated by Greek culture and thought, and both fascinated by, and suspicious of, their medical expertise. The Roman encyclopedist and doctor Aulus Cornelius Celsus (c. 25 BC–AD 50) is the key figure here. In *De medicina* ('On Medicine'), he basically latinized Hippocratic medical terms, taking Greek words and giving them a Latin form; so, for example, Greek *stomakhos* (στομαχος), 'gullet, stomach', became Latin *stomachus*. Other Greek terms he replaced with the Latin equivalent. Hippocrates called cancer *karkinos* (καρκινος), Greek for 'crab'; Celsus then gave it the Latin name for 'crab', *cancer*, the term we use today. Apparently it got its name from the look of a malignant tumour which had had its top sliced off.

At the same time there was a degree of suspicion that Romans felt about Greek medicine. It is most sharply put by Cato the Elder (second century BC). Plutarch reported:

> It was not only Greek philosophers that Cato hated, but he was also suspicious of Greeks who practised medicine at Rome. He had heard, it would seem, of Hippocrates' reply to the Great King of Persia, who offered him vast sums for his services, that he would never put his skill at the service of barbarians who were enemies of Greece. Cato said all Greek physicians had taken a similar oath, and urged his son to beware of them all.

Pliny the Elder took the view that medicine was a very dodgy profession. To his way of thinking, Greek doctors were nearly all charlatans who could get away with any crime in the name of their 'art', and charge monumental sums for so doing. He much preferred good, honest Roman herbal medicine. When he did suggest a number of cures for ailments, all Greek, he was simply highlighting what a good Roman could safely and properly take over from the vast store of potentially dangerous and corrupting Greek medical lore.

Celsus himself reflected this caution. His eight-volume *De medicina* covered a huge range of medical issues: healthy and unhealthy constitutions and times of the year; diseases and how to spot and treat them; the internal organs (the first ever description in Latin); specific ailments in a head-to-toe sequence; prescriptions; wounds, bites, skin disorders (very sound on swellings); surgery; the human skeleton; and surgical techniques, especially concerning bones (dealing with fractures, etc.). But at the same time, he never admitted that he was a practising doctor, coming across more as an encyclopedist; and he took the view that, since Greek medicine was invented to counteract the effects of 'indolence and luxury' that were evident in the Rome of his own day, medicine could 'scarcely protract the lives of a few of us to the verge of old age'. So what was required most of all for a long life was a modest and decent lifestyle.

After the collapse of the Roman Empire in the West in the fifth century AD, knowledge of Greek died out, and Latin (the language of church and education) in its medieval form came to dominate the terminology. Muslim doctors, who after the advent of Islam in the seventh century AD spread east into the Greek Near East and west into North Africa and Spain, were fascinated by Greek medicine, and translated much of it into Arabic. Indeed, much of the work of the great Greek doctor Galen (second century AD) survives only in Arabic and is yet to be translated into English. But despite impressive work in many areas, Muslim practice made little impact on Western medicine, let alone its language, which remained resolutely Graeco-Latin.

From the eighteenth century, people started translating Graeco-Latin terms into their own vernacular. For example, *ulcus ventriculi* became for the English *gastric ulcer*. But more recently, as we have come to know more and more about the body and how it works, thousands of new terms have been invented. Greek and Latin have been used where they could be. 'Adrenalin' (see p. 1) is a good example.

But English is now the global language and dominates the new terminology. Inevitably, one consequence is that drugs and brand names reveal nothing of their purpose. Take Viagra: what on earth could one guess that meant (let alone its technical name sildenafil)? Still, that did not prevent it getting a universal thumbs-up, despite claims that it was not supposed to have side effects.

To end with two words of warning. First, the subject is a vast one, and the selection of topics covered here can be nothing but a taster. Second, it is often extremely difficult to match what the ancients say about any named illness with what we know about it. So what the ancients call *cancer* can cover a multitude of conditions that bear no relation at all to what we know as cancer.

SCIENCE AND MEDICINE

Latin *physicus*, taken from the Greek *phusis* (φυσις, 'nature, natural world'), meant 'someone interested in the workings of the natural world'. But a *physicus* did not think as a modern scientist does. Latin *scientia*, 'knowledge, understanding', is the source of 'scientist', and our scientists work by hypothesis and repeated and repeatable experimentation. This was a sixteenth-century invention. Many ancient 'scientists' were in fact more like what we would call lifestyle gurus, with an interest in how best to lead our lives, though their recommendations were tied to their understanding of how the natural world worked (see p. 172).

HEALTH AND HYGIENE

Hygi(e)a was a goddess of health, daughter of the healing god Asclepius (also in Latin Aesculapius). Both are derived from Greek: *hugieia* (ὑγιεια), 'health, soundness of body', and *Asklêpios* (Ἀσκληπιος). Latin provides us with *sanus*, 'healthy in body or mind', and *insanus*, 'out of one's mind'.

Nero provided a splendid example of insanity. When he heard that the Spanish provinces had revolted against him and were preparing to cross through Gaul into Italy to depose him, Suetonius reported:

> It is believed that he formed many plans of monstrous
> wickedness, but in no way inconsistent with his character: to
> depose and assassinate the commanders of the armies and
> the governors of the provinces, on the grounds that they were
> all united in a conspiracy against him; to massacre all exiles

everywhere, to prevent them from joining the rebels, and all men of Gallic birth in Rome, because they might be implicated in the uprising; to turn over the Gallic provinces to his armies to pillage; to poison the entire Senate at banquets; to set fire to the city, first letting the wild beasts loose, to prevent citizens dealing with the blaze... He later declared, as he was leaving the dining-room after a banquet, that on setting foot in Gaul he would immediately present himself before the soldiers, unarmed, and weep and weep again; this would win back their loyalty, and next day he would stroll among his rejoicing troops and sing paeans of victory, which he really ought to be composing right now.

Nero did none of this, but fled and was helped to commit suicide.

DOCTORS

The Latin *doceo* (*doct-*) meant 'I teach', and a *doctor* was simply a teacher or trainer. The term was applied generally across Europe where, after the fall of the Roman Empire in the West in the fifth century AD, the church became the main deliverer of education. So monks were all *doctores*. They also delivered healthcare.

However, in the Middle Ages the church refused to allow monks to do surgery. This therefore fell to their barbers, whose job was to keep the monks' tonsures well shaven and who had a handy way with sharp instruments. Over time, a distinction between titles developed: monk *doctores* delivering general healthcare continued to be called 'doctors' even if they did not teach, while barbers became surgeons (see below) and have been called 'Mr' ever since.

Academic 'doctors' are different altogether. Increasingly since the nineteenth century, those wishing to teach in universities have had to produce a piece of original academic research in their field of interest to qualify for a university post. If their work is accepted, they become a PhD (*Doctor Philosophiae*, 'of philosophy'), which entitles them to the title 'Dr'.

SURGEONS

Celsus talked of lesions that could not be cured by medicines needing 'the help of hands'. What he meant was surgery. The Greek for a surgeon was *kheirourgos* (χειρουργος), which meant a hand (*kheir*) worker (*ergon*, 'work', → energy), i.e. an expert in handiwork. In Latin it became *chirurgus*. Our 'surgeon' comes from this word, via French for a surgeon, *chirurge*.

Ancient surgery could be a rough-and-ready business: 'whatever you do, do it quickly' was the main ancient advice. Friends of the patient needed to be on hand both to present the part to be operated on and to hold the rest of the body still, 'staying silent and obeying their superior'. The Hippocratic treatise on surgery talked mostly about bandaging. It said nothing about cleanliness, let alone anaesthetics.

The Roman satirical poet Martial dwelt on the theme of the incompetent in a number of poems:

Doctor Diaulus changed his trade:
He runs a mortuary.
Results were much the same as when
He lived off surgery.

OBSTETRICIANS

Seneca described a man 'running anxiously after an *obstetrix* to attend
to his daughter in labour'. Obstetricians were not only midwives but
also female (the *-ix* ending denotes 'female'). The word is based on
Latin *obstô*, basically 'I meet face to face', but, more importantly,
with strong overtones of keeping people (especially men) away; it
also meant 'I form a barrier to, block the path of, form a screen for' –
surely essential at this most vulnerable time of a woman's life.

In his *Gynaecology*, the great Greek doctor Soranus (second
century AD) described the qualities of an *obstetrix* (Greek *maia* [μαια])
as follows:

> We call a person the best midwife if she is trained in all branches of
> therapy (for some cases must be treated by diet, others by surgery,
> while still others must be cured by drugs); if she is moreover able
> to prescribe hygienic regulations for her patients, to observe the
> general and the individual features of the case, and from this to
> find out what is expedient... she will be sympathetic... She will be
> well disciplined and always sober, since it is uncertain when she
> may be summoned to those in danger... She must also keep her
> hands soft, abstaining from such wool-working as may make them
> hard, and she must acquire softness by means of ointments if it is
> not present naturally.

DELICIOUS NURSES

The derivation of 'nurse' is Latin *nutrix* (*nutric-*), a word
derived from *nutrio* (*nutrit-*), 'I nourish, bring up' (→ 'nutrient',

'nutritious', etc.). It probably derives from a Proto-Indo-European word meaning 'suckle'. The *nutrix*, in other words, was primarily a wet nurse. In the case of Romulus and Remus, the mythical founders of Rome, the *nutrix* was a wolf. Celsus insisted on the importance of a suckling nurse helping to ensure that ulcers in a baby's mouth did not spread by staying fit, visiting the baths to have hot water poured over her breasts, eating well and so on. Ovid talked of night as the 'most powerful *nutrix* of anxieties' – nourishing them and encouraging them to grow.

'Nurse' came to mean someone concerned generally about health in the sixteenth century.

PATIENTS

Anyone who is 'patient' puts up with things. We may feel this well describes what patients have to do in hospitals. The word comes from Latin *patior*, 'I am subjected to', and in Latin *patiens* meant 'able or willing to undergo, bear, support, stand up to' an experience. You certainly had to be able to do that under ancient medical care, though *patiens* was not used of patients then. The ancients did not pull their punches: the Latin for 'the patient' was *aeger* – 'the sick'. A long time ago there was a degree called an *aegrotat* ('[s]he is ill'), which was bestowed on those too ill to sit finals.

CLINICS

Romans did not have clinics, but they did have clinical physicians (*clinici*), who attended patients in bed. The Greek *klinê* [κλινη] meant something you lay on, such as a bed or couch, from the verb *klinô* (κλινω), 'I lean' (→ Latin *reclino, declino*, etc.). This verb also provides the *klim-* stem in 'climax' (p. 164) and 'climate' (p. 213).

The meaning 'clinical' as in 'coolly dispassionate' is a twentieth-century usage; the language of the medical profession is also called on in order to soothe the effect of killing people with 'surgical' strikes.

GERMS

For us, a 'germ' can be good or bad: medically bad, the 'germ' of an idea is good. It is this latter meaning that Romans would have understood, since *germen* (*germin-*) meant in Latin 'shoot, sprout' (whence our 'germinate', etc.). Its use in the bad sense dates from as late as 1871; but doctors, consulting their Latin dictionaries, realized this was a mistake and in 1880 invented the term 'pathogen' to replace it. This is based on Greek and is supposed to mean 'producing suffering'.

VIRUS

A *virus* in Latin meant a poison, from snakes or plants, or concocted by a poisoner; an acrid taste (for example, citrus peel); or a secretion from a plant or body. Doctors define it as 'an infectious agent that replicates inside living cells' (first used of venereal disease in the eighteenth century).

Roman poisons could be pretty *viru*lent. Here the epic poet Lucan described what happened to soldiers bitten by an especially nasty little snake:

The skin nearest the wound broke and shrank all round, revealing the white bone, until, as the opening widened, there was one gaping wound and no body. The limbs are soaked with corrupted blood; the calves of the legs melted away, the knees were stripped of covering, all the muscles of the thighs rotted, and a black discharge issued from the groin. The membrane that confines the belly snapped asunder, and the bowels gushed out. The man trickles into the ground, but there is less of him than an entire body should supply; for the fell poison boils down the limbs, and the manner of death reduces the whole man to a little pool of corruption.

It goes on in this agreeably epic vein for some time.

INOCULATION

'Inoculation' was originally a botanical term. Pliny the Elder described the process as follows:

It consists in opening an 'eye' [Latin *oculus*] in a tree by cutting away the bark with a tool resembling a shoemaker's punch and enclosing in it a seed that has been removed from another tree by means of the same tool. This was the method of inoculation used in old days in the case of figs and apples; the method described by Virgil [in *Georgics*, his treatise on farming] is to find a recess in a knot of bark burst open by a shoot and to enclose in this a bud obtained from another tree.

Getting your eye in, in other words.

That was then. Nowadays, it is a medical term, referring to a system of preventing disease by introducing into the skin a very small sample of material from the disease in question. In fact the eastern king Mithradates (first century BC), who ruled northern Turkey and gave the Romans terrible trouble as they expanded into that part of the world, experimented with the idea himself. We are told he took minuscule quantities of poison every day in order to 'inoculate' himself against its effects. He was so successful that, when he realized he could not defeat Pompey and the Romans, he found he was incapable of poisoning himself! So he ordered a slave to kill him.

Vaccination (the injection of dead bacteria) is technically a different process. Its inventor Edward Jenner, working on the story that milkmaids never got smallpox, inserted pus from a cowpox pustule (Latin *vacca*, 'cow') into a boy's wounded arm.

MITHRADATES' TREACLE

Pompey found and brought to Rome the recipe for Mithradates' 'universal antidote' (Greek *antidotos* [ἀντιδοτος], 'given (*dot-*) in place of, as a remedy for (*anti-*)', Latin *antidotum*). The recipe was given the Greek name *thêriakê* (θηριακη), 'to do with wild animals'), as a remedy against their bites. We get our word 'treacle' from *thêriakê*. The linguistic journey was as follows: Greek *thêriakê*; Late Latin *theriaca*, with an assumed diminutive form *thêriacula*; Vulgar Latin *triacula*; Old French *triacle*; Middle English 'treacle'.

STICK AT IT

Bacteria and bacilli are all over the place. The Greek *baktêrion* (βακτηριον), latinized in the nineteenth century to *bacterium*, meant 'staff, cane'. Every year the Athenian council met to assess the disabled for state benefits, and in one case the claimant, arguing that he was entitled to them, pointed out that he need two *baktêria* to walk, not just one.

The Latin *bacillum*, a type of *bacterium*, meant 'small stick, staff'. Umbricius, a figure in a satire about the ghastliness of life at Rome, talked of leaving the city for the countryside while 'I have life left in me and can walk on my own two feet without the need of a *bacillum*'.

These bugs that stick it to us all the time were given their names because they looked like rods. Purists will note that scientists have turned the Latin neuter noun *bacillum* into a masculine one, *bacillus*. Impurists may wonder if our 'imbecile' (Latin *imbecillus*) derives from *in* (negative) + *bacillum*, meaning someone too weak even to hold a stick. Almost certainly not.

PENICILLIN ENVY

You would imagine the distinction between 'penis' and 'tail' was fairly obvious, but Latin *penis* referred to both. In a letter Cicero said that *penis* meaning 'tail' was originally used of the penis as a euphemism, 'but nowadays it is an obscene word'. *Penicillus* meant 'small tail', referring to an artist's brush; 'penicillin' was so called because the mould cells looked like small tufts of hairs, or paintbrushes.

HORMONES

A hormone is a chemical 'messenger', issuing from endocrine glands such as the pancreas, regulating various body systems. It was so named by its discoverers in 1905 from the ancient Greek *hormê* (ὁρμη), meaning 'a setting in motion, arousal, excitement'. They imagined the glands sending the hormones whizzing about their work.

NUCLEUS AND CHROMOSOMES

Under a microscope (Greek *mikros* [μικρος], 'small' + *skopô* [σκοπω], 'I see'), chromosomes looked like coloured bodies. So they should: Greek *khrôma* (χρωμα), 'colour' + *sôma* (σωμα), 'body'. Chromosomes are held within a nucleus. 'Nucleus' means for us, in general, the central heart, crux or nub of something, and in physics it refers to the central core of an atom, charged with neutrons and protons. Nuclear physics is the study of how that central atomic core is made up and behaves. It has implications not just for weaponry but for medicine (for instance, magnetic resonance imaging) and archaeology (radiocarbon dating). *Nucleus* derives from Latin *nux* (*nuc-*), 'nut', and *nucleus* meant 'inside of a nut, pip, central part of anything'. It was used of 'the central point of an atom' by Michael Faraday in 1844, and in its modern sense by Ernest Rutherford in 1912.

Latin also had the form *nucula*, 'small, young nut'. Consequently, *nucleus* also appeared as *nuculeus*. This explains why former US president George W. Bush always said 'nuculer': he had classical blood in him. Though there may be another explanation.

BODY PARTS

Our main body parts are good, honest Anglo-Saxon – arm, finger, leg, toe, body, head and so on. In order to describe other anatomical structures, we sometimes take over from Latin and Greek words that Romans used to identify something else. So Latin for 'pipe', *tibia*, gives us our shinbone; *tuba*, a straight trumpet, gives us 'tube'; Greek *thôrax* (θωραξ), 'breastplate', describes the chest region from neck to abdomen; Latin *galea*, 'helmet', describes dense, fibrous tissue atop the cranium; and Latin *tragus*, from Greek *tragos* (τραγος), 'goat', refers to the hair growing at the entrance to the ear because it resembles the tuft on a goat's chin.

SYRINGE

The beautiful nymph Syrinx (*Surigx* [Συριγξ]) was known for her chastity, but that merely encouraged the lecherous god Pan (Παν) to go after her. She was off like a shot, but found her path barred by a river. As she prayed to the water nymphs to help her, they changed her into tall reeds. Finding himself showering ardent protestations of love on an armful of wetland plants, Pan sighed, and his breath stirred the plants into a soft whistle. He was utterly enchanted. 'We shall be in unison for ever,' he said, and promptly waxed together reeds of different length to make the pan pipes, *syrinx*, named after the girl. *Syrinx* was not only the word for 'shepherd's pipe' but anything like a pipe, for instance, a spear-case, and ducts and channels in the body.

In the fifteenth century the word was used to mean a tube for injecting liquids. Now it refers to the hypodermic syringe, which is not known to emit a merry song, though the patient might (see *cannula*, p. 236). Greek *hupo* (ὑπο), 'under' + *derma* (δερμα), 'skin' shows how the modern term 'hypodermic' was generated. That might have come as a considerable surprise to an ancient Greek in a modern hospital, since *hupodermis* (ὑποδερμις, 'underskin') meant 'clitoris' (*kleitoris* [κλειτορις]). That may possibly suggest that *kleitoris* originated from Greek *kleiô* (κλειω), 'I shut, enclose, confine'.

MODEL SKELETONS

In his famous *Satyricôn*, Petronius mocked the wealthy parvenu Trimalchio by describing the ghastly feast and entertainment he laid on for his chums. Part of it featured a jointed, puppet-like silver skeleton, brought on to remind the diners of their mortality. Could ancient doctors have used such models to educate their trainees? It seems not, though there is a small, jointed bronze example (nearly three inches tall) in the Getty Museum. Greek *skeletos* (σκελετος) meant 'dried up, withered', which led to 'skeleton' in the medical sense. Romans took it over as *sceletus*.

SKELETAL LARVA

Sceletus was not the only Latin word for 'skeleton'. There was also Petronius' word – *larva*. In the modern world, *larva* is the term given to the juvenile form of an insect, which is very different from that of the adult, such as a caterpillar before it becomes a butterfly. Books will correctly tell you that the term is derived from Latin *larva*, but meaning 'ghost'. *Larva* did mean 'malevolent spirit', 'demon' or 'devil', especially of those who had died a violent death, but it also had a much more appropriate meaning: 'mask'. The poet Horace mocked a buffoon for having a wart-covered face and said that 'he could do the dance of the one-eyed giant shepherd Cyclops, without needing a *larva* or actor's boots'. That surely is the *larva* as biologists mean it: it is a 'mask' that is eventually cast off to reveal the real thing. So too, perhaps, the *larva* is the consequence of the body casting off its 'mask', to reveal the real thing, the skeleton beneath.

NO LAUGHING MATTER
THE FOUR HUMOURS

If the meaning of the word 'humour' had not changed radically over the past 2,500 years, a humorist would be someone with a deep interest in bodily fluids. 'Humour' derives from ancient Greek *khumos* (χυμός), via the Latin version of the word, (*h*)*umor*, 'moisture, bodily fluid, sap' (whence 'humid', etc.).

Hippocrates was responsible. He drew on earlier theories of the nature of the cosmos, especially that the world was made up of four constituent elements (earth, air, fire and water) and that four 'powers' – hot, cold, wet and dry – were at work everywhere. We may guess that he observed that plants and the body survived on liquids, sap and blood. At the same time, other liquids regularly appeared on certain occasions: phlegm during colds, bile (black and yellow) during sickness, sweat when hot, and so on. Further, on occasion the body seemed willing to get rid of blood, its main life force, during nosebleeds and menstruation, for example. That surely justified bloodletting.

Putting all this (and much more) together, Hippocrates and later doctors matched these four 'humours' (blood, yellow bile, black bile and phlegm) with the four main 'powers' – hot, dry, cold and wet; the four main elements – earth, air, fire and water; the four seasons – spring, summer, autumn and winter; the four ages of man – infancy, adolescence, adulthood, old age (and so on, even unto the four gospels!), to produce an impressively comprehensive, internally consistent theory of everything. The conclusion was that balance was the key to health: the balance of liquids within the body kept it healthy, while the 'monarchy' of a single one made it ill. So when you fell ill, the doctor attempted to find out in which 'humours' you were deficient or excessive and rebalance them. Your age, the time of year and so on would all play into the analysis.

HUMOROUS DIET

Take diet (though note that Greek *diaita* [διαιτα] meant 'way of life, regimen'). Given that winter was cold and moist, you should eat as much 'hot' food as possible (but only few moist vegetables) and drink as little as possible; all meat and fish should be roasted. This would keep the body warm and dry. In summer (warm/dry), take a diet consisting entirely of soft cereals, boiled meat, and vegetables both raw and boiled, and a lot of liquid.

DISEASE ANALYSIS

Humour theory dominated medicine till well into the eighteenth century, because it was 'rational' in this sense: that the assumptions were made on the basis of empirical observations which, taken together, looked reasonable and seemed to have explanatory force. After all, since dead bodies were sacred and not to be cut up, Greek doctors were severely limited in what they could learn about the body from the living (though surgery and wounds on the battlefield helped). All they could do was to observe the externals and try to draw conclusions. In one of his most important works, Hippocrates emphasized the role patients could play in helping doctors understand disease (*nosos* [νοσος], as in 'nosology', the study of the classification of diseases and so their names):

> Internal diseases have not been mastered, but they have been mastered as far as possible for the present. The future depends on how far the intelligence of the patients permits the drawing of conclusions, and how far the abilities of future investigators are fitted for the task. If the nature of a disease cannot be perceived by the eye, its diagnosis will involve more trouble and certainly more time than if it can. What escapes our vision we must grasp by mental sight, and the doctor, being unable to see the nature of the disease nor to be told of it, must have recourse to reasoning from the symptoms with which he is presented.

The point about intelligent patient input into the diagnosis is of great importance, as important today as it was then. If a patient with a stab wound is asked where he is bleeding from and answers, 'I'm from bleedin' Romford', the diagnosis may not get very far. It was no different in the ancient world. We get a good idea from the Hippocratics of the sort of questions doctors asked, but could the patient answer them? The doctor Galen, for example, said that certain types of pain actually felt by patients could not be described by them when they were asked.

DIAGNOSIS AND PROGNOSIS

The *gno-* root in Greek (γνο-) is related to our '<u>know</u>' and implied knowledge by observation. Our 'diagnosis' derives direct from Greek διαγνωσις, which meant 'seeing through (*dia* [δια]) to the nature of a condition'; our 'prognosis' (Greek προγνωσις) meant 'seeing in advance (*pro* [προ]), foreseeing the course of a condition'. Given the Greek four-humour theory, their diagnostic ability was (to say the least) limited; but Greeks were sharp, careful observers, and their tracking of the course of a condition was impressive.

SYMPTOMS

Greeks knew all about the chance occurrence, and they called it a *sumptôma* (συμπτωμα). At one end of the scale, it could mean something inexplicable, a one-off mischance or mishap; at the other end, it meant something that might be hard to explain but could be associated with certain conditions – and so a 'symptom' of an illness, or a property or attribute of a comprehensible phenomenon of some sort or other.

Aristotle, for example, argued that, if we wanted to praise someone, we must show that he always acted purposefully, knowing what he was doing. However, his strokes of fortune and other chance happenings (*sumptômata*) should also come into that category, just as long as many examples could be cited. In other words, Aristotle was suggesting that a man got lucky because he was lucky. It is a notion with which we are familiar.

CHARACTER-FORMING PATTERNS

As well as dealing with physical conditions, the four-humour theory was also pressed into service to help with psychological ones. The Greek *kharaktêr* (χαρακτηρ) meant an engraver or engraving tool, especially a die-stamp, used for impressing designs on coins; and from there it came to mean the distinctive mark or impression that differentiated one person from another, and so 'character'. Your character could be revealed as much by the balance of your humours as your health could. Our own language draws on the analysis in the way that Greek does:

Greek *kholos* (χολος), '[yellow] bile, anger'; Late Latin *cholericus*; English 'choleric, furious'.

Greek *melas* (μελας), 'black'; combined with *kholos*, 'melancholy, gloomy'.

Greek *haima* (αἱμα), 'blood'; Latin *sanguis*; English 'sanguine, confident'.

Greek *phlegma* (φλεγμα), 'heat, phlegm'; Late Latin *phlegma*; English 'phlegmatic, cool'.

TEMPERAMENT

Latin *tempero* meant 'I mix' and your *temperamentum* was your personal 'mixture' of these humours. You were 'good-humoured' if the balance was right; if you acted absurdly, it indicated the balance of humours was wrong, and you became 'humorous'. 'Temperament' and 'temper' originally meant the same thing; 'distemper', implying the mixture had become unbalanced (*dis-*, apart, separate), meant you were angry. 'Complexion' derives from *cum* ('together') and *plecto*

('I weave') – your temperament, it was believed, was shown by the 'weaving together' of colours in the face.

NERVES

The climax of Homer's *Odyssey* was reached when Odysseus strung the bow with which he was to kill his wife's 108 suitors. Before he did so, he checked it was still in good working order by twanging the *neuron* (νεῦρον), i.e. the bowstring, which gave off a 'lovely note, like that of a swallow'. A *neuron*, in other words, was a tough object: it meant 'sinew, tendon, string of a lyre'. Latin *nervus*, related to *neuron* (whence 'neurotic'), had the same meaning (in addition to 'penis, virility, strength of mind'). It gives us 'nerve' as well as 'nervous' – nerves tight as a bowstring.

The ancients also associated *neuron/nervus* with sensation. For example, the Greek doctor Galen distinguished sensory and motor nerves by experimenting, especially on pigs. He cut their nerves to see what happened, but on one occasion he accidentally severed the laryngeal nerve, and the pig immediately stopped squealing. He looked further into the problem, and his patron Boethus suggested he put on a public demonstration. Many scholars turned up, and Alexander from Damascus expressed great doubt, saying that even if it was true of pigs, it would not necessarily be true of humans. Galen walked out, saying that he 'did not realize he was addressing a collection of ill-mannered pessimists'. But there was an outcry about this, and Galen finally agreed to go on with the show. He later said:

The meeting lasted several days in which I showed them [nerves controlling the breathing] and how damage to the nerves activating the muscles of the larynx (λαρυγξ) resulted in the loss of voice. All my detractors were thrown into confusion...

This was extremely important. Followers of Aristotle, like Alexander, believed that nerves came from and were controlled by the heart. Galen showed 'that the source of the nerves, of all sensation, and of voluntary motion, is the brain and that the source of the arteries... is the heart', and that the spinal cord, for example, was an extension of the brain.

CANCER

Greeks thought of cancers (see p. 272) as a form of accretion of 'humours'. As Greeks did not cut up bodies, only visible cancers were acknowledged, for example, of the skin and breast. When it came to what they assumed were hidden cancers, Hippocratics were against treatment: 'this causes speedy death, but to omit treatment is to prolong life'. Later doctors used the term 'cancer' to describe conditions such as herpes and gangrene.

FLOWS (1): HAEMORRHOIDS

Greek *haimorrois* (αἱμορροις) meant a vein likely to discharge blood. The roots of this word are very common: *haima* (αἱμα), 'blood' (latinized to *haema-*) + *rhoê* (ῥοη), 'flow'. The Hippocratics, who commited a small book to the subject, were rather eye-watering on the method of dealing with them:

> Have the person lie on his back and place a pillow under the lower
> part of it. Force the anus out as far as you can with the fingers, heat
> up the irons till they glow and burn the haemorrhoids until you dry
> them off completely. See that you leave nothing uncauterized...
> your assistants must hold the man down by his head and arms
> while he is being cauterized so that he stays still, but otherwise let
> him scream during the process, since that makes the anus stick out
> more.

I'll bet it does. Boiled and mashed lentils and chickpeas were then
to be applied as a plaster for five or six days, followed by a honey
compress. That said, some doctors thought haemorrhoids beneficial,
a natural way of releasing 'excess' blood in the body. Blood-letting
was a very common treatment in the ancient world.

Today haemorrhoids are often called 'piles'. This word probably
derives from Latin *pila*, 'ball', as 'pills' do. A haemorrhage described
blood 'breaking violently out' (*rhag-* [ῥαγ-] from the Greek 'break,
shatter, burst').

FLOWS (2): GONORRHEA

Ancient doctors got this badly wrong. What we know as an infection
involving inflammation and discharge from the urethra and vagina,
the ancients thought of as the flow (*rhoê*, see above) of *gonos* (γονος),
'seed'. Celsus surmised:

> There is a complaint involving the genitals, an excessive emission
> of semen. This is produced without intercourse or wet dreams.
> Over time, a man slowly wastes away. Helpful remedies include:

vigorous rubbing-downs, cold water showers, swimming in cold
water, and only cold food and drink...

And so, pointlessly, on. Incidentally, 'ejaculate' is based on Latin
iaculum, 'javelin'; *eiaculor* (*eiaculat-*) meaning 'I shoot out'.

FLOWS (3): DIARRHOEA

Given that 'diabetes' means 'passing through' (see below), diarrhoea
ups the game a little: 'flowing through' (διαρροια, Late Latin *diarrhoea*).
Classical Romans experiencing a dire rear called it *deiectio* – and who
would not feel dejected (literally 'cast down') at that? But they also
took over Greek *dusenteria* (δυσεντερια), our 'dysentery', meaning
'lousy (*dus-*) insides'.

FLOWS (4): CATARRH

Here the *rhoê* ('flow') is one that comes down (*kata* [κατα]) from the
head: a cold. Celsus described it rather well:

> The nostrils close up, the voice becomes hoarse, accompanied
> by a dry cough. The saliva is salty, the ears ring, the head throbs,
> the urine is turbid... These symptoms do not usually last long, but
> if neglected may last a long while. None is fatal, except that which
> causes ulcers in the lung [see below].
>
> Whenever we feel this coming on, we should keep out of the sun,
> avoid the bath, wine and sex. Anointing and customary food are
> allowable. The patient should walk, but only briskly and under
> cover; after that the head and face should be rubbed more than
> fifty times. We normally get better if we take care of ourselves for

a couple of days, three at the most. When the nostrils are more open, resume bathing, soaking head and face in hot, then luke-warm, water.

Next, along with more food, wine may be taken. But if on the fourth day the phlegm is still thin, or the nostrils still stuffed up, the patient should take dry wine from Aminea [in Campania], then for a couple of days water; after which he can return to the bath and his usual habits.

Nevertheless, even during those days, when some things are to be avoided, one should not treat the patients as if they were sick. They are to do everything as if they are healthy, unless these symptoms have been liable to cause more prolonged and severe trouble; for then a somewhat more careful attention is needed.

FLOWS (5): RHEUMATISM

Here is another disease that goes with the 'flow': *rheuma* (ῥευμα). It meant 'current, river' and medically a 'flux, flow, discharge from the body'; whence *rheumatismos* (ῥευματισμος) and *rheumatikos* (ῥευματικος), both duly latinized into *rheumatismus* and *rheumaticus*.

But this raises the question — what has rheumatism got to do with morbid discharges from the body? In the seventeenth century, any joint pain was ascribed to the flow of bodily fluids *into* the joints, and 'rheumatism' was the term chosen to describe it, even though it was not what the ancients meant by it. It covered everything from what we call rheumatism to gout.

FLOWS (6): GOUT

The soldier-historian Xenophon talked of hunting deer with foot-traps, the word for which was *podagra* (ποδαγρα). Very painful too. This was the word which the Greeks used for something equally painful, gout, and it was taken over in that form by the Romans.

We probably call it 'gout' after the Latin *gutta*, 'drop' (thirteenth century), because it was believed it was caused by blood 'corrupted by bile and phlegm' dripping into the joint. Hippocrates called it 'the most violent of all such conditions of the joints, as well as the most chronic and intractable'. He also said that the inflammation subsided within forty days, but those who are 'old or have hardened joints or life without exercise and are constipated are all incurable by human art, as far as I know (but dysentery will help)'.

Pliny the Elder claimed that wet seaweed was the sovereign remedy for gout and all joint problems. Pliny the Younger wrote of the suicide of his friend Corellius Rufus:

> In his thirty-third year (as I have frequently heard him say) he was seized with the gout in his feet. This was hereditary; for diseases, as well as possessions, are sometimes handed down by a sort of inheritance... as it grew upon him with advancing years, he had to manfully bear it, suffering meanwhile the most incredible and undeserved agonies; for the gout was now not only in his feet, but had spread itself over his whole body.

The doctor Aretaeus (second century AD) expressed the same view in rather more dramatic terms: 'No pain is more severe than this, not iron screws, not cords, nor the wound of a dagger, nor burning fire.'

As Pliny suggested by his comment on Rufus' sober life, it was known to be a rich man's disease. Celsus said: 'Some people have obtained lifelong security by refraining from wine, mead and sex.' Galen associated it with a life of debauchery. Seneca, the Roman emperor Nero's adviser (first century AD), went into full moralist mode:

> Hippocrates remarked that women never lost their hair or suffered from pain in the feet... yet now, in rivalling men in licentiousness, women rival them also in the ills to which men are heirs... No surprise, then, that we can prove wrong the greatest and most skilled doctor of all, when so many women are gouty and bald!

Incidentally, Scribonius Largus (who accompanied Claudius to Britain in AD 43 when the Romans began provincializing the island) was the first to use electrification for medical purposes: he recommended torpedo fish (an electric ray) to cure gout.

FLOWS (7): ARTHRITIS

An *arthron* (ἄρθρον) was a 'joint', and arthritis (*arthritis* [ἀρθριτις]) technically meant an inflammation thereof. This disease was again analysed in terms of a flow into joints and confused with what we know as rheumatism and gout. The -*itis* suffix indicating inflammation and attached to *arthr-* is a very early example of its use in English. This usage has since become very common.

Cicero wrote to his chum Papirius Paetus on 22 November 46 BC saying that he had heard that Paetus had foot problems, but that he would come to visit him anyway because at least he did not suppose his cook was *arthriticus*. Rheumatism? Arthritis? Gout?

FLOWS (8): INFLUENZA

A word that has the same roots as 'influence', influenza is a common illness that is all about inflows. It derives from Latin *influo*, 'I flow in', especially of rivers, the sea and so on, but also of words and ideas. Cicero agreed with Plato that 'nothing flows so easily into youthful and impressionable minds as different forms of music'.

This 'inflowing' image appealed strongly to those who believed in astrology and the 'influence' of the stars; and, at least from the sixteenth century, Italian *influenza* was used of epidemics thought to arise from astral forces.

FLOWS (9): HONEY KILLER

Sugar cane was well known in India long before it came to Europe. The Crusaders came across it ('sweet salt') in the twelfth century, but it was only after the Americas were opened up that sugar cane, brought there from the Canary Islands, was turned into sugar and became a luxury product in Europe. No sugar, then, in the classical world.

And no diabetes? Not quite. There was a sweetener: honey (Latin *mel*, *mell-*). When that became relatively common, diabetes was recognized as a disease. The doctor Aretaeus (second century AD) seems to have been the first to name it *diabêtês* (διαβητης). The Greek meant, literally, 'passing through'; the Latin *diabetes* meant 'siphon' (the agriculturalist Columella described trees drawing up water 'passing through the pith of the stem as if through a *siphonem*'.) Aretaeus, arguing that with diabetes the body became like a siphon, helping liquid to pass through it, described the dreadful consequences of type 1 diabetes (type 2 is quite different) as follows:

> The patient never stops making water, but the flow never ceases, as if from an aqueduct... death is rapid and his life disgusting and painful... it is a thirst like fire... it is impossible to stop him from drinking and urinating.

The doctor Galen asserted that it was 'a genuine disease of the kidney, resembling an unquenchable appetite'.

The ancients, of course, knew nothing about insulin, the crucial ingredient in diabetes. It derives from Latin *insula*, 'island', because of the three million or so little islands ('islets') distributed about the pancreas, some of which produce the hormone. The most common form of diabetes today gets its name from the Roman experience: *diabetes mellitus* – 'honeyed', from the Latin stem *mell*-! How did they know? Doctors checked for its presence by tasting the urine.

ANGINA

For us, angina is a chest pain, but it often radiates to the neck. (Modern doctors can still become confused by pain from the gullet and from the heart.) For the ancients, it was all about the throat. Greek *agkhonê* (ἀγχονη) meant 'strangulation, hanging', and Latin *angina* was an acute infection of the throat, involving choking or suffocating (we are told it could be caused by drinking wine, something that England's Chief Medical Officer seems to have missed).* Celsus again:

---

* The *angkh*- (ἀγχ-) root is related to our 'anger' and 'anguish', via Latin *angustus*, 'narrow', as if anger made one 'choke' with rage (and 'rage' derived ultimately from Latin *rabies*, 'ferocity, frenzy, rabies').

A fatal and acute disease is located in the throat. We call it angina.
Sometimes no redness or swelling is apparent, but the skin is dry,
breathing is difficult and the limbs relaxed... sometimes the tongue
and throat are red and swollen, the voice indistinct, eyes rolling,
face pale and hiccups...

This illness of the throat was called in Greek *kunagkhê* (κυναγχη),
'dog-strangle', from which derives our 'quinsy', when an abscess
forms around the tonsils. Latin *abscessus* meant 'departure': the
theory was that the 'humours' (see p. 287) departed from the body
via the pus in the swelling (Latin *pus*, Greek *puón* [πυων]).

DIVERTICULITIS

Romans would have been amused to learn that 'diverticula' are
pouches usually formed on the colon, or large intestine, in the bowels.
When they become inflamed, diverticulitis is the result. This can be
painful and lead to complications.

For a Roman, a *diverticulum* was a turning off the main road, or
a place for turning aside, a port of call. To judge from the graffiti
with which such places tended to be graced, they were expected to
offer 'services' of the sort associated with houses of ill repute. We are
told that Nero, dressed as a slave, used to enjoy visiting brothels and
diverticula with an armed escort, stealing goods and getting into fights.
Cato of Utica (first century BC), renowned for his ascetic lifestyle,
was sent to bring Cyprus under control, and though returning loaded
with money 'through Greek cities, veritable *diverticula*, where he had
to stop', he remained untempted.

Presumably the pouches in the otherwise straight colon looked like turnings off or diversions from the main road.

SCIATICA

The sciatic nerve runs from the back of the pelvis, through the buttocks and down both legs to the feet. It is the longest nerve in the body. If it is interfered with in any way, such as by compression − a slipped disc is often responsible − it can cause pain or numbness.

'Sciatica' derives from Greek *iskhiadikos* (ἰσχιαδικος), which meant 'relating to the hips' (medieval Latin turned it into *sciatica*). The ancients confused the condition with hip dislocations, gout, tuberculosis and so on. Caelius Aurelianus (*c.* AD 400) did better: he described it as a pain in one or both hips, making it difficult to move, causing numbness, skin irritation and pain extending from the groin and lower back through the buttocks into the feet, which he associated with lifting heavy objects or a sudden shock, for example, a fall ('common in the middle-aged') or compression of nerve tissue.

EPILEPSY

Known as the 'sacred disease' in the Greek world, because it seemed beyond human comprehension and must therefore be a divine sign, epilepsy was in Greek *epilêpsis* (ἐπιληψις), 'an act of seizure'. In fact, the Hippocratic treatise 'On the Sacred Disease' began:

> I do not believe the 'sacred disease' is any more divine or
> sacred than any other disease but, on the contrary, has specific
> characteristics and a definite cause... it is my opinion that those

who called this disease 'sacred' were the sort of people we now call witch-doctors, faith-healers, quacks and charlatans, pretending to be pious and particularly wise.

The writer did not reject divine influences across the board, however; instead, he saw them as part of the comprehensible and intelligible *natural* order of things. It was irrational superstition that he rejected. His conclusion was that epilepsy was a disease of the brain: it arose because the passage of phlegm through it was blocked and was diverted into the blood vessels. The Hippocratics recorded a classic case:

> Wintertime, giving himself a rubdown, Anekhetos' boy, warming himself at the fireplace in the bathhouse, suddenly got epileptic convulsions. Once the convulsions subsided, he started looking around, not yet conscious, but the next morning, after coming to, he was again seized: a convulsive state, but not much foaming at the mouth; the third day, only sonic bits of speech; and the fourth, he could only express himself by movements of the tongue, his voice faltered, he was unable to speak and stopped at the beginning of words. On the fifth day, his speech was very disturbed; the convulsions came on, and he was not in possession of his senses; then, when all that ceased, his speech only barely returned to a normal state.

Romans, however, were so convinced of the divine nature of the terrifying condition that they did not adopt the Greek terminology, perhaps regarding it as ill-omened. While some called it *morbus sacer* ('sacred disease') or *maior* ('greater' disease), others preferred what looks like the most mysterious epithet of all for it, *comitialis*, 'connected with the *comitia* (a Roman assembly)', i.e. days on which the assembly met! (See p. 190.) The theory is that if anyone in an assembly was struck with epilepsy, the assembly was immediately suspended.

LEPROSY

The ancient Greek *lepros* (λεπρος), 'scaly, scabby, rough', produced a noun which Romans took over as *lepra*, 'leprosy', a scourge of the ancient Mediterranean. Aretaeus (second century AD) left a harrowingly accurate account, of which this is part:

> Tumours prominent, not continuous with one another anywhere, but thick and rough, and the intermediate space cracked, like the skin of the elephant. Veins enlarged... The hairs on the whole body die prematurely... The skin of the head deeply cracked; wrinkles frequent, deep, rough; tumours on the face hard, sharp; sometimes white at the top, but more green at the base... veins on the temples elevated, and also those under the tongue; bowels bilious; tongue roughened with eruptions, resembling hailstones; not unusual for the whole frame to be full of such... Cracks on the feet and heels, as far as the middle of the toes; but if the ailment still further increases, the tumours become ulcerated, so that on the cheeks, chin, fingers, and knees, there are fetid and incurable ulcers... Sometimes, too, certain of the members of the patient will die, so as to drop off, such as the nose, the fingers, the feet, the privy parts, and the whole hands; for the ailment does not prove fatal, so as to relieve the patient from a foul life and dreadful sufferings,

until he has been divided limb from limb... faced with those in
such a condition, who would not take flight, or who would not be
repelled by their predicament, even if he were a son or a father or
a brother?

CREEPING UP

'Fevers in which the lips are ulcerated abate at intervals, with chills
on the third day', said a Hippocratic. This must refer to cold sores,
a type of spreading skin condition living in the facial nerves (though
not causing fevers), known in Greek as *herpês* (ἑρπης), as in Latin.
It derived from Greek *herpô* (ἑρπω) meaning 'I creep'. This can take
many forms and affect many parts of the body.

Herpês zôstêr (ζωστηρ), which meant 'belt, girdle', is different, being
caused by the chicken-pox virus. Romans translated *zôstêr* into their
word for 'belt', *cingulum*, which gives us 'shingles'. Hippocratics said
it was one of the most difficult diseases to get rid of. Greeks classified it
under the term ἐρυσιπελας – literally (probably) 'red-skinned' – taken
over directly by the Romans as *erysipelas*, a form of skin infection
of quite different cause from *herpês zôster*. Hippocrates also mentions
such rashes in the womb and the lung 'usually from drunkenness or
eating too many grey mullets and eels... or eating meat or a change
of water'.

TUBERCULOSIS

Tuber in Latin meant 'swelling, hard tumour'; *tuberculum* was a smaller
version. The ancients called it *phthisis* (φθισις), *p*(h)*thisis* in Latin
('consumption'), which is what tuberculosis (TB) was called until

microscopes revealed the little tubercles. It is a disease primarily of the lungs, on which small pustules form. Ancient doctors recognized the classic symptoms: chronic coughs, bloody sputum (Latin, 'spittle'), fever, sweating, weight loss and so on. Celsus summarized it as follows:

> It arises in the head, flows down into the lung, where it produces ulceration, from which a slight fever develops, which comes and goes. The patient coughs a lot and spits out often bloody pus.

A Hippocratic doctor wrote of it in greater detail:

> Fevers with shivering, continuous, acute... sweats continual... severe chills... bowels dysfunctional... continued spitting of crude sputa... throat painful and inflamed... delirium as death approached.

Doctors also noted it could be associated with physical deformity, especially curvature of the spine. Hunchbacks were commonly depicted in ancient art.

TYPHOID FEVER

The '-oid' ending indicates 'similarity to': 'typhoid fever' is therefore a fever resembling a *tuphos* (τυφος). Some ancients claimed that this meant 'smoke, haze', but this is not true. It meant 'delusion'. Hippocratics mentioned five varieties of *tuphos*, but none of them bears any relation to what we mean by typhus or typhoid.

The Hippocratics preserved a powerful account of the course of what seems like typhoid fever, though it was not so named:

The wife of Hermoptolemus, in the winter, had fever and headache. Whenever she drank she sat upright because of difficulty swallowing. She said that her heart had been damaged. Tongue livid from the outset. The cause seemed to be a chill after a bath. She was sleepless, night and day. After the first days, when asked, she no longer said that her head hurt, but that her whole body hurt. Thirst, sometimes insatiable, sometimes moderate. On the fifth and sixth days and up to the ninth, almost constantly delirious. Later, she babbled to herself half-intelligible things in the midst of drowsiness... On the last day, the twenty-third, her eye was large in the morning and her vision short. She was quiet at times, without huddling under covers or drowsiness. Towards evening there was movement of the right eye, as though seeing or seeking something, from the outer corner towards the nose. She showed recognition and answered what was asked. Her voice lisping after much talking, and broken and hoarse from the shouting.

DELIRIUM

Proto-Indo-European (PIE) had a root *leis-, meaning 'track' or 'furrow'.* From this, via its Germanic links, comes English 'learn'. The image is one of finding and keeping on a track. A different meaning came into English via the Latin connection. PIE *leis- became *lira* in Latin and meant a ridge between two furrows thrown up by a plough. The purpose of this, said the agriculturalist Columella, was to provide 'a dry bed for grain'. The grammarian

---

* An asterisk before a word indicates that it has been reconstructed by working back from existing words to the presumed Proto-Indo-European root.

Velius Longus made the linguistic point: that bulls swerving off the straight line of their ploughing 'are said to *de-lirare*', i.e. to 'de-ridge', whence Latin *delirus*, and our 'delirious', 'mentally deranged'.

TETANUS

Romans took *tetanus* directly over from Greek *tetanos* (τετανος), 'stretched, rigid'. A Hippocratic doctor provides a classic description of a case:

> In the commander of the large ship, whose right forefinger,
> bone and all, had been crushed by the anchor, an inflammation
> appeared, a bone-gangrene, and some fever. He was mildly purged
> on the fifth day. The bouts of fever subsided then, as well as the
> pain. A part of the finger fell off. After the seventh day, a pus came
> out properly. Afterward, he said that with his tongue he wasn't
> succeeding in explaining everything. Prediction: the backward
> spasm is on its way. The jaws began clenching, then it went to
> the nape of his neck; on the third day, he was totally convulsed
> backward, with sweating; on the sixth day after prediction, he died.

BOTANY

INTRODUCTION

B otany – from Greek *botanê* [βοτανη], 'herb, weed, plant' – is the
study and classification of plants. It was invented by the ancient
Greek Theophrastus (372–287 BC), who was a brilliant observer
and the first to classify plants by their physical features – sap, roots,
leaves, buds, flowers and fruits. But his work was not continued. The
ancients were a practical people and more interested in what plants
could do for them, especially as remedies for illness. So ancient
descriptions tend to concentrate solely on their medicinal properties.
Our 'panacea' derives from Greek *panakês* (πανακης – *pan*, 'all' + *ak*-,
'cure'), the name given to plants of this sort.

During the scientific revolution of the sixteenth century in Europe,
botany took off, and since Latin was the language of education
and scholarship, it was natural that botanists should turn for their
terminology to medieval and classical Latin and to ancient Greek.
The man responsible for our system of naming plants is the Swede
Carl Linnaeus (1707–78). His lasting achievement was to impose

order on the naming chaos that existed at that time, most importantly through his binomial ('two-name') system of classification.

The principle of the botanical naming system is quite simple. It identifies a broad, generic type of plant (*genus*, Latin 'birth, kind, class'), and then gives it a specific name (*species*, Latin 'appearance, special nature'). Here, for example, is the genus *Rhododendron* (which can be abbreviated to *R.* if used more than once). This species has blood-red flowers, so we shall call it *Rhododendron haematôdês* (Greek 'αἱματωδης, 'bloody'); this species has felted leaves, so we shall call it *R. lanigerum*, 'wool-bearing' (Latin *lana*, 'wool'). Note that the genus always begins with a capital letter, its specific name with a lower-case letter. Other descriptors can be added to make further distinctions.

So, where do the names of plants come from?

- Many are lifted direct from Latin or Greek, e.g. anemone, asparagus, crocus, cyclamen, rose, lily, violet, herb, together with genus names such as *Daphne* and *Narcissus*.
- Names also commemorate the famous: *Fuchsia* was named after the sixteenth-century German herbalist Leonhart Fuchs; *Forsythia* after William Forsyth (1737–1804), superintendent of the Royal Gardens of Kensington Palace (note the latinized *-ia* endings).
- Names, often in Latin forms, can tell us where plants come from – for instance, *persica* 'from Persia' (modern Iran) and *japonica* 'from Japan'.

- They can help us visualize a shape, colour, texture or size
  – for instance, *fusiformis*, 'spindle-shaped', Latin *fusus*,
  'spindle', i.e. thick in the middle, thin at either end.
- They can celebrate the person who first identified them,
  e.g. *forrestii*, in honour of the Scottish plant-collector
  George Forrest (1873–1932), who scoured western China
  for specimens.

One could, of course, use English throughout – thus *Anthriscus sylvestris*, for instance, is simply cow parsley. But the full Latin naming system is universal and international. This system provides an efficient, economic, unambiguous and universal means of naming that transcends all modern languages and colloquial names, as vital for botanists today as universal medical terms are for doctors.

It has recently been put about that the International Botanical Congress intends to abandon the use of Latin in the description and naming of plants. This is not true. What in fact was agreed (in 2011) was that from now on the official *descriptions* of new plant families do not have to be in Latin. But the *names* of the various plants, going back to the great Linnaeus, will continue to be latinized in accordance with the traditional system. So *nil desperandum* (literally, 'nothing [is] to-be-despaired-of '): the latinized names are here to stay.

VEGETABLES

Vegetables used to be staid and boring. If we vegetate, we slump into stagnation and mental torpor. Worse still is a vegetative state, where there is no response to external stimuli.

But the etymology of vegetables shows they are anything but, let us say, sluggish. Latin *vegetus* meant 'vigorous', and *vegeo*, 'I enliven, fill with vigour'. So too did *vegeto*, rather bewilderingly the source of our 'vegetate', which means the very opposite! Presumably that meaning arose when invigorating vegetables were felt to be just dull plants.

Some would claim that cabbage derives from Latin *caput* (head) via medieval Latin *caputium* (a 'head-cabbage') and Old French *caboce*. If the derivation from *caput* is true, when you ask your greengrocer for a head of cabbage, you mean a head of head-cabbage. Still, cabbage was considered good for heads with a hangover.

PEONY

Paeonia, peony, is named after the mythical Greek healer Paeon, who used it for medical purposes. The species *P. officinalis* is very appropriately named – and has nothing to do with offices or officials in our sense of the words. The Latin *opificina*, shortened to *officina*, meant a place where a product (*opus*, whence 'opera') was made (*facio*, 'I make, do') – in other words, a workshop or studio. In the Middle Ages *officina* came to be used of monastic store-rooms, and so of herb stores and pharmacies. Consequently *officinalis* means 'originally used for medical purposes', and is used to describe many species.

LILIES

Holidaying in Greece, we wield our phrase book and say *kal' hemera*, 'good-day', to appreciative locals. We could be talking about the day lily. This has its good day too, as its *genus* name indicates. It is made up of exactly the same elements as the greeting: *Hemerocallis* –

hêmera (ήμερα), 'day' + *kallos* (καλλος), 'beauty', indicating a plant that is supposed to flower in all its glory for one day only. The day lily is a member of the *Liliaceae*, the *-aceae* being a common Latin ending meaning 'belonging to the family of'. Other genera of the lily family include *Hyacinthus*, a pre-ancient Greek name thousands of years old, and *Aspidistra*, because the stigma is like an *aspidion* (ἀσπιδιον), Greek for 'little shield'. Hyacinthus (Ὑακινθος) was the handsome young man with whom Apollo fell in love, but who was accidentally killed with a discus (δισκος). The flower was formed from his blood.

OX-EYES

The yellow daisy-flower *Buphthalmum salicifolium*, which is borne throughout the summer, also looks the part – literally. *Bous* is 'ox' (βους) and *ophthalmos* (ὀφθαλμος) 'eye' in Greek, and you could indeed see the flower as a long-lashed ox's eye. *Salicifolium* describes its willow-like leaves: Latin *folium*, 'leaf', and *salex* (*salic-*), 'willow'. The family name is *Asteraceae* (Greek *astêr* [ἀστηρ], 'star').

GERANIUMS

The popular cranesbill is quite properly named *Geranium*, which derives from the Greek *geranos* (γερανος), 'crane'. This meant the bird, but also lifting machinery, such machinery being tall and stooped over. The tall, stooped-over carpels of the geranium give it its name. The flowers are similar to the *genus Erodium*, another ornithological plant, 'heron's bill' or 'stork's bill', from the Greek *erôidios* (ἐρῳδιος), 'heron'.

Scabious, *Scabiosa*, is a much-loved flower but with a less than lovely name. It derives from Latin *scabies*, 'roughness of skin', of the sort accompanied by eruptions and itching (→ 'scab'). The plant is so called because of the roughness of its leaves, though its popular name 'pincushion' derives from the appearance of the flower's centre. It was believed to cure the itch. Is this why it was also known as 'mourning bride'?

STACHYS

Stachys (σταχυς, 'ear of corn', and so 'spiky') is one of many plant types to which the *descriptor officinalis* is added (see p. 312). The flowers of the genus *Stachys* are indeed like spikes, and English 'spike' derives from Latin *spica*, whence the adjective *spicata*, 'spiked'. There is a *Stachys spicata*, which rather overdoes the spikiness; it is the same flower as *Stachys macrantha*, Greek *makros* (μακρος), 'big' + *anthos* (ἀνθος), 'flower', which has the equivalent Latin name *Stachys grandiflora* – no explanation required.

NIGELLA

Nigella damascena is also known as 'Love-in-a-mist'. *Nigella* comes from the Latin *niger*, 'black', with the added -*ella* termination, which means 'little'. It refers to the colour of its little black seeds. The species name *damascena* refers to its eastern origins, 'from Damascus'. The family to which it belongs is the jaw-breaking *Ranunculaceae*, 'Little-frog-family' (Latin *rana*, 'frog'), referring to the fact that many species grow in marshy places. Perhaps someone has already grown, or soon will grow, a *Nigella domestica* in honour of TV's domestic goddess (*domestica*, 'often used as a house plant', from Latin *domus*, 'house').

HYDRANGEA

Hydrangea looks as if it should have something to do with water (Greek *hudr-* [ὑδρ-]), but it is the second half of the word that is the important part, Greek *aggeion* (ἀγγειον), 'vessel for holding liquid'. The reference is to the plant's fruit, which looks like a cup. *Hydrangea* is one of the extensive *Saxifragaceae* family, Latin *saxum*, 'rock, stone', and *frango*, 'I break'. In what sense can such plants be 'rockbreakers'? No one is absolutely certain, but one theory is that the herb saxifrage grew in rock crevices – it must, therefore, have been able to break rocks, and so was prescribed to break up stones in the bladder!

SNAPDRAGONS

The snapdragon or *Antirrhinum*, 'resembling an animal's snout', should not really be spelled like that. Words in ancient Greek *beginning* with 'r' are always followed by 'h' (e.g. 'rhododendron' [ῥοδοδενδρον]) and Greek *rhin-* (ῥιν-), 'snout'). But *Antirrhinum* does not begin with r! In such cases Greek dropped the 'h' but doubled the 'r' to make up. Where, then, did the rogue 'h' come from? Blame the Romans, who put the 'h' back in order to be 'correct'.

HELIANTHUS

Helianthus, the sunflower, is precisely named: *hêlios* (ἡλιος) is Greek for 'sun', and *anthos* (ἀνθος) Greek for 'flower'. One explanation of its name is the way many such plants turn to face the sun. The name ends in *-us* and not Greek *-ος* because plant names tend to be latinized, and *-us* is the proper Latin ending. *Anthemon* (ἀνθεμον) is another word for 'flower' in Greek and has been latinized into *anthemum*. *Chrysanthemum* is a gold flower (Greek χρυσος, 'gold') and *Helianthemum* is the sun-rose. An anthology is, literally, a selection of flowers.*

RUBUS

The season of berries is full of *Rubus*, from the Latin for 'blackberry' (it is probably connected with Latin *ruber*, 'red'). *Rubus fruticosus* is the blackberry (*fruticosus* means 'bushy, shrubby' and has nothing to do with 'fruit'), and *Rubus idaeus* is the raspberry ('from Mount Ida', overlooking Troy!). Do not confuse *Rubus* with *Ribes*, 'currant'. These two words are not connected: *Ribes* apparently comes from a word of Arabic or Persian origin, meaning 'acid-tasting'. *Ribes nigrum* is the blackcurrant, and *Ribes sativum* the red and white currant (*sativum*, 'cultivated, sown').

PRUNES

October sees the last of the prunes, or rather, of the ancient Greek *proumnê* (προυμνη), 'plum tree', which the Romans took over in Latin to give us the genus we know as *Prunus*. Originally confined to plums, the genus now embraces a wonderful range of exotic, often eastern, fruits. *Prunus avium* ('of the birds') is, appropriately enough, the

---

* Warning: 'anthem' derives from Greek *antiphonos* (ἀντιφονος), 'answering sound'.

common sweet cherry; *Prunus cerasus*, 'the cherry plum tree', is the sour cherry (e.g. morello) for which, again, the Romans plundered ancient Greek, turning *kerasos* (κερασος) into *cerasus*. *Prunus persica* ('from Persia') is the peach, while *Prunus armeniaca* ('from Armenia') is the common apricot.

CLEMATIS

Clematis is (as we have often seen) a Roman name lifted directly from ancient Greek, *klêmatis* (κληματις). In Greek *klêma* meant 'twig, branch' and was especially associated with the vine, so *Clematis* is properly a genus of various climbing plants. One late-flowering example is *Clematis apiifolia*, a deceptive species name. The *folia* element is easy (Latin *folium*, 'leaf'), but what of *apii*? This looks as if it might have something to do with bees (Latin *apis*, → 'apiary'), but in fact comes from Latin *apium*, 'celery'; so *Clematis apiifolia* has celery-like leaves. *Clematis chinensis*, also spelled *sinensis*, comes from China.

ACHILLEA

What has the ancient Greek hero of the Trojan war, Achilles, got to do with *Achillea*? Achilles was brought up by a half-man, half-horse centaur called Cheiron, who (Homer tells us) taught him all about medicine, presumably concentrating on treatment appropriate to the battlefield; and from ancient times, *Achillea millefolia* ('many-leaved'), yarrow, was laid on wounds to help them heal. All very well, but what about *Achillea ptarmica*, sneezewort ('wort' is Old English for plant or herb; ancient Greek *ptarmos* [πταρμος] meant 'sneezing')?

We are told that it was used as a kind of snuff, but it was more usefully employed against toothache.

ECHINOPS

Echinops is a splendidly accurate term for the globe thistle. *Ekhinos* (ἐχινος) is the ancient Greek for 'hedgehog', and *ôps* (ὠψ) for 'face', 'appearance', perfectly describing the look of the plant's spiny, metallic-blue flower heads. The silvery-grey species is *E. sphaerocephalus*, which emphasizes the 'globe' element: *sphaira* (σφαιρα, → 'sphere') is Greek for 'ball', and *kephalê* (κεφαλη) Greek for 'head'. Now and again you will come across an 'acephalous' feature in plants, and the '*a-*' is Greek again, meaning 'without' or 'no' – a headless wonder. This '*a-*' prefix appears in words like 'anaesthetic' ('no feeling') and 'atom' ('not cuttable').

COTONEASTER

Cotoneaster derives from Latin *cotoneum*, the quince. As usual, Latin has taken the Greek for 'quince', *kudônion* (κυδωνιον), meaning 'from Kydon' (a town in Crete), and latinized it. The *-aster* termination has nothing to do with stars. It is a shortened form of Latin *ad instar*, 'towards an equivalence', and indicates that the plant is wild, or somehow inferior (compare 'oleaster': wild olive; 'poetaster': inferior poet). Thus *Cotoneaster* means 'false quince'.

Of the various *Cotoneaster* species, *C. horizontalis* clings to rocks and *C. microphylla* has 'small leaves' (Greek μικρος, 'small', φυλλον, 'leaf'), while *C. rotundifolia*, 'with round leaves', comes from Latin (*rotundus*, 'round', *folium*, 'leaf').

HOLLY AND IVY

'The Holly and the Ivy', we sing at Christmas, which admittedly trips off the tongue more easily than 'The *Ilex aquifolium* and the *Hedera helix*'. English 'holly' is the same word as 'holm' (as in the holm oak tree) and ultimately derives from a very ancient word meaning, appropriately enough, 'prick'. So does the Latin. *Ilex* means 'holm oak', but *aquifolium*, interestingly, has nothing to do with *aqua*, 'water': it is a combination of *acus*, 'needle, pin' + *folium*, 'leaf'.

'Ivy' is *hedera* in Latin; and *helix* (stem *helico-*) means 'spiralling', as in 'helico-pter' – meaning 'spiralling wing' (Greek *pteron* [πτερον] means 'wing').

SNOWDROPS

The snowdrop's Latin name is *Galanthus nivalis*. As often, the Greeks provided the basis of the *genus* name *Galanthus* – Greek *gala* (ἀνθος) means 'milk' (→ 'galaxy' p. 188) and *anthos* (ἀνθος) 'flower'; the name was then latinized.

Nivalis is Latin from the stem *niv-* meaning 'snow': so the snowdrop is 'snowy milk-flower'. The *niv-* stem gives two other flower terms meaning 'purest white' and 'growing near snow' – *niveus* (whence Nivea moisturising cream) and *nivosus*.

Galanthus, with a small 'g', is also used as a species name, meaning 'with milky-white flowers'.

WINTER SWEET

Winter sweet is a shrub that flowers in winter. Its *genus* is *Chimonanthus*, latinized from Greek *kheimôn* (χειμων), 'winter' + *anthos*, 'flower'.

The winter sweet species *C. praecox* is 'very early, premature' (→ English 'precocious'), from Latin *coctus* meaning 'cooked, baked prematurely' (like English 'pre-cooked'), from *coquo* (*coct-*), 'I cook'.

This word is also the basis of 'apricot'. The apricot ripens earlier than the peach, and so was called *praecoquum* in Latin ('pre-cooked'). This word was picked up by Arabs in Syria, turned into Arabic *al-burquq* (*al* = 'the') and eventually became 'apricot'!

IRIS

The spectacularly coloured *Iris* (Greek Ἶρις), like the iris of the eye, gets its name from the ancient Greek goddess of the rainbow (who is also a messenger goddess). *I. foetidissima*, 'stinking iris', is so called because of the nasty smell it gives off when crushed (Latin *foetidus*, 'foul'; the *-issima* termination means 'very'). *I. xiphioides* (compare the Spanish iris, *Iris xiphium*) has broader leaves, like a lance or sword: Greek *xiphos* (ξιφος), 'sword' + the *-oides* (-οιδης) termination, which means 'like, resembling'. *I. unguicularis* (Latin *unguis*, 'fingernail, claw, talon') is named after the narrowed 'claw' of the petal.

CROCUS

The name *Crocus* (κροκος) is ancient Greek and one of the oldest unchanged plant names still in use (it is at least 3,000 years old). In Greek it meant 'saffron', a popular dye and fragrant foodstuff (often scattered in front of emperors to perfume their path). It was gathered from what we know today as *C. sativus* (Latin 'sown, planted, cultivated'). *C. angustifolius* has narrow leaves (Latin *angustus*, 'narrow'); *C. albiflorus* has white flowers (Latin *albus*, 'white', →

'albumen'); *C. vernus* (Dutch crocus) is spring-flowering (Latin *ver*, 'spring', → 'vernal'); while *C. serotinus* is late-flowering, in the autumn (Latin *sero*, 'late').

PRIMROSE

Primula, or primrose, is the 'first little flower [of spring]' (from Latin *primus*, 'first', with its diminutive form *primulus*, 'firstling'). The common primrose is *P. vulgaris* — not vulgar in our sense, but derived from the Latin *vulgus*, 'the ordinary people'. *P. denticulata* has teeth (Latin *dens*, 'tooth'), but only very fine ones, along the leaves; while the flowers of *P. capitata* grow into a dense head (Latin *caput*, 'head', → 'capital', 'decapitate'). *P. elatior*, Latin for 'rather taller', is the oxlip. The *Polyanthus* group has 'many flowers' – Greek *polu-* (πολυ-), 'many', as in 'polytechnic' ('many skills') and *hoi polloi* (οἱ πολλοι), 'the many'.

NARCISSUS

Narcissus (daffodil) is a latinized form of the Greek ναρκισσος. Myth tells us that Narcissus was a youth of great beauty who rejected all advances, male and female, and paid the price when one day he saw his own reflection in a fountain. He at once fell in love with it and wasted away there, pining to possess the reflection of himself. The gods took pity on him in death and turned him into a beautiful flower, drooping over to look at itself in the water. *Narcissi* are split into a number of divisions, one of which is *Narcissus poeticus* — a term reserved for plants linked with Greek and Roman poets (also found in the form *Narcissus poetarum*, 'of the poets').

EPILOGUE

The terms 'root', 'stem', 'prefix' and 'suffix' have occurred regularly in the preceding pages. 'Root' refers to the simplest, usually the dictionary, form of the word: so *scrib-* is the root of the verb *scribo*, 'I write'. But the verb has another 'stem', *script-* (used for different tenses and voices: so – *scribo*, 'I write'; *scriptum est*, 'it was written'). We get words from both of these, e.g 'scribe', 'scripture'.

These words are formed by the addition of prefixes attached to the front and/or suffixes to the end. Our 'scribe' derives from Latin *scrib-a* with the *-a* replaced by *-e*; 'scripture' from Latin *script-* + the suffix *-ura,* and again the *-a* replaced by *-e*. Our 'prescribe' derives from *praescribo*: note the pr(a)efix *prae-*.

Pedants moan endlessly about the 'corruption' of words formed from different languages – for instance, 'television' derives from Greek *têle* (τηλε, 'far off') + Latin stem *vis-*, 'seen'. Let them. Unless a word is taken directly from Latin without change, such as 'momentum' or 'consensus', it will inevitably use anglicized or at least non-Latin endings, such as the *-e* at the end of 'scribe' and 'scripture'. Technically, therefore, 'agendums' would break no 'rules' of English word-formation. It has simply become convention that we use the Latin plural *agenda*.

Romans regularly added *-io* to the alternative stem to make a noun, e.g. *scriptio*, 'the act of of writing'. One very fruitful source of English is to add an -n to that, making -ion. So the *script-* stem yields de- /pre- /in- /re- /trans-scrip*tion*; compare *duco* (*duct-*), 'I lead' + the prefixes de- /in- /re- /pro-duct with the suffix -ion.

But English also makes use of the root. Take *port-o*, 'I carry' and add the prefixes im- (= in-) /ex- /re- /trans- /de-. You can then add other English suffixes, such as '-er' or '-ing', to give 'reporter', 'reporting' and so on. Or you can add Latin suffixes such as *-abilis*, English '-able', meaning 'X can be done' – 'reportable', 'transportable'.

It would be possible to expand this list of prefixes and suffixes very considerably. But this explains why Latin roots and stems bulk so large in English (mostly via Norman French) and why those who learn Latin (and Greek, which works in just the same way) always talk about how 'useful' it has been. It is easy to see why: since Latin helps to explain words and their formation, it makes people understand more and so feel confident about their use of English as well as easing their learning of the Latin-based romance languages.

The structure of the Latin language also opens eyes to the way language actually works (see p. 123). The result is that reading Latin or Greek is an invaluable training in linguistic awareness. You must understand the function of every word, and how Latin marks it, in order to translate it into English.

Result: you will be able to say precisely what the function of the word 'of' is in the following utterances: 'a cup of tea', 'the pen of my aunt', 'he died of boredom', 'piece of cake' (and a few more could be listed). You may say, 'So what? I understand the English.' Of course you do. But that was not the isssue. To understand function gives a deeper grasp of, sensitivity to and awareness of language. Take the phrase 'the love of God'. That has two quite different meanings. Doesn't it?

Try it again with 'to'. What is the function of 'to' in the following utterances? 'To me, that makes no sense', 'I like to run', 'I'm off to Wales', 'To cross the line, use the footbridge', 'Donate to Classics for All'. All this is clearly of great importance if you want to learn a foreign language, which may work in a quite different way from English, but whether children as young as six should be put through it *for its own sake* is quite another matter.

Obviously, you do not *need* to learn Latin or Greek to understand precisely how language works. But if you do learn them, you will not only be able to read the magnificent literature composed in two of the West's most influential languages; you will also better understand your own language (its vocabulary and structure) as well as other languages, and you will be a far better communicator because of it.

This is no idle boast. A nationwide YouGov survey conducted in 2011 showed that classics provided lifetime skills, benefits and pleasure, not to mention employability, even to those who have studied them to no further than age sixteen. This is not an invention: it is what respondents themselves said – and they, after all, should know. It is striking how many people who never studied Latin will confidently say how useless it is.

The full survey report (the second of three surveys) can be found at http://classicsforall.org.uk/book-reviews/perceived-value-classics.

What is most striking of all is that, among those who studied Latin to age sixteen and did not study anything classical again, while just over 20 per cent found the exercise a waste of time, nearly 80 per cent rated their study to have been anything from beneficial to very beneficial. The reasons centred almost wholly on the sense that their understanding of English and their ability to use it clearly, accurately and persuasively had been considerably enhanced. Again it must be stressed that there are many ways to skin a cat. Winston Churchill, for example, a supreme master of the English language, would have been one of the 20 per cent. But not all of us are Churchills.

The plain fact is that Latin and Greek, through their unparalleled literatures, have spoken to generations of people down the millennia. That is why they have survived. The languages cross all barriers, enriching our own language and at the heart of many others (French, Italian, Spanish, modern Greek). In them, for the first time in the West, we hear the voices of epic and lyric poetry, history and philosophy, biography, tragedy, comedy and satire. On the walls of Pompeii, on scraps of papyrus, on grave monuments, from northern Britain to Egypt, the voice of each of us speaks out, with our loves and fears, jealousies and worries, hopes and failures, enmities, pleasures and jokes.

These are highly inventive and imaginative cultures: atomic theory, democracy, republicanism, aqueducts, history, concrete, geometry, logic, tragedy, the foundations of many legal systems, biology, rhetoric, rational medicine, our alphabet and the arch, with a range of other major architectural forms – all were either invented or radically developed on their watch.

Greeks and Romans were the first people in the West to discuss, intensively and at length, a range of concerns that we still grapple with: life, death, gods, sex, love, family, children, education, the natural world, our origins, history, money, health, property, respect, status, friendship, empire, power, politics, crime, justice, war. In the process they raise questions of slavery, heroism, citizenship, sexism, human rights, responsibility and blame, the just war, the uses of power, xenophobia, punishment theory, the good life, racism, inclusive (not exclusive) deities. Further, as people who were not Christianized, they provide a fascinating alternative mirror in which to look at ourselves and reflect on our world, its values and concerns. If their literature is 'dead', then so are Shakespeare and Mozart. Some achievements are immortal.

And the spin-offs! Latin and Greek demand especially close and accurate attention to linguistic detail; teach close linguistic reasoning (though they are no more 'logical' than any other language); provide, at a very basic level, a solid foundation for understanding how languages work; and make a superb introduction to English's Graeco-Roman linguistic vocabulary (often thought of as 'difficult').

For those of us with some knowledge of the ancient world, it is incomprehensible how 75 per cent of our school pupils can be kept from anything other than brief, casual contact with such riches. How fortunate for those that go to schools where something classical is taught in depth! If that is 'elitist', we want all our pupils to have a taste of it.

BIBLIOGRAPHY

Beard, M., North, J. and Price, S., *Religions of Rome: Vol. 2. A Sourcebook* (Cambridge, 1998)

Bricknell, C. (ed.), *Gardeners' Encyclopedia of Plants and Flowers* (Dorling Kindersley, 1994)

Celsus, *De medicina*, I–VIII (Loeb Classical Library, Harvard)

Cicero, Vols. I–XXVIII (Loeb Classical Library, Harvard)

Clackson, J., *Language and Society in the Greek and Roman Worlds* (Cambridge, 2015)

Columella, *De agricultura*, I–XII (Loeb Classical Library, Harvard)

Erskine, A., *The Hellenistic Stoa* (Bloomsbury, 1990)

Glare, P. G. W. (ed.), *Oxford Latin Dictionary* (Oxford, 1982)

Grafton, A., Most, G. W., Settis, S. (eds), *The Classical Tradition* (Harvard, 2010)

Grmek, M. D., *Diseases in the Ancient Greek World* (Johns Hopkins, 1989)

Harlow, M. and Laurence, R., *Growing Up and Growing Old in Ancient Rome* (Routledge, 2002)

Harper, D., *Online Etymology Dictionary*, www.etymonline.com.

Healy, J. F., *Pliny the Elder on Science and Technology* (Oxford, 1999)

Hippocrates, Vols. I–VIII (Loeb Classical Library, Harvard)

Hornblower, S. and Spawforth, A. (eds), *Oxford Classical Dictionary* (Oxford, 2003)

Johnson, E. L., *Latin Words of Common English* (D. C. Heath, 1931)

Jones, P., *An Intelligent Person's Guide to Classics* (Bloomsbury, 1999)

Jones, P. and Sidwell, K. (eds), *The World of Rome* (Cambridge, 1997)

Jones, P., *Veni Vidi Vici* (Atlantic, 2013)

Kay, P., *Rome's Economic Revolution* (Oxford, 2014)

Kenney, E. J. (ed.), *Cambridge History of Classical Literature*, Vol. 2, Latin Literature (Cambridge, 1982)

Keppie, L., *The Making of the Roman Army* (Batsford, 1984)

Martin, T. R., *Ancient Rome* (Yale, 2012)

Onions, C. T. (ed.), *Oxford Dictionary of English Etymology* (Oxford, 1966)

Partridge, E., Origins: *A Short Etymological Dictionary of Modern English* (London, 1958)

Pliny the Elder, *Natural History*, I–XXXVII (Loeb Classical Library, Harvard)

Riggsby, A., *Roman Law and the Legal World of the Romans* (Cambridge, 2010)

Rowland, I. D. and Howe, T. N. (eds), *Vitruvius: Ten Books on Architecture* (Cambridge, 1999)

Rüpke, J., *Religion of the Romans*, trans. Richard Gordon (Polity Press, 2007)

Seneca the Younger, I–XIII (Loeb Classical Library, Harvard)

Sidwell, K., *Reading Medieval Latin* (Cambridge, 1995)

Stearn, W. T., *Botanical Latin: History, Grammar, Syntax, Terminology, and Vocabulary* (Timber Press, 1992)

Wulff, H. R., 'The Language of Medicine', *Journal of the Royal Society of Medicine* (2004, April 97 [4]), 187–188

INDEX